THE GOLDEN AGE OF PRO FOOTBALL

THE GOLDEN AGE OF PRO FOOTBALL

NFL FOOTBALL IN THE 1950s

Mickey Herskowitz

A National Football League Book
Taylor Publishing Company
Dallas, Texas

The Photographers
AP/Wide World Photos,
Bettman Newsphotos,
Vernon Biever, David Boss,
Detroit Lions, Nate Fine,
George Gellatly, Fred Matthes,
NFL Photos,
New York Giants,
Darryl Norenberg,
Hy Peskin *Sports Illustrated,*
Philadelphia Eagles,
Pittsburgh Steelers,
Pro Football Hall of Fame,
Robert Riger, Frank Rippon,
Fred Roe, Dan Rubin,
Russ Reed, Vic Stein,
Tony Tomsic.

A National Football League Book

Creative Director **David Boss**
Editor-in-Chief **John Wiebusch**
Editorial Staff: **Jane Alexander, Phil Barber**
Managing Editor **Chuck Garrity, Sr.**
Art Director **Chris Mossman**
Production Manager **Brian Davids**
Editorial Offices **6701 Center Drive West,
Suite 1111, Los Angeles, CA 90045**

Herskowitz, Mickey
The golden age of pro football/Mickey Herskowitz
p. cm.
A revision of the book originally published in 1974
ISBN 0-87833-751-2 : $15.95
1. National Football League—History. 2. Football—United
States—History. I. Title
GV954.H47 1990
796.332'64' 0973-dc20
Printed in the United States of America
10 9 8 7 6 5 4 3 2 1

Contents

Foreword

Bear with us if this gets a little personal. This edition of *The Golden Age of Pro Football*, the one you are presumably holding in your hand, was fifteen years in the making and a story goes with it, as befits so long a wait.

The idea for a book about pro football in the 1950s originated with John Wiebusch and David Boss, two of the brains behind the National Football League's Creative Services Division. They also made a judgment, with which many observers, including the author, agreed: The age really was golden.

The hardcover version, with artist Lon Keller's superb portrait of Hugh McElhenny on the dust jacket, appeared in 1974. It received flattering notices, sold well if not wildly, became a work of reference for writers and hardcore fans, then disappeared from the bookstore shelves, which is what books do.

For most of the next year, I tried, and failed, to convince a New York editor to bring out a paperback edition. I proposed what seemed to me a foolproof idea. Take advantage of a long-running television sitcom by changing the name of the book to *Pro Football's Happy Days*, and invite actor Henry Winkler to write a foreword under his *nom de tube*, The Fonz.

The editor believed, quite wrongly as it turned out, that the book was dated. "It's too late," he kept telling me, "the fifties boom has peaked. It's over."

That view ran contrary to what has become Yogi's Law. A 1950s icon if there ever was one, although Yogi Berra easily could have had that decade in mind when he issued his famous proclamation: "It isn't over until it's over." In fact, we still were recycling the songs and the fashions of the '50s as the planet plunged into the 1990s.

Rock and roll will never die.

As the years rushed by, copies of *The Golden Age* were nearly impossible to find. People checked them out of libraries and never brought them back. From his office in Los Angeles, to my home in Houston, John Wiebusch and I regularly consoled each other, cursing the literary darkness.

John has his own credits as a writer, meaning that he brings to his role of editor a certain level of understanding. He cares about other writers as one would the lost children of the Third World.

When he encountered another fan of the book in Jim Donovan, of Taylor Publishing, *The Golden Age of Pro Football* was assured a revival, at last. In thanking John, and David Boss, for their commitment, I thank them as well for their friendship and the freedom they gave me to write what I thought and felt.

There is a risk that these sentiments will come off as self-serving. So be it. The intent was to demonstrate the loyalty not only to the words, but the deeds, of the great players and great teams of those years.

No one really can explain why there was, and is, such a longing for the 1950s, that decade of American graffiti. The American dreamhouse, three bedrooms, one-and-a-half baths, and a fireplace, sold for $15,000. We went to war to save South Korea from the Commies. We would mourn the passing of the big bands, train travel, and hand-cranked ice cream freezers.

But let's face it. Not everyone danced to Guy Lombardo, and the sandwiches they sold in day-coach would choke a great white shark. Do you ever wish that nostalgia would go back where it came from?

Not if you're a pro football fan, you don't.

Rereading these pages, one is struck by how long the list has grown of "absent friends," in Red Smith's phrase. Sadly, Red is one of those who is no longer around.

They were both subjects and sources when this book first appeared in the mid-1970s: George Halas, Bobby Layne, Buddy Parker, Bob Waterfield, Norm Van Brocklin, Alan Ameche, Gino Marchetti, Art Rooney, Carroll Rosenbloom, Buddy Young. It is like walking through a churchyard, picking out the names of friends on tombstones.

It may or may not have been easier to write about the figures of that time. The sports pages have long since ceased to be about fun and games. Today they tell stories about people who seem stranger than other people because they have no privacy.

For example, this about George Halas, from a piece I wrote a year or so before his death:

"A Chicago writer was talking one day about George Halas, as Chicago writers often do when they are not talking about Mayor Daley or Al Capone or Mrs. O'Leary's cow.

"I have always gotten along well with Halas,' the writer was saying proudly. 'He has never been uncivil to me.'

"To what did he owe this astonishing relationship?"

"Mostly,' he said, 'to the fact that I cover baseball. I've had no reason to criticize him. But I wouldn't have anyway. How can you criticize someone who has done what Halas has done for pro football?'"

We have just about covered over the last traces of the 1950s, not to anyone's surprise. When we left that decade, Pete Rozelle was about to succeed Bert Bell as commissioner of the National Football League, and Tom Landry was preparing to begin his career as coach of the Dallas Cowboys.

In 1989, Rozelle retired after guiding the league to new peaks of prosperity, and Landry became the first coach the Cowboys ever fired. Someone may put his fist through a coffin and surprise us, but as nearly as we can tell no one remains today in the same position he held in 1959.

The free-wheeling nature of this prologue allows us to remedy an omission from the hardcover copy of *Golden Age*. Well, perhaps not so much an omission—the point, after all, was to focus on the teams that made the decade glitter. But some mention begs to be made of a franchise that in defeat symbolized the vitality of the game.

Not everyone will remember the 1952 Dallas Texans, which isn't entirely a bad thing. The Texans left barely a footprint on the sands of pro football. They were formerly the New York Yankees, based in Boston before that, and owned by Ted Collins, the manager of singer Kate Smith. The team nearly bankrupted Collins.

Larger crowds turned out to hear Kate Smith sing "God Bless America."

The league moved the franchise to Dallas, and changed its name to the Texans. The new owners were the Miller brothers, Giles and Connell, heirs to a textile fortune. They were men of the cloth, so to speak, but they were quite unprepared to lose their shirts. At midseason they gave back the franchise, and the club finished on the road.

As a future prospect for pro football, Dallas seemed a dead issue. In January, 1953, Al Ennis, who had been dispatched from the home office of Commissioner Bert Bell to help organize the staff, wrote a sad, bitter letter to the club's executive secretary, Marilyn Cunningham:

Buddy Young

"It is almost certain that Baltimore will receive the franchise so nonchalantly thrown overboard by the Texas millionaires. They have already sold over 15,000 season tickets and are still going strong...This is the sort of civic interest which all of us in the league confidently expected Dallas to exhibit—but we were wrong.

"It will be a long time, if ever, before anyone outside of Texas will believe that any group of Texans would not quit COLD if the going got rough."

The Texans were not a team bereft of talent. They had Claude (Buddy) Young, an exciting little runner, and future Hall of Fame selections in Gino Marchetti at end, and Art Donovan at tackle. Plus a few tough, willing pros such as Dick Hoerner and Tom Keane, part of a carload of 11 players obtained from the Rams in a sensational trade for rookie linebacker Les Richter. But the Texans were a team in between.

The publicity man was Hamilton B. (Tex) Maule, who had quit a similar job with the Rams, the defending world champions. "I was convinced the Texans couldn't miss," Maule said. "I was hired by Frank Fitzgerald, Ted Collins's son-in-law. When I got to Dallas, I asked for Fitzgerald. He had been fired the day before. I was off to a great start."

Later, Maule would become the pro football authority for *Sports Illustrated*.

Ominous signs were present in training camp—an uncertain coaching staff, a team composed of strangers, and a city that hadn't really asked for this blessing and wasn't ready for it or attuned to it. Whatever else went wrong, the Texans at least struck a quiet blow for social justice. "There was talk of segregated seating at the Cotton Bowl," Buddy Young said, "but the Texans knocked out Jim Crow. I think that was a breakthrough."

For the final five weeks of the season, the team was based in Hershey, Pennsylvania, the league adopting the attitude that everyone has to be someplace. This was an exercise in running out the clock. Most of their practice time was spent playing volleyball over the goal posts.

The Texans were a mixed collection of styles and temper. "We had some characters," Young recalled. "[Forrest] Chubby Grigg, we got him in the Weldon Humble trade. Chub was mean as a snake, fat as a hog, on the downside of his pro career. His whole disposition was mean."

Once, when Young tried to break up a fight, Grigg picked him up and threw him into a phonograph, around which the team would gather and listen to Kay Starr sing "Wheel of Fortune" night after night. "We sure hated to lose that record player," Art Donovan said.

Young remembered the starting quarterback, Bob Celeri, as "almost uncoachable. He was the first guy I knew to do his own thing and he was doing it in 1952. He liked to throw on situations like fourth-and-twenty."

Art Donovan

The purest character of all, the one around whom the deeds of the season unwound like a fire hose, was the head coach, Jimmy Phelan, a handsome, whimsical Irishman.

"We had a good time in spite of everything," Donovan insisted, "mostly because of Phelan. He had a great line of bull. It was a picnic just being around him. One day we were working out at a field near the Rose Bowl, getting ready for the Rams, and we ran off a couple of plays without fouling up. Phelan stopped practice, loaded everybody on a bus, and took us to the racetrack. Jimmy loved the races."

Donovan was out of Holy Cross, in his third year as a pro and on his way to greatness with Baltimore teams still to come. He was Phelan's favorite, and, in the sight of his coach, in the midst of a season where little went right, he could do no wrong. "Phelan went to Mass every morning," Donovan said. "I'd be dragging in around six o'clock and he'd be waiting for me with a cab to take me to church.

"He cared about the game. If he thought you were laying down, he wouldn't stand for it. But football had passed him by. He was the only coach I ever knew who hated practices more than the players did."

The Texans made their Dallas debut on September 28, 1952, against the New York Giants in the Cotton Bowl. A gathering of 17,000—it was to be their largest home crowd—turned out to see the return of SMU heroes Kyle Rote and Fred Benners. The Giants won 24-6, and the Texans' only touchdown was set up on a punt fumbled by New York's return man, Tom Landry.

The team's only win, 27-23 over the Bears, came after the Texans had tapped out in Dallas. That was the game played in Akron before a crowd of around 3,000, in which Phelan suggested in his pregame pep talk that in lieu of the usual introductions, the players go into the stands "and shake hands with each fan." It must have loosened them up, or something, because they played the hell out of the Bears. "George Halas nearly croaked," Donovan said. In no other game that season did the Texans come within 17 points of a tie.

The week of what turned out to be their last game in Dallas, the Texans picked up Frank Tripucka, the former Notre Dame quarterback, from the Cardinals. When it was announced that Tripucka would start that Sunday against the Rams, Maxwell Stiles, a Los Angeles columnist, asked Maule how he could be ready on such scant practice time.

Maule, who was not your typical press agent, sighed heavily. "Well, hell," he said, "it only took Phelan thirty minutes to give him the offense, and it wouldn't have taken that long except Jimmy went over it twice."

The game was played in a blinding rainstorm. From the press box it was impossible to see any fans at all. Those who did attend had taken shelter under the overhang of the stadium roof. The Texans tried, but the Rams outgunned them 27-6.

So the adventure in Dallas ended, almost unobserved, on a day without sunshine. The day the franchise folded, Phelan canceled practice so the players could race to the bank before their paychecks bounced.

The Texans, pro football's Lost Battalion, went on to become the Baltimore Colts. When Lamar Hunt founded the American Football League in 1960, and purchased the franchise in Dallas, he renamed the team the Texans. After three years he moved them to Kansas City, where they became the Chiefs.

The publicity job that Tex Maule vacated in Los Angeles was filled by Pete Rozelle. In their wake, the original Dallas Texans left ripples that spread all through the 1950s...and far beyond.

1

Shake, Rattle, and Remember

It is remarkable how much of the 1950s stayed with us, like tar you picked up on the bottom of your feet at the beach. No matter how you rub and scrape you can't get it off and, after a time, you no longer *want* to get it off.

Once, late in the decade, a reporter for one of those awful fan magazines asked a dancer on *American Bandstand*, a bobby soxer, one of the regulars, about her plans for the future.

"We Bandstand kids have a crazy dream," she said, then hesitated. "It's a baby idea. Maybe I better not say."

"Oh, tell her," the cry went up.

"Well, what it is we all want is to get married and live on the same street in new houses. We'll call it...Bandstand Avenue."

Now that's, well, *sweet*. You will see that it isn't much different, as a vision, from the sentiment of a fellow named Robert Lawrence Layne. Years later, looking back on the 1950s, and looking back on his game, which was pro football, a kind of American Bandstand for reluctant adults, Layne said:

"I'll tell you what I really miss. What I miss is the guys. That's what I miss more than anything. I miss going to training camp. I miss the road trips and the card games. I miss the fellowship. The locker room, the places where it was a pleasure to be. The practice sessions. I miss the bar where we'd go for a beer after practice. I miss having that beer with the guys. I miss the ball games. I mean, when you've got a whole team looking forward to everything, when you've got guys showing up for practice early and staying late—well, you've got something there. We had that perfect thing for a while. What I miss now is my teammates."

Don't you *see* it? Don't you *feel* it? Bobby Layne and the Detroit Lions...no, Bobby Layne and every blessed fellow who played pro football in the fifties...all living in new houses, on the same street, and they call it Touchdown Avenue...

That outrageous suggestion, of course, evokes the very spirit of a decade that still again in the 1990s...if not in reality, in our fashions, our coffee shops, and in our imaginations, which is one of the best places.

Hula hoops and bomb shelters and 3-D; Elvis and Marilyn and Edward R. Murrow; "I Like Ike" and chlorophyll and McCarthyism; penny loafers and rock 'n' roll and the $64,000 Question; white sport coats and pink carnations; suburbia and Bridey Murphy; Big Daddy and the Dallas Texans and the Alley-Oop pass.

Of course, nostalgia is the art of remembering the things we *want* to remember, a kind of highlights film with the penalties and fumbles all left out. Not everyone remembers the fifties that way. To some, under Ike, America simply went to sleep for eight years. We still had our sexual guilt, social injustice, a cold war, and a Red-under-every-bed mentality. No nostalgia there, buster.

But the simple truth is this: In the first year of the middle decade of the 20th Century, life was getting sweeter and softer for more Americans. Personal income was rising. The country babbled about full employment. Factory workers were making it. The idea of women holding jobs had grown more acceptable, and a man did not have to feel himself a failure if he allowed his wife to work.

American families fled to the suburbs, to a new kind of existence built around power mowers and barbecue pits and patios and cocktail parties. The boom was on: in new cars and television sets and, of course, babies. *La Dolce Vita*—the good life—came into the vernacular in the fifties.

All of these factors, but notably television and the new leisure, conspired to renew a sport that by the end of the decade would be on its way to becoming the new national obsession. Professional football not only reflected the times, but benefitted mightily from them. It was the only sport, we can see now, that kept changing for the better through those years.

There was one other circumstance that overlaid the era and gave it texture. The generation that came to young adulthood in the 1950s was the generation that learned to live with The Bomb. We learned to live with it so well, of course, that football appropriated the phrase, and the long touchdown pass—the game's most picturesque play—became The Bomb.

In the early fifties, suburban real estate ads emphasized the fact that a particular piece of property was "out of the radiation zone."

What with a continuing drum roll of military, political, and scientific debate over A-bombs, H-bombs, and radioactivity, the apocalypse didn't seem so far away. All of which helped encourage the impression that America in the fifties was celebrating the so-called Test Pilot Syndrome ("eat, drink, and be merry, for tomorrow...").

That was part of it, part of the romance, the reaching for new games and thrills and heroes. There had to be some serious rationale. I mean, the decade wasn't all *"Howdy Doody Time"* and watching Annette Funicello's sweater filling out.

In 1950, we began to disconnect ourselves from the past, from grandpa's America, a development at least suggested by a list of some of the prominent obituaries of that year: Al Jolson, Edgar Rice Burroughs, who created Tarzan; Frank (Bring 'em Back Alive) Buck; Kate CrossEyes, widow of the Apache chief Geronimo, and Mrs. Mabel Young Sanborn, last surviving child (among 56) of the Mormon leader Brigham Young.

The poetess Edna St. Vincent Millay also died in 1950—it was not a bad year to die, but a better one to be born. She left behind a collection of memorable verse, including these lines:

"...I cannot say what loves have come and gone, I only know that summer sang in me a little while, that in me sings no more."

She might have been writing about the fifties. She wasn't, of course, but let's pretend we don't know that. For those years do indeed remain fixed in the chamber of our mind, a summer song, reminding us of our swinging youth when, yes, we had all the answers.

And pro football fits into this, a chorus of that summer song. You'll have to trust us on that, for a while. It will all become clear as you see it join, how the years and the game and the people interlock. As much as any decade has ever been, the fifties were all of a piece, as perfectly formed as a gold wedding band.

But it wasn't stuffy. Some of it was the kind of lunatic doings that you knew, at the time, no one would believe 20 years later.

For example, with the possible exception of Communism, do you realize that the biggest threat to national morality in the fifties was Elvis Presley? Right. Elvis.

It was a national scandal when the ex-truck driver wiggled, bumped, and gyrated his way through "Heartbreak Hotel" and "Blue Suede Shoes" in a voice that quivered as if it were suffering from an electrical short.

When Ed Sullivan signed Presley for three network appearances—after first insisting he was unfit for a family audience—he tried to protect America's virtue by refusing to allow his cameras to show Elvis from the waist down. Even so, Sullivan was criticized by a righteous public.

Good looking, soon to be rich, adored by ladies of all ages, Elvis was not a young man a father could easily like. But he was soft spoken, polite, and disarmingly honest. When asked if he intended to marry, Elvis answered, "Why buy a cow when you can get milk through the fence?"

If we read Elvis correctly, this would mean that, contrary to popular belief, Joe Namath did not discover sex in the sixties. Now it might be noted that the fifties people were not necessarily more open, or more honest, in what they did (although they could afford to be, because the communications art was not yet as sweeping or as demanding). But, somehow, the trespasses of the time did not come across as *hard-core*.

Then, as now, pro football players knew how to have a good time, but their efforts so often ended like some kind of Tom and Jerry cartoon.

There was the summer the Los Angeles Rams played a preseason game in Little Rock, and the players found a party, a live one, in progress in a downtown apartment building after the game. One player called back to the hotel, to a buddy, but, on orders, the switchboard operator hooked the call into head coach Joe Stydahar's room.

"Hey, Mac," the exuberant player said, "get your ass over here...Everybody's here...greatest party of the year."

"No, you get *your* ass over here," thundered Stydahar, "and that goes for the rest of the team." Instantly, the player sensed that something had gone wrong.

On the plane home the next day, Stydahar gathered the press around him in the curved bench seat in the tail and announced he was fining every player on the squad $500 for breaking curfew. Bob Oates of the *Los Angeles Examiner* quickly calculated the fine times 35 players and said, "Joe, do you realize you've fined the team $17,500?" Stydahar pointed at Oates and said, "*That's* off the record!"

There was a casualness about the era that extended even to the mayhem they visited upon each other. The symbol of the fifties was not the soaring touchdown pass or the broken-field run or the field goal in the gloaming, but two guys down in the bloody pits with clenched fists. So routinely ferocious was the action at the line of scrimmage, one writer was moved to observe: "Pro football is getting like atomic war. There are no winners. Only survivors."

One of the survivors was Tex Coulter, out of West Point, that rare article—an offensive lineman who dealt out punishment. As an offensive guard and tackle for the New York Giants, Coulter, who sometimes played defense on an important series, earned a reputation for toughness that the Gestapo would have envied. Rams linebacker Don Paul always could tell which lineman would be playing opposite Coulter simply by picking out the one holding his head in his hands before the game, dreading the kickoff.

Once, when a last-minute lineup switch moved Oklahoman Stan West across the

So routinely ferocious was the action at the line of scrimmage, one writer was moved to observe: "Pro football is getting like atomic war. There are no winners. Only survivors."

13

Tex Coulter

line from Coulter, West caught Paul looking at him in the Rams' locker room. "Well," he roared, "I'm not going to let the big blankety-blank intimidate me."

On the first play of the game, West hauled off and hit Coulter in the face. Paul said he could hear Coulter's deep, bass voice: "THAT'S THE WAY IT'S GOING TO BE, HUH, OKIE?"

On second down, a sweep to the other side of the field, Don Paul heard a weird, terrifying, keening scream. He looked around and there was West, holding his mouth. Coulter's hard shot had knocked Stan West's teeth through his upper lip.

Paul rushed over to his stricken teammate. Blood drenched his jersey. "The Rams had a rule that the defense could never call time out, and there wasn't any officials' time out for injury unless you'd used up all your time outs," Paul related. "So I pulled West's lip loose from his teeth and told him, 'Hold it right there, Stan, and if we stop 'em this down you can get to the sidelines.'"

It is important to understand that there was nothing really personal about such encounters. The linemen of the day, most of them, considered it their job to hurt each other and often they did so in the friendliest spirit.

Coulter was an orphan, a product of the Masonic Boys Home in Fort Worth, Texas. That may have been the only orphanage in America to produce two professional football players in the same decade. The other was Hardy Brown, of the San Francisco 49ers, who is one of the bona fide legends of the National Football League.

Hardy Brown hasn't made the Pro Football Hall of Fame, but teammate Y. A. Tittle called him, "Pound for pound, inch for inch, the toughest football player I ever met...he was so tough he was damn near illegal." He was no classic specimen at 6 feet and 180 pounds, and he compensated for his size by being slow. Yet from 1951 through 1955 Hardy Brown was the scourge of pro football.

Whatever the demons that propelled him, whatever inner frenzy it was that gave him his strength, Brown wrecked people and teams. One day in 1951 he knocked out the entire starting backfield of the Washington Redskins, leaving only quarterback Harry Gilmer in one piece. He laid them out stiff with shoulder tackles, hitting high, in the face if he could manage it. He kept the stretcher bearers busy.

That same year he hit the Rams' Glenn Davis coming through the line, met him so hard, head-on, that ligaments were torn in Davis's knees. Now that is the kind of result you expect to get if you club a fellow on top of the head with one of those circus sledge hammers, the kind they use on the test-your-strength machine. Davis, Army's famed Mr. Outside, was never the same again and shortly thereafter quit. Davis had dated Elizabeth Taylor and married actress Terry Moore, and his departure was a loss to the league's prestige.

Brown's techniques were uniquely his own. He never used his arms to tackle. He hunched down in a crouch like a panther about to spring, and when the runner got close he would drive his shoulder up toward the ball carrier's head. He hit Pittsburgh's Joe Geri so hard that one of Geri's eyes popped out and literally was hanging on his cheek. The incident took place in Kezar Stadium, in 1951, and did nothing to increase Brown's popularity or diminish his legend.

Rival clubs often sent a representative to the 49ers' dressing room before the game to check Brown's shoulder pads. They suspected that he reinforced them with sheet metal (an echo of stories that had circulated about the immortal Jim Thorpe). In the 1951 season alone, Brown kayoed 21 opposing players, surely a league record, if only such interesting categories were tabulated. The 49ers' head coach, Buck Shaw, would not allow Brown to take part in the team's scrimmages or practice games. Those were the days before everyone wore facemasks, and Shaw was unwilling to expose his own team to Brown's style.

Brown was ideal as a linebacker in the 49ers' 5-3 defense, filling holes in the line. But when the 4-3 came into vogue his effectiveness suffered. He couldn't make open-field tackles, because he never used his arms. Tittle, his roommate, tried to save his job in a training camp game in 1956, by which time Frankie Albert had taken over as coach. Tittle tipped him to the plays with hand signals as he broke out of the huddle. Even after Albert put in Earl Morrall, Tittle knelt on the sidelines by his coach, who was sending in plays, and kept signalling Brown. But then Albert had the teams switch ends of the field, and Brown got confused about right and left in Y. A.'s signals.

Brown ran the wrong way on a series of downs, and Albert pulled him. That afternoon he was cut, a sad, swift ending for a fellow who had terrorized the league.

Having made reference to broken lips and missing teeth and a dangling eyeball, it might seem a bit incongruous to speak now of fun. But the fifties were. Everybody says so, especially those who look back on them from the perspective of the 1990s.

It was a decade when people began to take life—and each other—a little less seriously. A new irreverence crept into our national humor. Cartoonist Jules Feiffer invented the sick joke. Mort Sahl poked fun at the growing Red menace: "Maybe the Russians will steal all our secrets. Then they'll be two years behind."

And a young satirist named Mike Nichols spoofed all the pretentious southern writing of the day with one wicked line about an imaginary heroine: "She has taken to drink, dope, prostitution—and puttin' on airs."

By 1953, our lives had been invaded by something called chlorophyll, a plant extract credited with promoting freshness. It turned up in our chewing gum, toothpaste, deodorants, cough drops, and dog food.

"You had it in everything," Bobby Layne remembered. "It was chlorophyll this and chlorophyll that. So we had a slogan that year: 'Chlorophyll will put more sock in your jock.' We went on to beat Cleveland in the championship game, and all our wives sat up there in the stands, wearing hats that they'd made from jock straps dyed green."

At this point perhaps a distinction should be made. We celebrate the fifties as a turning point. We do not mourn it as the passing of a way of life. Somehow it all came together, the explosion of pro football against a backdrop of social and political quiet. We had problems, but we didn't want to know about them, and television had not yet been handed the keys to all our living rooms. Beyond that, there was something paternal and uncomplicated about Eisenhower that inspired calm. The country was ready, they said, for a president who didn't interfere in the affairs of government.

Pop psychologists have had a field day with this yearning for the fifties, this flight to a sunnier time. Some see it as a bridge across the generation gap, a backdoor way for fathers and sons to rediscover each other. Others see it as a rejection of the misspent energy and burned-out hopes of the 1960s.

Of course, the answer may be simpler than that. We are a nation of round numbers and cycles and gross public sentimentality. We cry over empty gum wrappers. Few of us can resist a headline in small print that says, "Ten Years Ago Today"...or 20, or 50. If one must rummage around in the attic of the past, the 1950s were

Teammate Y.A. Tittle called Hardy Brown, "Pound for pound, inch for inch, the toughest football player I ever met...he was so tough he was damn near illegal."

Chuck Bednarik

simply splendid years to do so. Colorful. Wacky. Secure. There was no tendency, as there is today, to analyze things to death. We sensed that not everything was meant to be understood.

Out of these times, and this attitude, grew a movement known as the Beat Generation...beatniks...the hippies of the fifties. One of their prophets was Jack Kerouac, whose book *On the Road* became their Bible. "We love everything," Kerouac said. "Billy Graham, the Big Ten, rock and roll, Zen, apple pie, Eisenhower—we dig it all. We're in the vanguard of the new religion."

That new-time religion spilled over into the world of the National Football League in the fifties. They were years of evangelism, of glamour, of prosperity for a game that had begun in the 1920s, a game played largely by vagrant athletes on dirt fields on the tough side of town. The fifties were a bridge between the years when the sport would be watched by few, and when it would be watched by multi-millions who would rearrange their lives—their weddings, funerals, Bar Mitzvah receptions—around the home team schedule.

There is a temptation to think of the period as the Golden Age of Professional Football, for approximately the same reasons that Paul Gallico anointed the twenties, his decade, as the golden age of sport. In a best selling book, *Farewell to Sport*, Gallico rhapsodized over the feats of Ruth, Grange, Dempsey, Jones, Tilden, and Gertrude Ederle. "What a world!" he gurgled. "What heroes and heroines!"

A similar spirit attaches to professional football in the fifties. What heroes! What characters! Mostly, the attraction was in the quality of football that was played, and in the unreconstructed men who played it. It was, in a sense, the last pure football, played in only 12 cities by a select few who endured not so much for the money—$20,000 salaries were the exception, $6,000 salaries were the rule—as for that most romantic of reasons: love of the game.

It was a prime example, we suspect, of something else the 1950s reflected: *la innocenta vita*. The innocent life.

On many teams, an almost familial feeling existed. The skirmishes for more money often were reduced to upmanship, a test of wit and nerve, rather than the oppressed workers-versus-capitalist wolves mood of today. Tex Schramm, who later would build a model organization in Dallas, was publicity man and acting general manager of the Rams in the first half of the fifties. "The game was important then," Schramm said. "For everyone. The players. The coaches. The owners. It's not that way anymore...."

As late as 1955, the Los Angeles Rams employed a coaching staff of four. Head man Sid Gillman was paid $22,000 that year, his first in the NFL. Norm Van Brocklin, the quarterback, was the team's highest paid player at $19,000. Don Paul, the punishing linebacker, earned $8,500.

It seems unthinkable now, but most assistant coaches in the early fifties still worked part-time. That is, they required other jobs in the offseason to support themselves. Tom Landry, beginning a career in New York coaching defensive backs, sold insurance in Dallas.

A spirit of give and take existed between players and ownership that, for better or for worse, will never be quite the same again. It was a time of mutual sacrifice. Huge corporate profits and dazzling rookie bonuses were in the future. In a way that now seems hopelessly outdated and even naive, the players and owners did not regard the sport as an investment. They *cared*.

In Detroit, it was the proud boast of Bobby Layne that he never took longer than

30 minutes to sign a contract. The general manager of the Lions, Nick Kerbawy, "treated us right. He put us up at first-class hotels. When we'd go to the West Coast on a two-game trip, the club would slip us a hundred or two hundred dollars for spending money."

Keep in mind that this was in an era when the size of a team's monthly phone bill might determine whether or not it broke even.

As one of the league's high-salaried stars ($20,000 and change), Layne attracted a reputation for free spending that he consciously supported. "For one thing, I was making more money than anybody else on the club. So I always allocated a certain part of my salary to spend on the players. I called it play money. I mean, I didn't try to pick up every tab, but I tried to pick up more than my share.

"I tipped good when I got good service. When I didn't get good service I didn't tip. I never owned a Cadillac. I never owned a boat. I never had a diamond ring in my life and never wore any rings or stickpins or crap like that. I don't think I dressed fancy. But I did carry around a little spending money."

It was, of course, a different lifestyle that the players pursued, and a different code by which they existed. The evidence suggests that no decade produced more of the very special people: Half of the 16 players on pro football's all-time team played major portions of their careers in the fifties: Jim Brown, Elroy Hirsch, Chuck Bednarik, Gino Marchetti, Leo Nomellini, Night Train Lane, Em Tunnell, and Lou Groza. Three others began their careers during the period: Jerry Kramer, Ray Nitschke, and the most famous graduate of the Bloomfield Rams, Johnny Unitas.

If any single characteristic could be said to represent the fifties, it would be this: there was no conformity. No two boxes alike. They were superbly gifted, like Jim Brown, and joyfully physical, like Chuck Bednarik, and wonderfully dedicated, like Raymond Berry, the frail Baltimore end who took a bride between seasons. When a teammate, fullback Billy Pricer, asked if Sally could cook, Berry hesitated. "I don't know," he said, "but she can run a film projector."

It was a decade in which science came to the sport, and many of the concepts of the new modern era were conceived and refined. The glamour that previously had been reserved only for the college game began to reverse itself. "The postwar years," Schramm said, "had ended the prewar stigma of a college player going into the pros. And in the 1950s, being a pro football player was something.

"We weren't reaping much money but we were gaining exposure. Everyone started doing things professionally. Instead of using *Street and Smith* and a phone call to scout players, clubs began establishing scouting departments."

But the computer age was a long way from taking command. The human element still prevailed. There was still time, and room, for the makeshift, the spur-of-the-moment, the splendidly unrehearsed.

And that's how the Alley-Oop pass was born.

The Alley-Oop was the feature of the 1957 season, when Tittle was voted player of the year in the NFL. This is the story of how it came to happen:

It begins with R. C. Owens, 6 foot 3 inches and 200 pounds, out of Idaho, a reformed basketball player. The 49ers had been upset in their season opener by the Chicago Cardinals 20-10 and had to face Los Angeles in the second game. Having bombed against an inferior team (the Cardinals), the 49ers were not enthused about their chances against the talented Rams, and the week's practices were flat and sloppy. Receivers dropped the ball. Linemen swarmed upon Tittle before he

Raymond Berry took a bride between seasons. When a teammate asked if Sally could cook, Berry hesitated. "I don't know...but she can run a film projector."

Big Daddy Lipscomb

could throw. Finally, late in the afternoon, as he was again about to be trapped, Tittle flung the ball high into the air, in sheer disgust.

It went up and up and seemed to hang there, before floating down gently to Owens, who leaped up and grabbed the ball while three defensive backs just stared. End coach Red Hickey yelled: "Hey, there's our Alley-Oop play." For the rest of the week Tittle and Owens worked on the maneuver after practice. The newspapers were full of it, but the Rams thought it was a gimmick and ignored the playful press reports.

The 49ers thought it was great fun. It made their practices lively, snapping them out of their defeatism. Leading the Rams 9-7 near the end of the first half, Tittle threw from the Rams' 46, a high, arching shot to the goal line. Owens outjumped Don (The Blade) Burroughs for the touchdown, and Kezar Stadium vibrated with cries of "Alley-Oop!" (The actual origin of the phrase is vaudeville, where acrobats would cry out "Allez-Oop" before a catapult stunt.)

The Rams recovered their composure, rallied, and went ahead 20-16 with three minutes left. The 49ers had their last chance. Hugh McElhenny and J. D. Smith broke long runs to move to the 11-yard line, and, on second down, Tittle winked at his breathless teammates and announced in the huddle, "We'll go for the Alley-Oop."

Y.A. described the play:

"R. C. jogged into the end zone and stood next to Jesse Castete, the Rams' defensive halfback. I dropped back, waited for a count of two, and then heaved the ball almost straight up in the air. It must have looked funny from the stands. Both teams were just standing there, waiting for the damned thing to come down. Nobody was moving. Owens didn't even appear concerned. But just at the right instant he went up that invisible ladder of his. Castete jumped with him and there must have been two other guys on his back, but they didn't get high enough. R. C. came down with the ball and we had a twenty-three to twenty win."

Later in the season, one of the officials, during a game against Green Bay said, "Hey, Y. A., when are you going to throw one of those big Alley-Oops? I never have seen the thing."

The obliging Tittle said, "How about the next play?" Whereupon he called it. This time Owens batted the ball out of reach of two Packers, caught it on the rebound and fell over the goal line, making the final score 24-14.

There was a casualness, a looseness, about the era that encouraged free enterprise. In 1950, in Los Angeles, a thief walked up to the cashier at a movie house, poked a pistol through the window and said to the girl inside, "I didn't like the movie. Give me everybody's money back." He walked off with $212.

In Dansville, New York, a classified ad appeared in the local newspaper: "WANTED—Farmer, age 38, wishes to meet woman around 30 who owns a tractor. Please enclose picture of tractor."

No one typified this sense of adventure more than Bobby Layne, the blond prodigal from Texas. Layne delighted in making up little trick plays, and he saved a beauty for the New York Giants, one he was confident would work against the defense they liked to use. He called it the "wait-a-minute" play.

As he bent over the center, halfback Tom Tracy suddenly shouted, "Wait a minute." Without moving from his crouch, Bobby looked around.

"What's the matter?" he called.

On the word "matter," the center snapped the ball directly to John Henry

Johnson, who fled for a touchdown. Unfortunately, an official, faked out of the play, called them offsides.

But the fifties were not all candy for our soul. Integration was a new, uneasy word. It was happening, but it required patience and courage and the answers were never quick or simple. After the war, Cleveland's great Marion Motley and Bill Willis were two of the first four blacks to come into pro football, simultaneously, with Kenny Washington and Woody Strode, at Los Angeles, in 1946.

They were the first blacks to enter the league since 1933. Given the temper of the times, pro football had four Jackie Robinsons. Washington, who had been Jackie's college running mate at UCLA, played only three years. Strode lasted just one, and became an accomplished character actor in Hollywood.

The steps taken to erase the traces of the color line were small ones, and slow. But they also were the hardest and the most meaningful, because they were the first. On the Cleveland Browns, head coach Paul Brown had a rule. Whenever a rookie from the South reported, he had to first look up Marion Motley and Bill Willis, introduce himself and shake hands. It broke the ice, and it worked.

One of the most identifiable names of the fifties—colorful, popular, and tragic—was black. Whites as well as blacks mourned in 1963 at the death of Eugene (Big Daddy) Lipscomb, who died in circumstances much less attractive than those he usually traveled.

The name was part of his appeal. He sounded like a character out of a Tennessee Williams play. But he was a proud, complicated giant of a man, 6 feet, 6 inches and 285 pounds. Once, wrestling in the offseason, he went on a crash diet when his weight climbed to an even 300. "I don't want to look sloppy in my tights," he explained. People were constantly asking him if his wrestling matches were fixed. "All I know is," he said, "I just do the best I can and nobody has yet told me whether I should win or lose. I don't know about the other guys. I don't ask, either."

He quit wrestling when the promoters suggested he switch from the good-guy image to the bad-guy role. "That ain't Big Daddy," he said. His friend, John Unitas, believed that he couldn't see himself facing the kids if he had to be a villain in the ring. He cared, honestly cared, in the way that only a fellow who grew up an orphan can appreciate, about the way kids looked at him.

He never knew who his father was and he lived his early years with his mother in a furnished room in Detroit. One night, when he was 11, a policeman came to the room and told him that his mother was dead. She had been stabbed 47 times, by a man she knew, while waiting at a bus stop. Eugene lived with his grandfather and worked to pay for his room and board. He worked as a dishwasher and, when he grew a little, he shoveled sand and gravel on a construction job. "There was a time," he told his teammates, "when I worked the midnight-to-eight shift in a steel mill and then went home and put on a clean shirt and went to school."

Lipscomb never went to college. After high school, in Detroit, he enlisted in the Marines and made his football reputation playing for the Camp Pendleton team. The Rams signed him as a free agent late in 1953, but he never established himself and, in 1956, they put him on waivers.

Baltimore claimed him for the $100 waiver price. Three times he went on to make all-pro for the Colts, and, with his size and sweeping defensive style, to capture the public's affection.

Ironically, Big Daddy was one of those people who lived in fear, the kind born of

One of the officials said, "Hey, Y.A., when are you going to throw one of those big Alley-Oops? I never have seen the thing." The obliging Tittle said, "How about the next play?"

19

Tex Schramm

a lifetime of insecurity. "I've been scared all my life," he told Unitas. "You wouldn't think it to look at me, but I have been."

The night he died, Unitas thought, was typical of the way he kept looking, and needing someone to be with all the time. He had been traded to the Steelers two years previously, in 1961, and he planned to drive to Pittsburgh the next morning to sign a new contract, for a reported two years at $15,000 per year. He had played in a softball game that night—it was early in May—and after the game he went partying with another fellow and two girls.

At around 3 A.M. they dropped off the girls in Big Daddy's yellow convertible, then drove down to what Baltimore called "The Block," which was where most of the late-night action was in those days. They wound up in a second-floor apartment on North Brice Street. His companion bought $12 worth of heroin for them, according to what he told police, and Big Daddy began to froth at the mouth moments after he took it. He keeled over on the kitchen floor. The police were called. An ambulance came and took him away. He died in minutes. He was dead when they got to the hospital.

Unitas called it a particularly sad and useless way to die. "I've never been convinced," he said, "that Big Daddy took heroin willingly. For one thing, he was right-handed all the way, yet the needle marks were on his right arm. For another he was like Jim Parker. They hated needles like poison. We'd have to back him into a corner to get him to take a tetanus shot."

Thousands attended Big Daddy's funeral, including all three of his former wives. Of one of them, he had said: "I don't mind losing her so much, but I sure minded losing my 1956 Mercury to her. I loved that car. It was the best car I ever owned."

The poignant story of Big Daddy Lipscomb was part of the fabric, too, part of the bittersweet search for what?—for more? for something? for anything?—that kept pulling so many fifties children.

James Dean played a troubled teenager in a movie called *Rebel Without a Cause*, and when he died in his car at dusk, on an open road in California in 1955, he became the spiritual leader of a new generation of young men who were not meant to be understood. Boys who, as John Dos Passos put it, stood before the mirrors in the restroom looking at themselves and seeing James Dean.

Still, there was a freedom in the 1950s, a freedom to try, to fail, risk and take it. We were not yet, not by a long shot, a nation of drawing room spectators.

Which brings us to television, whose influence—in our lives and on professional football—has been almost beyond computing. "It was the decade everybody became watchers instead of doers," was the way Tex Schramm put it. "Television meant the end of minor league everything. Not just minor league baseball. Minor league entertainment was out. People couldn't put together a stage show with one big name and no other talent and expect to draw people to the theater. They were seeing the best in entertainment every night right in their living rooms. It was the end of regionalism. Everyone started thinking on a national scale."

Schramm was one of the pro football people, early on, to see the ultimate power of television, and the wisdom of the policies created by Bert Bell and distilled by Pete Rozelle. Between tours with the Rams and Cowboys, Schramm watched it evolve as an executive with the Columbia Broadcasting System.

"In 1954," he said, "the Rams were paid $100,000 for the rights to their telecasts from CBS, which negotiated with each team individually. Four years later, when I was with CBS, I know that Green Bay got $5,000 at the insistence of Bert Bell.

"George Preston Marshall [of the Redskins] had the whole South in his network. He had no black players and, for the pregame ceremonies, he had the Redskins' band march down the field playing 'Dixie.' Marshall made more money off television in the early fifties than anybody else, even though he had a losing team."

The point is that, in an uneven and improvised way, pro football was going national. The speed with which it got there amazed even the game's most devout supporters. Its ticket to ride, of course, was television.

What you have to remember is that in 1950, only nine percent of the families in the United States owned television sets. But that year, a Los Angeles television station, network affiliated, bought the rights to carry the Rams' home games, guaranteeing to pay the club in cash for all empty seats *and* an amount equal to a five percent increase in attendance.

That year, with a winning team, the Rams' live attendance suffered a 50 percent drop. So significant was this piece of evidence that it led, several years later, to a decision by a federal judge approving the entire home blackout feature of the league's television contracts. It is the test case against which every threat to the NFL's television policy has been defended, and it turned out to be one of the most fortunate things that ever happened to pro football, involving as it did a championship team.

Another who sensed the potential of the 21-inch eye was the irrepressible George Halas, whose Chicago Bears appeared on the DuMont Network in 1951, live to 11 midwest stations. Boasted Halas: "More people have seen the Bears play this year than the first thirty years of our existence put together."

Halas lost money on his network arrangement that year. So eager was he to get his team on the air, he assumed the liability for all unsold time and line charges. This was not exactly in character for Halas, who had a reputation for throwing dollars around as though they were manhole covers.

But Halas was on to something. In 1952, he switched his games to ABC and cleared a profit of $4,468. Due largely to that connection, ABC became the National Football League network for the next three years. CBS won the contract in 1956.

Today the league's television contracts are somewhere off in the financial stratosphere. Team shares equal some countries' gross national products.

It took an incredible amount of timing, luck, vision, and perseverance to reach those kind of chips. But it was a case of the absolutely perfect game for the right medium at the exact moment when the nation was getting ready for it.

But pro football was no fad. It was a good product going on great. It is safe to say that it has outlasted hula hoops, droodles, panty raids, the Bunny Hop, and fallout shelters, and has held its own with rock 'n' roll.

Speaking of hula hoops, American kids were spinning 30 million of them in 1958. A year later, people were poking around in garages, trying to find one to complete their scavenger hunt lists.

The decade began with the war in Korea, and ended with the beginnings of one in a place called Vietnam. It began with Harry Truman. It rallied around a slogan, "I Like Ike." It produced both Richard Nixon and John Kennedy.

Another national hero was fired from his job, but came home to a tumultuous welcome. In April, 1951, General Douglas MacArthur addressed a joint meeting of the House and Senate. At the end of his speech, he said:

It is safe to say that pro football has outlasted hula hoops, droodles, panty raids, the Bunny Hop, and fallout shelters, and has held its own with rock 'n' roll.

Paul Brown

"Since I took the oath at West Point, the hopes and dreams of my youth have all vanished. But I still remember the refrain of one of the most popular barracks ballads of that day, which proclaimed most proudly that old soldiers never die, they just fade away.

"And, like the old soldier of the ballad, I now close my military career and just fade away, an old soldier who tried to do his duty as God gave him the light to see that duty."

Many of the players and coaches of the fifties had served in World War II. In the peak years of pro football's expansion, it became fashionable to compare the sport to war itself. No matter how one compares them, pro football is a better alternative.

The literature of the sport is filled with old soldiers who did their duty and, sometimes, faded away.

In the National Football League, the decade began with Sammy Baugh throwing his last passes, and marked the exit of pioneers such as Curly Lambeau and Steve Owen. It ended with the death of Bert Bell and the entrance of the men who would shape pro football in the sixties: Vince Lombardi, Pete Rozelle, Johnny Unitas.

And all across the fifties stretched the shadow of the most dominant team that sport has known, the Cleveland Browns, and the coach whose name they carried, Paul Brown. If any one man could be said to have left his imprint on the decade, it was Brown. He gave the league its standards of excellence. He showed them how to scout, how to organize, how to demand more than a player thinks he has to give.

He could inspire a team with one dryly sarcastic line. On the night the Browns, four-time champions of the belittled All-America Football Conference, were to make what some observers were calling their professional debut against the Philadelphia Eagles in 1950, Brown suddenly paused at the locker room door, stacking up his anxious team behind him. He turned and said in a clear, slow voice: "Just think. Tonight you're going to get to *touch* Steve Van Buren."

The Browns wrecked the Eagles and Van Buren, their star running back, 35-10.

Brown also could dismiss a player, an entire career, with one biting but ruthlessly correct observation. Sideline observers at one Cleveland camp were impressed with a young halfback who was receiving punts during a kicking drill. Brown's eyes never left the field. "He runs pretty good against air," he said. The young halfback wasn't around long.

It wasn't until late in the decade, of course, that pro football came to be thought of as a part of the American culture. If you could freeze any one moment and say this is when it happened, you probably would be looking at the 1958 championship game, and Baltimore's sudden-death win over the Giants—certainly the most important game ever played to that time.

It was two weeks later that Johnny Unitas realized he had it made. He had returned to New York to receive a Corvette on the "Pat Boone Show," over network television, as the game's most valuable player. Afterward, Unitas and his wife stopped for dinner at the Harwyn Club. And there, as a courtesy to the hot new celebrity, the head waiter led them to the corner table where Eddie Fisher and Liz Taylor had their last rendezvous, the night before Eddie flew home to Hollywood to tell Debbie Reynolds he wanted a divorce.

Now *that* was the 1950s.

What We Listened To

That is how we remember the stadiums of our youth, helmets glistening in the sun, shadows playing across the lush emerald sod, real grass, not some outsized bath mat.

One needn't tax the imagination to see, in the music of the decade, messages that could apply to the prevailing moods of pro football. "The Great Pretender" clearly referred to the Chicago Bears, who finished second four times. "So Rare" described how the Steelers felt about any winning season. And "Crazy Otto Rag" could only be a musical tribute to the Cleveland quarterback.

You could make whatever you wished of "It's All in the Game," or "I Can Dream, Can't I," or "Twilight Time," and most especially, Kay Starr's big number, "Wheel of Fortune."

There is no device that tells us more about ourselves, or the times, than the songs that filled our heads and our radios. It was George M. Cohan who said, "Other men can write the nation's laws, let me write her music." An army of composers wrote the music of the fifties, and if you get a sense of anything it is infinite variety.

It ranged from Liberace, whose piano solos and ever-present candelabra melted the hearts of middle-aged ladies, to Mitch Miller, the bearded guru of sing-along folk tunes to Harry Belafonte's erotic Calypso beat.

And, or course, there was Elvis, about whom no living American could be neutral. In Cincinnati, a used car dealer advertised this special: "WE GUARANTEE TO BREAK 50 ELVIS PRESLEY RECORDS IN YOUR PRESENCE IF YOU BUY ONE OF OUR CARS TODAY." He sold five cars.

By mid-decade, the big beat was rock 'n' roll, a phrase coined by a New York disc jockey, Alan Freed, and taken from the lyrics of a slightly raunchy old blues number: "My baby rocks me with a steady roll." The pop ballads America had danced to, and the big bands that played them, began to fade.

It was kicky to hear the dignified, established singers of "Your Hit Parade" as they tried nobly to get through "You Ain't Nothin' But a Hound Dawg," one of Presley's immortal hits. By mid-1967 the show left the air, a casualty of the rock 'n' roll explosion and teenage taste.

The song that started the breakthrough was called "Sh-Boom." In 1955, Bill Haley and his Comets recorded "Rock Around the Clock." And the stage was set for the guitar-twanging, torso-twisting style of Elvis Presley. By the end of the decade, he had sold $120 million worth of records, sheet music, movie tickets, and merchandise. The uniform of his salad days in Memphis—the T-shirt and tight dungarees—had given way to gold lame suits that reportedly cost $10,000. His face, with that original baby fat look, was now a world-famous face.

Elvis Presley

By 1958, teenagers, mostly girls, were buying 70 percent of all records, in the process creating overnight idols out of the new breed of rock singers. The guitar found its way into homes all over America, another plot to confound poor old dad.

But still there was something for everybody. Exactly what it indicated no one knew, but in 1955 some 35 million people attended classical music performances—more than twice the attendance at that year's major league baseball games.

There even was a spiritual revival, of sorts, as witnessed by such songs as "The Man Upstairs," and "The Bible Tells Me So," and a haunting song that sold a million copies, "Vaya Con Dios."

The great crooners—Nat Cole, Tony Bennett, Frankie Laine—were still in business, and after five years of near obscurity, Frank Sinatra made it back, scoring high on the charts with a song called "Young at Heart." But his comeback, ironically, had been triggered by a supporting role in the movie, *From Here to Eternity*, in which Sinatra did not sing a note.

Some of the artists who cashed in were, in that vague way that can only be explained as chemistry, exclusively a product of the fifties, a piece of the tapestry. It was the decade of Eddie Fisher, who was to have a series of hits, and a romantic wedding to actress Debbie Reynolds. He would divorce her for Liz Taylor, and before the decade was out that marriage would fail. Eddie Fisher had more fun failing than most guys did succeeding.

Johnny Ray's tearful inventory of songs ("Cry," "The Little White Cloud That Cried") somehow touched our glands, and listeners were fascinated at the high, scraping quality in Ray's voice. But no one vanished faster.

Julie London made it big with "Cry Me a River," as we appeared to be on some kind of a national weeping jag. But we first discovered her as the bride of Jack Webb, who gave us "Dragnet." ("Just the facts, ma'am.")

And Rosemary Clooney. Now there was a fifties name. She was best known for happy, bouncy, meaningless tunes such as "Come On-A My House." One way or another, we all did.

The best-selling records of the 1950s:
1950—Goodnight, Irene, *The Weavers and Gordon Jenkins.*
1951—Tennessee Waltz, *Patti Page.*
1952—Cry, *Johnny Ray.*
1953—Song From the Moulin Rouge, *Percy Faith.*
1954—Little Things Mean a Lot, *Kitty Kallen.*
1955—Rock Around the Clock, *Bill Haley and the Comets.*
1956—Don't Be Cruel, *Elvis Presley.*
1957—Tammy, *Debbie Reynolds.*
1958—Volare, *Domenico Modugno.*
1959—Mack the Knife, *Bobby Darin.*

3

Color Them Brown

Ray Renfro agreed with the accepted picture of Paul Brown in the 1950s: a man of cool reserve, in perfect control, icily calm on the sidelines. And his always dapper attire reinforced the impression: trousers with a knife-edge crease, camel's hair topcoat securely buttoned up, a snap-brim felt hat squared away on his head.

"But there was another side of Paul," Renfro said, "that only the players knew about. He was tough. And he could be brutal in what he said to you. He could say things that would stick with you the rest of your life."

In fact, Brown said one such thing to Renfro.

"It was 1959, toward the end of the season, and as usual we were in a race with the Giants to get into the title game. We were tied for first place and we had four games left, so things were really tight. This Sunday we were playing Pittsburgh, which was maybe another thing that added pressure to the situation. The Steelers were coached by Buddy Parker and he had Bobby Layne at quarterback. Parker had beaten us out of two championships [1952 and '53] when he was at Detroit, and one time he'd held about a seven-game win streak on Paul.

"This didn't mean he was a better coach. It was just one of those things that get strung together in football. But Paul was a competitor, I mean a burning competitor, and all the sportswriters had made a big thing out of it.

"I had one of the best days of my career that game against the Steelers. It was *the* best day in terms of touchdowns. I caught three, all of them bombs. Milt Plum would just haul off and throw that day and I'd run under them. Except we messed up one of the extra points, a bad snap or a fumbled snap, whatever, and we only had a six-point lead, 20-14, when we had to give the ball over to Layne. He started way down at his end of the field, one of those two-minute drives, and he was using every bit of the clock. It was like working for the last shot in a basketball game—win or lose in the last second. He wasn't going to leave us any time to come back, and he didn't. Layne took them on down for a touchdown and they kicked the extra point and we only had time left for one play, from our twenty.

"Everybody in the park knew what our play would be, a long pass and most likely to me. I just streaked down the left sideline—and Plum heaved it as far as he could throw. Counting his dropback, it must have gone about seventy or seventy-five yards in the air, and it came down just about perfect, just on my fingertips. But when I hauled it in, I was running so hard, my knee came up and hit the ball and it went flying. It might have gone in the end zone seats. The game was over. I was just standing there and Paul grabbed me by the arm. He had run down the field to get to me. 'Renfro!' he said—he seldom yelled at you. But it was like electricity in his voice. 'Renfro!' he said. 'You're through... *You can't make the big play anymore!'*

Paul Brown

"I saw a Cleveland press book not long ago that had the team records in it, and nobody has ever caught more than three touchdowns in one game for the Browns. Seven guys did it, but still....What shook me up, of course, was this: I was conditioned to believe anything that Paul said. We lost our next two games and finished second to the Giants, and I spent all the offseason worrying about being washed up."

The power of Paul Brown and the Cleveland Browns made believers out of a lot of other people in the 1950s, as the man and the team achieved a record of consistent excellence that may never be equaled. "They talk about Super Bowl records today," Paul Brown said, somewhat wistfully. "The NFL Championship Game was our Super Bowl and we played in it seven times the first eight years we were in the league. And we won four straight in our old league before that. Perhaps all that doesn't count for much. It makes me sigh to think about it."

The Browns had come into being in 1946, midwifed by a famous sports editor, Arch Ward of the *Chicago Tribune*, who conceived baseball's All-Star game, then the College All-Star game, and, finally, the All-America Football Conference. The fellow who took the baby and ran with it was Mickey McBride, the owner of a taxicab company, a fanatic smitten with football because his sons went to Notre Dame. Later, when Paul Brown insisted on keeping more players than the allowable limit of 33, McBride circumvented league rules by putting the extra players on his company payroll—thus originating the terms "taxi squad" and "cab squad" for handy reserves.

McBride, always promotion-minded, elected to choose a nickname for his team via public contest. "Panthers" won, until the owner of a semipro club in the area threatened to sue. McBride paid off the winning suggestion and gladly conducted a second contest, won by an entrant who suggested "The Brown Bombers," in honor of heavyweight champion Joe Louis. The name was shortened to Browns, not without some admiration held by McBride (and most of Ohio) for Paul Brown.

Elmer Layden was the commissioner of the NFL at the time, and he uttered a line about the new league that challenged Marie Antoinette: "Let them get a football." Before the AAFC played its first game, however, Layden was out and Bert Bell became commissioner. Of the AAFC teams, only Cleveland, San Francisco, and Baltimore (a brief season) survived the "merger" from the AAFC. The bitterness from this union was traumatic, particularly when Baltimore had to agree to pay the Washington Redskins $150,000 for "territorial rights." The rivalry between the two cities was so intense that a Baltimore disc jockey punctuated the announcement of a losing Redskins' score with a three-minute laugh record. The Baltimore NFL team was doomed, as it turned out, but the Cleveland Browns would apply a salve that would last forever.

"It was almost a storybook plot the way that 1950 season worked out," Brown says. "Bert Bell believed in starting out the season with the strong against the strong, and the weak against the weak, to get everybody down to a closer level. His plan was that everyone should finish with a seven-seven record. So he scheduled our first NFL game against the NFL champions of the year before, the Philadelphia Eagles."

The Browns, in fact, embarrassed the Eagles 35-10 in that classic opening game. "And," says Brown, still the bitter competitor four decades later, "we had three touchdowns called back on dinky little things."

The "plot" had a perfect denouement in matching Cleveland in the 1950 title game against the Los Angeles Rams, the team that had deserted Cleveland after winning the NFL title in 1945—and the championship game was played in Cleveland. The Browns won it 30-28.

Aside from the technical innovations Brown introduced—the draw play, the sideline pass, the face bar—he had an essential quality going for him to which he attributed all his successes. The winning record followed him from Massillon, Ohio, High School through Ohio State, from the Great Lakes Naval Air Station to the Cleveland team. Brown has a simple two words for what carried him: Eternal Truths.

"You can't violate them and be very successful," Brown says. "That's in living, or in the project of a football team, or business, or anything, and I believe it."

Brown's truths were embodied in The Speech he gave at the beginning of every training camp. It never changed, essentially, from 1946 to the end of his coaching career—only the names changed—and he has always required that his players take notes. The language was crisp, and blunt:

"We're going to be as good a football team as the class of people you are. We intend to have good people because they're the kind that win the big ones. If you're a drinker or a chaser, you'll weaken the team and we don't want you. I'm talking to the veterans as well as the rookies here today. If you're an older player and have reached the point where you can't concentrate on what I have to say, maybe you've reached a point where you ought to be looking for other work. If you think about football only when you step on the field, we'll peddle you. A year ago one of my players was talking while I was telling you this. I traded him.

"I like to think that the Cleveland Browns are somewhat different from the average professional football team. I want to see some exuberance in your play, some sign that you play for the sheer joy of licking somebody. We're the Ben Hogans, the Joe Louises, the New York Yankees of our game and that's the way we want to keep it."

Make your blood percolate? Make you want to go out and whip somebody? You understand the Browns.

"I expect you to watch your language, your dress, your deportment, and especially I expect you to watch the company you keep. That pleasant guy who invites you to dinner may be a gambler.

"Here in training camp I don't want to see a player in the dining room in a T-shirt. I expect civilized table manners and table talk. There have been people who have failed to make this team simply because they were obnoxious to eat with."

The talk was more extensive, but that's the important gist. For its time and place and audience, it is a classic speech, the kind you can't get anywhere else, anymore. It is about pride, an echo of the speech Patton made to the Third Army on the eve of D-Day, which included this deathless message: "...when you are sitting at the fire with your grandson on your knee and he asks you what you did in the Great World War II, you won't have to say: 'I shoveled shit in Louisiana.'"

Which, at bottom, is the essence of Brown's "Good People" speech, and the essence of what the championships were all about. Otto Graham always believed that it did. "Give me eleven players who are top-notch people," Graham said, "and who have some amount of talent, and I will take them over eleven guys who have more talent but maybe won't put out one hundred percent for you every game. And I'll beat that second eleven."

Graham was the quintessence of Brown's vision of a quarterback. Brown chose

McBride circumvented league rules by putting the extra players on his taxicab company payroll—thus originating the term "taxi squad."

Mike McCormack

him as his T-formation leader on the basis of one play as a collegian. "When I was coach of Ohio State," Brown said, "the only Big Ten game we lost was to Northwestern in 1941, fourteen to seven, and we lost it on a play where Graham ran left from the Single Wing, then threw back to his right to a man going lickety-split away from him, right on target, for the winning touchdown. I asked myself, 'What kind of player is this?' He was the first man I picked for the Cleveland team."

The stringent Paul Brown code of behavior was specifically pragmatic, related to the won-lost column. "You hear all this talk about 'freedom,'" he said. "Holy smoke, the reasons I asked my players to do things was not for moral reasons or to try to restrict their freedom. I did it because I wanted them to perform to the best of their ability for our project. This is just because I thought it gave us a better chance to win."

Brown had a quaint idea that his team should go out to a movie together the night before a game. "The players on the other teams used to laugh at us," an ex-Brown remembers, "but we would whomp their ass on Sunday."

Cleveland's mastery of the Eagles at the beginning of 1950 was rationalized by the end of the season, when Philadelphia had proved vulnerable to many others and had finished with a 6-6 record. The Los Angeles Rams, meanwhile, had been building an awesome team in the Western Conference. "They were like a Who's Who of pro football," Brown remembered, "with Glenn Davis and Elroy Hirsch and Tom Fears. It was glorious that we were playing them back in Cleveland, the town they left because the fans hadn't turned out—and we'd just finished a year averaging 60,000 paid admissions."

This classic contest was explosive from the first play to the last. "There never was a greater game," Brown said, and his quarterback, Otto Graham, agreed: "I never played in a greater game than that one. It had everything." What it had mainly was a passing duel between Graham and Bob Waterfield. Graham completed 22 of 33 passes; Waterfield hit 18 of 22.

The Rams' opening strike, the first play of the game, was an 82-yard touchdown pass from Waterfield to Davis. Fears had set an NFL record that season with 84 catches, and all Cleveland eyes were on him as he cut to the middle of the field. Davis hesitated two counts and sprinted out of the backfield into the area Fears had cleared. The linebacker who was supposed to cover Davis had gone with Fears, and Davis had an open road to the end zone.

The game symbolized the swing that pro football would take in the fifties, when the passing game would set up the run instead of vice versa. Both teams set their halfbacks out as receivers, leaving only the fullback to protect the quarterback.

They swapped points until a bad snap on an extra-point attempt left the Rams ahead 14-13. The Browns recovered the lead on a pass to Dante Lavelli, then fell behind again 28-20. With only 1:50 to play, Graham got the ball at his 32-yard line, trailing 28-27.

"Nobody knew about sideline passes, how to stop them," Graham said, "because this was our first year in the league and we had perfected it. Also, when a quarterback ran, there was no one to cover him, and you could pick up a few yards without anyone touching you." Graham began the series by running for 14. Then he threw to the left sideline to Rex Bumgardner, the right side to flanker Dub Jones, then to Bumgardner again. Bumgardner tumbled out of bounds at the Rams' 11. "Bumgardner made just one helluva catch right on his fingertips to set up the field goal," Graham said. When Lou Groza kicked it, only 28 seconds showed on the clock.

The Rams had one last shot. They called on Norm Van Brocklin, who had sat out the game because of rib injuries he had suffered in the previous week's playoff.

From his 46, Van Brocklin tried a bomb to Davis, and Warren Lahr intercepted.

The Browns' victory stunned everyone except the bettors, who had made Cleveland a three-point favorite. It was the beginning of a string of six championship game appearances by the Browns, who were to win half of them. It was as if no one else in the Eastern Conference knew how to play this game. Everyone wondered what Paul Brown's winning secret was.

Mike McCormack, who came to the team in 1954 and eventually became one of the all-time great offensive tackles, thought he knew what the secret was. "Or at least what most of it was," McCormack said. "Paul was a great detail man, great in organization and in teaching fundamentals. We'd start off with fundamentals every year as if we'd never seen a football before. But the key thing that made Paul stand out was his confidence. He was so absolutely sure. You just believed that the way he told you to do something was the final, the best way to do it. Now what this means to a team is considerable. It means you go out on the field to play a ball game supremely confident that you're prepared. Confident all the time that you're going to win." Brown, as always, would leave it to others to analyze his success, but he laughed and acknowledged McCormack's view. "When I think back," he said, "it sort of scares me a little bit. But I was so filled with the game that it never entered my mind I wasn't right, either. The game was such an obsession with me. I could go into a game and actually visualize ahead of time the things that would happen—I suppose you get that way when you are involved in calling the plays. Obsessed is the word for it."

One of the things Brown was most certain about was the wisdom of sending in plays to his quarterback. "It was never because Otto wasn't bright, because he certainly was," Brown said. "But nobody under pressure of performing can give as much thought to play selection as he should. We were feeding in information from all our coaches in the press box—and we always had a coach sitting in the end zone. I was a quarterback myself—not a very good one—and in those days when you couldn't think of anything else, you'd run off tackle. What does a quarterback see when he makes a handoff? What part of the defense does he see? He doesn't see much. Field level is the worst vantage point in the stadium. Besides, a coach calling the plays takes a lot of heat off the quarterback—and a lot of coaches don't want this responsibility. I didn't care. The players perform and get the credit. If people wanted to blast me for a dumb call, I could take it."

Brown also had one tangible asset for that string of championships: the championship quarterback. When Otto Graham defeated the Rams again 38-14 in 1955 and retired, the record he left behind—10 consecutive title games and seven victories—would be his legacy. It is possible the record never may be contested.

"I think Graham had the finest peripheral vision I've ever witnessed," Brown said, "and that is a big factor in a quarterback. You know, he was an All-America in basketball and he played with Rochester in the NBA. He was a tremendous playmaker. I watched him in a game one night and I wasn't aware of him scoring, yet he scored twenty points. And he'd helped everyone score. His hand-and-eye coordination was most unusual; he was bigger than you think, and faster than you think. Find another quarterback who took his team to as many championships.

Brown requested his players go to a movie together the night before a game. "The players on the other teams used to laugh at us," an ex-Brown remembers, "but we would whomp their ass on Sunday."

Otto Graham

"Otto was my greatest player because he played the most important position. He was the crux of how we got to things. I don't discount Marion Motley, Dante Lavelli, or Jim Brown. But the guy that was the engineer, the guy with the touch that pulled us out of many situations was Otto Graham."

Graham didn't always agree, however, with the way Brown ran the team. He chafed at times under the play-calling system, and he resented the discipline measures the coach installed—until years later when Graham became a head coach himself, with the Washington Redskins.

"Even though we were grown up and thought we were mature men," Graham said, "we found out later we weren't as mature as we thought we were. I was a clean-cut kid. I went to bed nights and got my rest, didn't drink, didn't smoke. When they came around to check my room I resented it. They knew I was in there. But what I didn't appreciate is that you have to check every guy—as an equal. You've got to have discipline to the lowest common denominator. If you've got an animal on the team you have to keep in a cage, then everybody has to be confined to a cage. I found out you have to crack down on guys—and that if you didn't have a curfew there'd be a dozen guys who would go out the night before a game and get loaded."

Graham has a sharp image of pro football in the fifties: "Every oldtimer will always tell you how things were different in his time, but one thing I'm convinced of—we were more of a team. We cared about our teammates. Nobody was selfish. There was none of this, 'Well, I gained a hundred yards so it was a great game and too bad we lost.' There was a span of thirteen years, later, when I coached the College All-Stars, and it was an upward scale—every year there were more prima donnas than there were the year before. All talking about the money they had. Money wasn't the prime factor when we played in the fifties. We played mostly because we liked to play.

"They used to say about me, if I had a killer instinct I would have been a better quarterback. I never saw it that way. I was a competitor, I played to win, but if we lost a game I didn't brood about it. I'd start planning to win the next one.

"I would have played just for the fun of it, and a lot of guys played that way then. I'd be out there hunched over the ball and before calling the signals I'd wink at a guy across the way, somebody I knew, letting him know we were coming right at him. One time after Don Shula was traded to Baltimore, I looked at him and winked and nodded—and then I completed a pass right over him.

"But I was never this relaxed before a game. My stomach was twisted in knots, and I went to the bathroom every five minutes. Our pregame meal used to be steak and potato, no butter, dry toast with no butter, and I'd choke on it. Never could get it down. So I'd have a Hershey bar and an orange.

"Only one game in my life, I didn't get excited. That was the year I came back in 1955. I'd retired after the 1954 season, but Paul called me up the next summer and I came back. I woke up the morning of my first game back and I told myself, 'You're doing the Browns a big favor, so relax and enjoy it.' I ate the pregame meal with no trouble—and then I went out and played the worst game of my life."

Graham doesn't feel there was any mystery ingredient that made him and the Browns a winner. "We just had the greatest coach, a lot of great players, and a lot of luck—particularly, luck that we all came together for those ten years."

Leaders of the Packs

In terms of the quality of the quarterbacks it produced, the decade was more than golden: it was platinum, titanium, and blue diamonds.

Over the years many lively arguments have been inspired by the issue of which quarterback was the most heroic. To illustrate, take a random night in the early 1970s.

On this night a man named Howard Cosell, who has been known to talk a little, was handed a telephone. This was at one of those night-before-the-kickoff parties where, when the hour gets late and the bottle low and the mood indigo, people start waking up their friends all over America.

At the other end of the line was a West Texas rancher, Bobby Layne. Instantly, Cosell swung into his staccato, on-the-air delivery:

"Let's face it, Bobby," he began. "There was Waterfield. And Graham. And Van Brocklin. And Unitas. Now some say Bart Starr. Others say Tittle, but he never won the big one. But for those of us who know the game, there was only one quarterback—Bobby Layne."

"Howard," said Layne, momentarily overcome by emotion and a little bourbon, "you're only telling it like it is...."

Well, that is precisely the point. There were all these great quarterbacks, each with a fan club willing to proclaim their man the best. And all of the names Cosell mentioned had one thing in common: Their careers either ended, spanned, or began in the 1950s. Even the immortal Sammy Baugh went out at the end of the 1952 season.

There is, of course, no disagreement on how a quarterback is graded. Coaches are notoriously partial to the one who wins the most games. For example:

Red Hickey: "People ask me about the great quarterbacks and I'll start with Otto Graham. 'He won a lot of championships,' I'll say. Then I mention Layne and Waterfield and Van Brocklin, and before I can get to Unitas or Starr, they'll say, 'But you left out Y. A. Tittle.' And I'll say, 'But Tittle never won a championship.' That's what a championship quarterback does: win championships. Now Layne, as bad as he looked throwing the ball, was a winner. You'd work him out and you wouldn't want him. But you'd want him in your huddle. Players feel that way about a quarterback. When a leader is in there, they'll perform, they'll go."

Buddy Parker: "You can't win a championship without a great quarterback. You may win five or six games with an ordinary player at the position, but as far as a title is concerned you might as well stay at home, if you don't have a real big guy at the spot...Layne was hot-headed, explosive. He went all out every minute of the game and expected all others to do the same."

Paul Brown: "Otto was the greatest of all quarterbacks. For ten years he pro-

There is no way to put this delicately. In 1947, playing for LSU against Ole Miss, in front of 40,000 fans, including his fiancee, Tittle lost his pants.

pelled his team to ten championship games. That's the real test of a quarterback: Can he move his team?"

They seem to be saying—and they're right—that winning is a quarterback's excuse for living. You could hear the trumpets in his voice when Bobby Layne said:

"There's something about being a winner—it's, well, it's the greatest thing in the world. You can spot a winner by the way he walks down the street. When you're a winner you don't have to park your car yourself; somebody parks it for you. When you're not a winner you have to stand in line for picture shows, but when you're a winner you go in the back door with the manager."

It is a pity Y. A. Tittle never put the arm on a championship. He tried mightily. For 15 years he tried, an Ahab pursuing his great white whale. A photograph appeared in papers all over the country the day after Tittle retired, a photograph that seemed as symbolic of defeat as the flag-raising on Iwo Jima was of victory. It showed Tittle, kneeling, dazed, his uniform dirty and torn, blood dripping from a wound high on the side of his bald head and streaking his face. You didn't have to be told the score to know that Tittle, and his last team, the Giants, had lost that day.

You could not dislike Y. A. Tittle. Even when he was beating your team, which he did so often in those games where the fate of the universe was not at stake, you could never hate him. Maybe it was that kindly farmer's face, or that unlikely name, one of those names you never got tired of saying.

Phil Foster, a Brooklyn comic and sports freak, worked it into his night club act in the fifties. "I used to love the tough guys in pro football," he would say. "In my day we had real he-men—Bronko Nagurski, Alex Wojciechowicz, Mel *Heinnnnn.* Now what have we got—names like Milton *Plum...*Y.A. Tittle...Y.A. Tittle?" And Foster would throw up his hands, as if to suggest that the next step would be to let women play.

Tittle was no loser. But his legend was reduced by the fact that he never quarterbacked a team that ran the course. He is remembered best, ironically, for a gimmick: the Alley-Oop play. Yet he was a tough, persistent operator whose thoughts were often original, and as a passer he was nearly an artist. When he retired he owned four career records: most attempts, completions, yards passing, and touchdowns.

If you didn't know another thing about Y.A. Tittle, you would have to honor him as the semihero of one of the classic stories of football lore. It happened in his college years, but it no doubt helped build the character that sustained him through some of the trying times still to come.

There is no way to put this delicately. In 1947, playing for LSU against Ole Miss, on his home field at Baton Rouge, Louisiana, in front of 40,000 fans, including his fiancee, Miss Minnette DeLoach, Tittle lost his pants.

Y.A. was at left cornerback on defense when he intercepted a pass thrown in the flat. The Ole Miss receiver grabbed at him as he made his move, and in the process tore away his belt buckle. Football pants in those days were not the skin-tight stretch variety worn in the eighties. They were loose-fitting and baggy. Tittle tucked the ball under his right arm, and used his left hand to hold up his pants as he crossed the 50-yard line.

At the Ole Miss 20 he got hemmed in against the sideline by two Rebels, and tried to shift the ball from his right arm to his left, so he could stiff-arm the tacklers. When he made the switch, down came his pants, and he fell flat on his face,

Portfolio:
QUARTERBACKS

The 49ers' Frankie Albert was a plucky, lefthanded thrower who
played in the 1951 Pro Bowl, the first of the modern series.

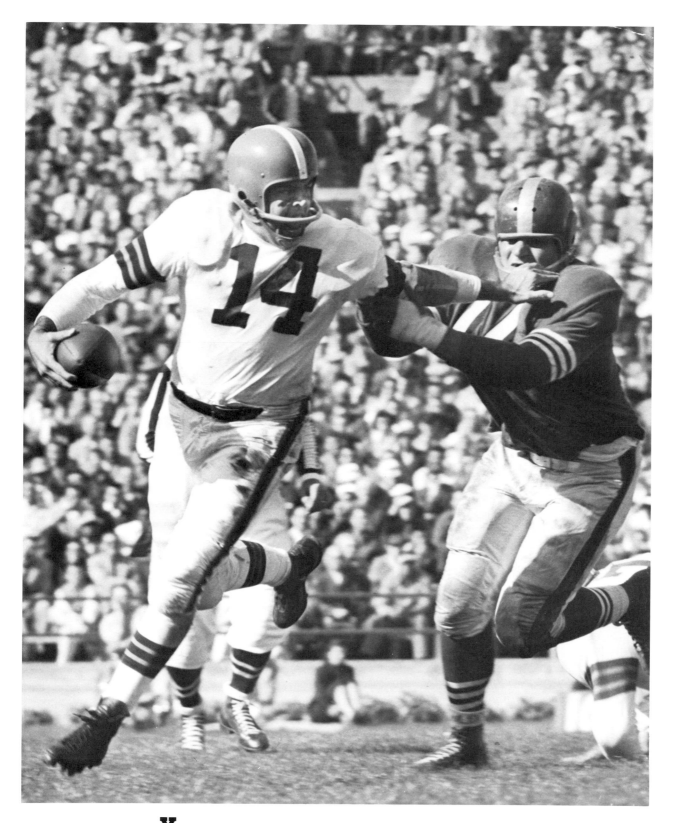

Y.A. Tittle and Otto Graham were two all-time standouts who came to the NFL via the AAFC. Tittle (opposite) played with the ill-fated Baltimore Colts before setting records with San Francisco. Graham (escaping Bob Toneff, above) led the Browns to 10 consecutive championship games.

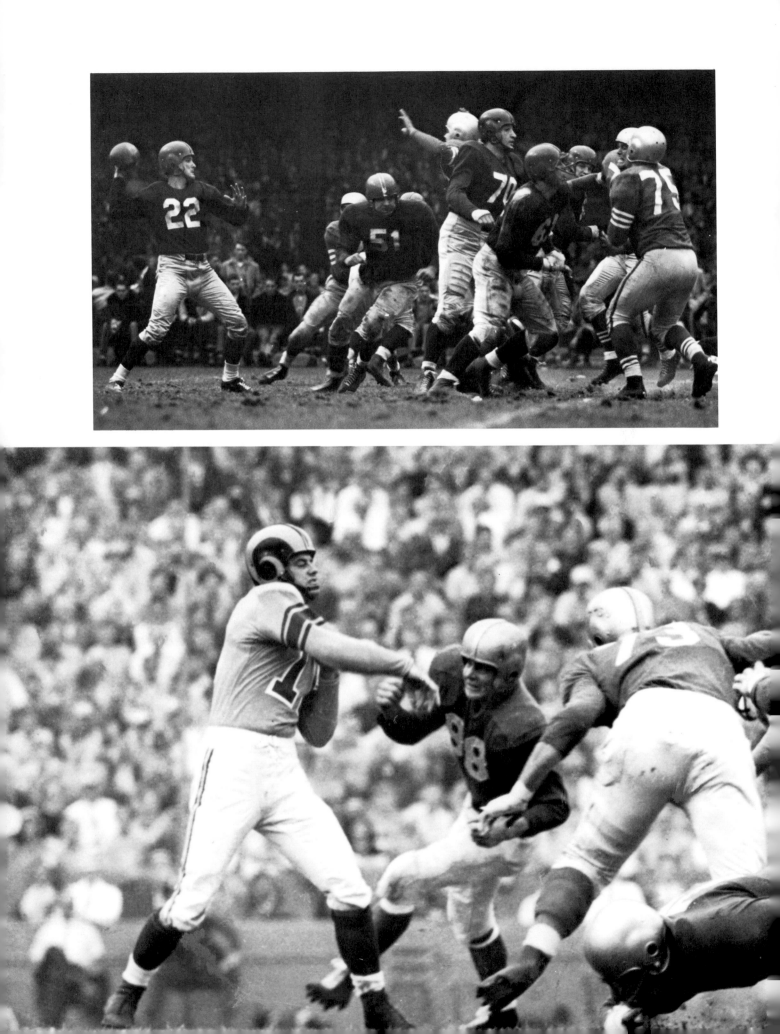

Detroit's Bobby Layne (opposite, top) was a rebellious idol of the 1950s. This photo was take in 1954, the year Layne made the cover of Time magazine. Norm Van Brocklin (below, far left) was an explosive—and often abrasive—pure passer who made things tough for his opponents and his coaches. Cleveland's Paul Brown once called Jim Finks (right) "the best quarterback in the NFL." He also has done pretty well as a football executive.

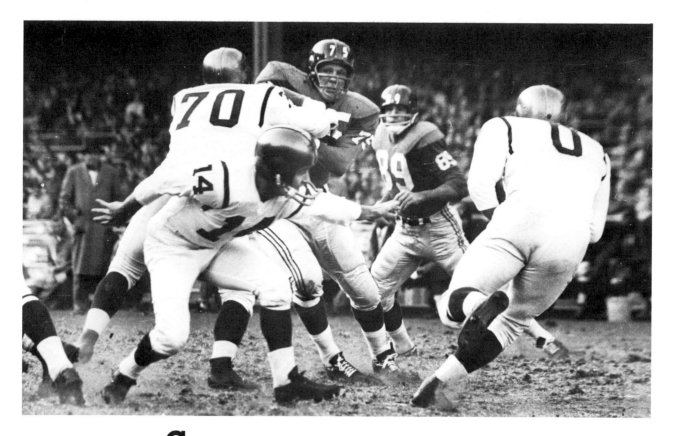

Giants quarterback Charlie Conerly (opposite), was the original
model for the Marlboro Man character; little Eddie LaBaron (above)
was the NFL "midget magician" in the late fifties; Tobin Rote (below)
was an NFL castoff who led the Lions to the 1957 title.

Johnny Unitas's career was a bridge between the 1950s and the big-business 1970s. Unitas entered the realm of legend after guiding Baltimore to an overtime victory over the Giants in the 1958 NFL Championship Game (above).

20 yards from what would have been the winning touchdown. Tittle staggered to his feet, trying to pull up his pants, and fell flat on his face.

There was a time when Hollywood could have made a full-length movie out of a scene like that, starring Jack Oakie.

Y.A. Tittle

Few doubted that Tittle, if he could keep his pants on, would make it in the pros. After his 1947 season at LSU he signed with the Cleveland Browns for a $10,000 salary and a bonus of $2,000, and was promptly traded to the Baltimore Colts.

There, his passing philosophy was established as a rookie by Baltimore head coach Cecil Isbell, who had thrown all those passes to Don Hutson at Green Bay. "Depend on yourself to complete the pass," Isbell told Tittle. "Throw the damned ball. The only one you can count on for help is your receiver. Don't wait for a pass pattern to spring a guy open so you can lay it in his lap. Your mother-in-law can do that."

Tittle was traded to the 49ers in 1951, and spent the rest of the decade working for coaches who did not exactly turn the game into a science. In training camp, in 1951, he approached Frankie Albert and asked about some minor point on a play. Albert made a face and said: "Hey, Tittle, don't you know you're after my job?"

For most of the fifties, the looseness of the game, the willingness to improvise on the field, made it possible for coaches such as Buck Shaw to prepare their teams without a playbook. "The game was so different," Tittle said. "We did not study two sets of films before each game. We did not take frequencies on the red dog. We never studied automatics; we didn't even *have* automatics. There was none of the preparation we know today. We did not have to face the great defensive stars who now play in the National Football League. In those days, the average life-span of a pro was two or three years; today quarterbacks have to contend with defensive specialists who have seven, eight, nine years experience."

In fact, the only part of the game as complicated in the fifties were the signals, which then as now sounded like something out of a CIA codebook. Example: In 49ers terminology, left end was "port," right end was "rip," and the tight end was X or Y, depending on which side of the line he was positioned. So Tittle's call for the Alley-Oop in the huddle would go: "Fifty-one [pass pattern]...Y right ...rip...Alley-Oop!" (R. C. Owens was the right end, "rip.")

The country wasn't as big nor was pro football, and college wasn't yet available to all. So it does not seem odd that lives and careers so often overlapped, and sometimes became a tangled ball of yarn. Born in Marshall, Texas, Tittle enrolled at Texas University, but sized up the competition—another Single-Wing tailback named Bobby Layne—and transferred to Baton Rouge. In 1947, Y. A.'s senior year, Bernie Moore put in the T-formation at LSU, the same year Blair Cherry was introducing it to Layne at Texas.

Exactly what one coach would have done with two talents such as Layne and Tittle on the same team isn't known. But no doubt he would have smiled a lot, and felt good all over.

The summer of his senior year in college, Layne and his wife were driven by Cherry, to the camp of the Chicago Cardinals, so Bobby could study the T. At every gas stop, Layne would hop out of the car to work on his techniques. He would make his wife bend over and snap the ball while he pivoted and went through his motions. Coach Cherry observed and offered small criticisms.

All through the Midwest, they left behind a trail of service station attendants who concluded that they had now seen everything.

41

Bobby Layne

There always seemed to be an extra dimension to Bobby Layne, to his moods, his actions, his words, all of it summed up by his old high school and Lions buddy, Doak Walker: "Bobby never lost a game in his life. Time just ran out on him."

Yale Lary, the fine Detroit safety, explaining how the Layne brand of leadership worked, said, "When Bobby said block, you blocked. When Bobby said drink, you drank."

That, too, was part of the legend. Layne once beat a drunk-driving charge when his attorney persuaded the judge that the arresting officer had mistaken Bobby's Texas drawl for drunken slurring. The incident, which involved an early morning collision with a parked car, led to some hilarious stories, one of which had the attorney claiming that Layne's condition was also affected "by a case of laryngitis."

From the rear of the courtroom came a stage whisper: "What? A whole case?" It was probably one of his teammates.

The next week, Friday Macklem, the Detroit equipment manager, posted a sign in the locker room: "AH ALL AIN'T DRUNK, AH'M FROM TEXAS."

Layne was not insensitive to his reputation. He defended his late habits on the grounds of an inner time clock that had to be served. "I'm the kind of guy," he said, "who can't go to bed early. I don't need more than five hours sleep. If I go to bed early, I wake up early, maybe five o'clock, and if there's a game to play that day I play it over in my mind maybe a dozen times before I even get out on the field. When the Lions played the Browns for the championship in 1954, we all went to bed at ten o'clock and we got beat fifty-six to ten. That's no excuse for losing, but I think it shows it takes more than an early bedtime to win a ball game."

Ravaged by clean living, Layne did not often repeat the mistake of getting to bed too early.

With Pittsburgh in 1958, Layne and his then roommate, Tom (The Bomb) Tracy, stayed out late the night before a game against Philadelphia. The next day, Layne handed off to Tracy 18 times. When Tracy scored his second touchdown of the day he was hurt diving into the end zone. He limped off the field and, sucking air, slumped heavily on the bench. Layne kicked the extra point and came walking by Tracy on the sidelines. He glared and said, "Dammit, Bomber, why don't you stay in shape?" And he kept right on walking.

Reunited in Pittsburgh with head coach Buddy Parker near the end of both their careers, Layne fought relentlessly to instill in the Steelers his own pride and passion for winning. He was incapable of sanctioning defeat, even in the preseason. After one such loss, Parker and Layne stoked the fire for several hours over drinks. Then, arms around each other's shoulder, they rode like vigilantes through the halls of the team's dormitory, Buddy pounding on doors and shouting at whomever was inside: "You yellow son-of-a-bitch, come out here and tell me why you can't play football."

Behind one of the doors was Charley Bradshaw, a large offensive tackle with hands like catcher's mitts. Rising out of a sound sleep, Charley sat up in bed and slowly, coldly, said across the room: "If I have to get up, I'm going to open the door and kill whoever is out there." Parker and Layne, weaving slightly, continued down the hall.

Of course, in the field of human relations, Bobby's most creative work came on the field. "I get a little irritated," he said, "because I want to win. One year, at Detroit, I quit getting on the ballplayers and they went to the coach and asked him to get me on them. They said it made them play better. I was trying to be a good guy that year—the guy with the white horse and the white hat. But it's more fun being on the black horse and wearing the black hat."

Layne drove, pushed, threatened and shamed. At times he used a needle, and at times a machete. "Beatty," he once castigated Steelers center Ed Beatty, "once, just once, take out your man and we'll all declare a damned holiday."

Layne was the quarterback people hated to bet against. A muffin-faced blond, handsome in a rugged, western way. Unselfish, unsparing of himself, almost schoolboyish in his devotion to his teammates. The early Lions were the love of his football life. "We had a team of leaders," he said. "The fellowship between our players was legendary. We all thought the same way. You could have all the fun you wanted to, but when you went out to play, you had to win. We looked forward to practice, we looked forward to games. We even looked forward to training camp. God damned, it was like going on a vacation when we went to training camp. Guys got there early, just to get up there and get their hands on the football."

The game Bobby Layne knew and revered is gone. So are the Bobby Laynes who played it. Once, after a disappointing season, Layne offered to take a $2,500 cut in his next year's contract. The Lions knew it was no stunt, no grandstand play. Nor did it embarrass the management to accommodate him.

He was an endangered species, one of a kind, the last pro football player to play without a facemask. In fact, except for a helmet and a set of almost wafer-thin shoulder pads under a short-sleeved jersey, he wore no protective paraphernalia: no face guard, or pads on his ribs, thighs, hips, or knees. "I like freedom," he said.

He was a free spirit with an incurable sentimental streak. "I went up to New York, years later, to be inducted into the College Hall of Fame," he remembered, "and I looked around and Bob Smith had come there from Tulsa and Cloyce Box had showed up from Dallas and Harley Sewell from Arlington, Texas, and Doak Walker and Dorne Dibble from Detroit, and I mean just a whole bunch of guys I'd played with. Guys I didn't expect to see. They'd gone there to be with me."

He paused to let that sink in. All these great guys, all those great football players, taking time out from their busy lives, maybe leaving the wife at home alone with the kids, or breaking a business date, to share a memory and a toast with Bobby Layne. Touchdowns in the sky, old timer.

The one endless vexation of Layne's career seems to have been the sportswriters. Like Ted Williams, baseball's stormy petrel, he regarded them as a menace to freedom, meaning his freedom. They were always hovering, like the fruit fly. Myron Cope of Pittsburgh was one of the few who won Layne's confidence. But Myron knew that such friendships were fragile. This is Cope, explaining Bobby Layne:

"He saw the press as one great mass of gossip-mongers, waiting to feed on his traffic tickets and nightclub celebrations. His argument was that the press had no consideration for the feelings of his wife and two sons.

"On one occasion, while the two of us sat in a parked car outside his apartment at 3 A.M., he stated his argument plaintively, keeping a grip on his temper. But at the table in Dante's [a team hangout in Pittsburgh] he sometimes would turn on me, remembering that I was a member of the press, and denounce me in the strongest possible terms. He would ask me to leave the table, and when I refused, he would insist. Finally, I would approach the table. He would utter the beginnings of an apology, but then his pride would stop him and again he would explode with a denunciation of me. I would return to the bar. Even at those times, I always liked him. One does not expect even temperament from genius."

Yale Lary, explaining how the Layne brand of leadership worked, said, "When Bobby said block, you blocked. When Bobby said drink, you drank."

Bob Waterfield

In Los Angeles, in the early 1950s, a quiet genius named Bob Waterfield was at work. Waterfield was an emotional opposite of Layne—slow to temper, serious, low-keyed, reserved. There was a romantic quality about him, a California campus hero who married a movie star—Jane Russell.

Waterfield had the committed athlete's craving for the open, natural life, hunting and fishing, hours of solitude, the company of other men under a high sun, sitting on a grassy bank. The Hollywood lifestyle was alien to him. He coped with publicity, his own as well as Jane's, but he didn't require it, and strangers made him fidget.

It couldn't have been easy for him. Jane Russell was a sex symbol, the heroine of a movie called *The Outlaw*, which sent the national temperatures rising. Waterfield had let her continue acting, one gag went, because he didn't want her bending over a hot stove and endangering her career.

Waterfield had it all going for him—looks, manners, wife—but none of it would have counted, of course, if he had not performed. He was the ultimate triple threat, a storybook player who was the last quarterback in history to win the NFL title and the most valuable player award in his rookie year. That was 1945, when the world was young (and the Rams were still playing football in Cleveland).

That year, in the championship game in six below zero weather, the Rams razor-edged the Washington Redskins 15-14 on a Waterfield extra point that hit the crossbar and tumbled over. He threw two touchdown passes.

Waterfield was a pressure player who did things like that, fictional things, of a kind we once read in pure-at-heart sports novels by people such as John R. Tunis, books we grew up on in the late forties and early fifties.

In 1952, Waterfield brought the Rams from 22 points behind in the second half at Green Bay. Down 28-6 at halftime, they had scored (28-13) and were moving again with eight minutes to play, at which point Waterfield kicked a field goal. In the press box, a Los Angeles writer, John Old, leaped to his feet, threw down his pencil and screamed, "How stupid can you be? That has got to be the dumbest call in the history of the game."

It was now 28-16, whereupon the Packers fumbled. Again, Waterfield took them in to score. Once more the ball turned over and, in the last 60 seconds, he threw a perfect pass to Tom Fears to win it 30-28.

In the dressing room, they asked Waterfield why he had kicked a field goal with eight minutes left, when he needed so many points? "Well," he said, "I had to have a field goal some time to win. I figured I might as well get it then."

Waterfield's ability to keep his turbines cool seemed to have a calming influence on his teammates. "He was great at sizing up the defense," Tom Fears said. "Cool as a deep freeze. He was the same one point ahead or fourteen behind. He'd look at me after the first couple of plays and say, 'Tom, any time you got it, let me know.' That meant, when I thought I could shake clear to tell him and he'd throw me one. And how he threw 'em. A country mile, and land in your mitts so soft you'd never break stride."

Success established Waterfield as a celebrity, albeit a reluctant one, in a town where people wore sunglasses at night, hoping to be mistaken for stars.

While appearing in a movie with Jane Russell, actor Vincent Price became a frequent visitor to the Waterfield home. He tried, without success, to befriend Waterfield. It became a challenge. "This is silly," he told Mrs. Waterfield one day, "I've just got to get your old man to like me."

His efforts to amuse the quarterback were met with coolness, and one night Price ran out of patience. "I want you to know," he snapped, throwing in the towel, "that I don't know anything about football...and I loathe what I do know about it!" A slow grin tugged at Waterfield's features. Warming up, Price proceeded to insult his host's manners, his vanity, and his intelligence, letting out all the frustrations of the past weeks.

From that point on, they were friendly. "Bob liked honesty in people," explained his wife. "It's a passion with him. He'd talk football all night with someone who knew what he was talking about. He hated to yak with people who were just trying to make an impression."

The opinion of his teammates meant everything to him, and he tried consciously to reduce the gap between his salary ($20,000) and status, and theirs. When he arrived in camp in 1951, he tossed the keys to his new convertible on the dresser in his room. "When I'm not using it," he announced, "that's where the keys will be. Any of the guys want it, can have it."

You have to understand what this meant as a gesture. The two-car garage still was a novelty, a convenience for the rich folks. Not only did few players bring their wheels to camp, not all of them even owned a car or could afford one.

Waterfield's career with the Rams was complicated by the team's penchant for encouraging two quarterbacks—to a point where not just the fans and sportswriters, but the players and the coaches chose up sides. In the fifties, the Rams were one of those teams that always seemed to be making the best of a bad situation. They got so used to it, some felt they went around creating bad situations so they could make the best of them.

First there was Jim Hardy, a Southern California product of later vintage than Waterfield, a happy-go-lucky sort whose disposition was in sharp contrast to the guy whose job he wanted. There was no ill blood between them, but Hardy was popular, and his friends resented his lack of playing time.

After Hardy was traded away, the competition was a rookie who had more or less hand-picked the Rams as his team of the future. He was Norm Van Brocklin, whose brilliant junior year at Oregon had led the school, in 1948, to entertain Rose Bowl thoughts. But the young Dutchman had higher ambitions. He wrote to Dan Reeves, the president of the Rams, and informed him that he had the credits to graduate a year early—if the Rams were interested. They were, drafting him on the third round and laying a bonus of $2,500 on him for his thoughtfulness. The other NFL teams, not to mention the state of Oregon, greeted the move as though it were the re-enactment of Pearl Harbor.

Van Brocklin played sparingly behind Waterfield as a rookie, until the last game of the season. On a hunch, Clark Shaughnessy let him do most of the quarterbacking against the Redskins, and Dutch threw four touchdown passes in a 53-27 win.

That was the beginning. By 1950, Joe Stydahar had taken over, with a plan to alternate his quarterbacks—Waterfield playing the first and third periods, and Van Brocklin the second and fourth. The city and the team were split, just as cleanly.

The arrangement reached a climax, of sorts, when Van Brocklin refused a play that Stydahar sent in from the sideline in the final game of the 1951 season. The coach summarily benched him, and Waterfield finished the game as a soloist, brilliantly, passing for five touchdowns and 256 yards. It was enough, by a fraction of a percentage point, for Waterfield to edge Van Brocklin for the league passing championship.

When Waterfield arrived in camp in 1951, he tossed the keys to his new convertible on the dresser. "When I'm not using it," he announced, "that's where the keys will be. Any of the guys ...can have it."

Norm Van Brocklin

Later, Dutch and Stydahar engaged in a rather earthy cussing match, with the result that Waterfield quarterbacked the first 50 minutes of the playoff game against Cleveland. The score was tied 17-17 when Van Brocklin was finally summoned from the bench, and from the doghouse. He immediately passed for 73 yards and a touchdown to Tom Fears and the Rams won 24-17 for their first world championship since moving west.

Van Brocklin never lost his resentment of the two-quarterback rotation in Los Angeles. It became a continuing news story. One writer, recalling the "foul" rumors of discord that had haunted Waterfield and Jim Hardy, observed: "The same thing is now happening with a nice kid and a great quarterback, Norm Van Brocklin."

Van Brocklin was torn between ambition and his respect for Waterfield. When a columnist in Portland wrote that there was friction between them, and that Waterfield's attitude was holding back Van Brocklin, the two of them got together, sat down at a table, and in longhand drafted a letter to the writer, telling him politely he was wrong and asking for a retraction.

The issue resolved itself after the 1952 season when Waterfield, weary of the constant battle, retired. Hampton Pool took over as the Rams' next coach, their third in four seasons. Pool was to confide later that his association with Van Brocklin shortened his life span by at least eight years.

What happened next? Dutch was to alternate with Billy Wade, a nice young man out of Vanderbilt, whose NFL career was undistinguished (until he led Chicago to the NFL championship in 1963). To share the position with Waterfield was one thing. But Billy Wade? Gads. Dutch felt like a husband whose wife had brought another man home for dinner.

And so it went. He could do things like put 41 points on the scoreboard in a single quarter—as he did against the Lions on October 29, 1950—and yet there was something about his skills that the fans disbelieved.

For one thing, he was slow, at a time when quarterbacks were being looked upon as a third running back. One opposing coach said of him: "All he has is an arm. He runs like a girl with her girdle slipping." Added George Halas, in a withering judgment: "Van Brocklin can throw. Period. In the full sense of the word, he is not a professional player."

Van Brocklin sneered at his critics. He compared it to faulting a hockey goalie "for not rushing out of his cage and throwing body checks all over the rink. Or a pitcher who wins twenty games is a bum, because he didn't hit three hundred. And Joe Louis wasn't a great fighter...all he could do was punch."

Still, the fans chanted for Wade at the Coliseum and, when Sid Gillman moved in as coach in 1955, he rotated them and won a division title. "Van Brocklin's speed," Gillman said, "was a terrible disadvantage in those years, when a quarterback had to run on the rollout. But he had the one thing that paid off in football—he threw the ball straight. There is no defense against a quarterback who can throw straight. That was Van's strong suit."

The Dutchman was a great passer because he always thought in terms of the receiver's problems. Once, on a bet, he passed a football downfield and then, after it had come to rest, hit it with 6 of 10 throws from 35 yards away. "The difference between a touchdown and an interception," he said, "is whether a ball drops over an end's right shoulder or his left."

His moods were volatile, his patience thin, and he loved a good argument, often taking either side. But he was also a perfectionist, consumed by the game. His wife Gloria would wake up at odd hours, hearing her husband mumbling in his sleep, wordless noises punctuated by strange yips. "Even at three A.M.," she finally figured it out, "he was calling plays."

In the heat of a game, when his acid tongue provoked a lineman into roughing him up, Dutch often invited the villain to meet him outside after the game. Those dates were never kept. Dutch would cool off in the locker room. No one ever accused him of being stupid.

Yet he could not resist baiting them. Once, against Cleveland, a tackle named Chubby Grigg nailed him for a loss on a pass play. When Dutch ordered him to "get off me, you big slob," Grigg reacted by silently dropping his fist, like a club, on the Dutchman's back. Grimacing with pain, Norm demanded, "Now why the hell did you hit me in the back?" Said Grigg: "If you don't like to get hit on the back, then take off your noseguard."

Nor did his teammates escape the lash of Van Brocklin. When Tom Dahms, a Rams tackle, missed a block that caused Dutch to be buried for a loss, he carried his anger with him to the sideline. There he picked up a Dixie cup filled with water and, wordlessly, flung it in Dahms's face. His teammates covered their ears and waited for the explosion. But Dahms, 50 pounds heavier, shrugged it off. The Rams understood. They knew that Van Brocklin's temper, and his urge to win, demanded expression.

He never lost either instinct, not through the rest of his career, which ended with the Eagles, or in his turbulent coaching years after that.

The cold war had eased, yielding to something called the "Geneva Spirit" in 1955, a promising year for the world and for pro football. Rock and roll had triumphed over pop music: The nation's number-one song was Bill Haley's "Rock Around the Clock."

In Montgomery, Alabama, a weary black seamstress defied the local law and refused to give up her bus seat to a white man, quietly touching off a social and civil revolution.

And a rookie quarterback was released by the Pittsburgh Steelers, which turned out to be a colossal error in judgment.

John Unitas had been drafted ninth by the Steelers in 1955, and signed to a contract worth $5,500. The head coach, Walt Kiesling, gave no real indication that he knew the rookie was in camp. If anyone else did, it was possibly the result of the one puff of publicity that came his way. A photographer, who needed someone who wasn't busy, posed him with a Chinese nun, demonstrating the correct passing grip.

No newspaper in America can resist a photograph of a Chinese nun looking at a football. Many of the captions even spelled the young man's name right: J-O-H-N U-N-I-T-A-S.

He was running behind Jim Finks and Vic Eaton in camp, so far behind that he never played a minute in five preseason games. Kiesling let him go, paid off the few dollars he had coming in pocket and bus money, and advised the disappointed Unitas to "try us another time." It was like being turned down at the post office. Unitas cashed his bus ticket and hitchhiked home to Pittsburgh.

He was married, soon to have a family, and his in-laws took in the young couple. Johnny got his old job back on a construction gang, as a pile driver, and signed on to play quarterback once a week for a local semipro team, the Bloomfield Rams.

One opposing coach said of Van Brocklin: "All he has is an arm. He runs like a girl with her girdle slipping."

Lawrence (Buck) Shaw

And thus began a story that was to become pro football's "Gift of the Magi."

The Bloomfield Rams played every Thursday night at the Arsenal Street school in the Greater Pittsburgh League. It was not exactly the National Football League. It was not even the University of Louisville, where Unitas had spent his college time, sometimes hurt, always outmanned, but making a losing team better than it was.

The Rams performed on a field with no grass, and the players had to get out and sprinkle it with oil before every game to keep the dust down. They never played before crowds larger than a few hundred, but Unitas was paid his price, $6, empty stands or not. After every game, Johnny collected his six bucks, in cash, in the basement of Parise's Dairy on Liberty Avenue. He would take the pay home and hand it over to his wife Dorothy.

In the light of later and historic events, that experience seems the height of irony. But it was never a fit subject for humor to Unitas, and it pained him whenever someone failed to understand what the money represented. "I was making a hundred twenty-five a week on my job," he said, "and we were still living with the in-laws, so we weren't starving. But what I needed was the chance to prove that I could play football. The six dollars that I gave to Dorothy every week was important, not because I had earned it but because I had earned it playing football."

It used to fracture his Bloomfield teammates when Unitas spoke, as he occasionally did, of going to camp the next summer with the pros. The only question in his mind was which team, Pittsburgh or Cleveland, where he felt Paul Brown had an interest in him. "It must have seemed comical," he admitted, "for a six-dollar-a-game quarterback on the sandlots to be talking about playing with the Steelers or Browns."

But the call that came was from Baltimore, inviting him to try out with the Colts. Colts head coach Weeb Ewbank had been touted on Unitas by Johnny's college coach, an old friend of Ewbank's. Unitas was offered a contract for $7,000, a $1,500 raise over the salary the Steelers never had to pay. Unitas said he thought he could work it into his schedule.

Today, that original Baltimore contract, calling for seven big ones, hangs in a frame in the Pro Football Hall of Fame, in Canton.

There is one other version of how the Colts happened to rediscover Johnny Unitas. They received a letter from a fan in Pittsburgh, rhapsodizing over the quarterback for the Bloomfield Rams, and urging the Colts not to let him get away. Ewbank always accused Unitas of writing the letter himself.

If Gary Kerkorian, the backup quarterback for the Colts, hadn't decided to become a lawyer, Johnny U. might have been just another hard hat. Kerkorian's decision resulted in Unitas's invitation to camp; an injury to George Shaw plunged him into the lineup. The Colts were trailing the Chicago Bears by a point when Shaw failed to rise from a pileup. And here came the sub quarterback, the fictional hero of so many books, the understudy pushed onstage to save the show.

Except that Unitas met the challenge by throwing an interception, which was returned for a touchdown, and he set up two more with fumbles as the Colts were blown out 58-27. It was not an auspicious beginning, but it would get a whole lot better.

Later that season, Weeb Ewbank went to George Shaw and "like a father, not a coach," urged him to be satisfied as number two behind John Unitas. "He might have lasted ten years," Ewbank said, "if he had listened to me."

Unitas was to lead the Colts to two world championships before the end of the decade, the first in 1958, in that historic sudden death, in the two most exciting finishes any game ever had. Unitas would go on to become the prototype quarterback of his time.

Perhaps this is the place to make a statement about the nature of the game. Pro football doesn't lend itself to Ruthian heroes; it depends too much on the group, so that often the one who orchestrates the effort—the coach, Brown or Lombardi or Shula—commands the attention. Which is why great teams are called machines.

Which brings us to Otto Graham, whose career may be said to have defined greatness for pro quarterbacks. He was the finest mechanic of his time. He led his team to the championship game every season he played, which doesn't sound quite legal. He wasn't flamboyant, but he had style, a quality that is beyond ability.

Graham didn't smoke or drink. His values were right out of the Eagle Scout Handbook. One of the rival coaches he most admired was Buck Shaw, then of the 49ers, for reasons that involved an order Shaw once gave his team.

Graham started against the 49ers one day despite a heavily taped knee that should have kept him on the bench. On Cleveland's first series, he threw a touchdown pass to Dante Lavelli and the Browns won easily. The 49ers sacked him at times during the day—he couldn't maneuver—but no one hit him unnecessarily hard. Later, he learned that Shaw had warned his team in the locker room, "The first guy who roughs up Graham gets fired."

His decent instincts did not prevent Shaw, himself, from being fired at the end of the 1954 season. But Graham recalls the incident warmly, because it suggests that there was still room in the game for the gentlemanly gesture. From his somewhat mellow viewpoint, Graham remembers the fifties, which means, mostly, remembering Paul Brown:

"The old Browns had two things going for them: We had one of the greatest coaches who ever lived, Paul Brown, and we had something else, an *esprit de corps* you find very seldom on a football team today. We didn't have the petty jealousies. It didn't matter who got the credit...who made the headlines...who scored. The important thing was, did you do a good job?

"The Browns stayed together. Paul Brown believed—he insisted—that we be a big, happy family. We'd bring our wives to camp, we'd hang out together, we had picnics, for heaven's sake. It worked because, for one thing, we didn't make the kind of money that allowed us to live like playboys.

"My first year with Cleveland, Paul Brown signed me to a two-year contract for seventy-five hundred dollars a year. I was a naval air cadet at Glenview Naval, at Evanston, Illinois, and Paul was at Great Lakes. I had played against his Ohio State teams while I was at Northwestern. I was making seventy-five a month as a cadet, and he offered me this two-year package, plus a bonus of one thousand dollars, but the big payoff was, if I signed right then, he'd pay me two-fifty a month for as long as the war lasted. Now, to a guy making seventy-five a month that was like being offered a piece of the mint. I said, 'Who you want killed?' and I signed the contract. The war lasted only a few more months.

"After we won the championship my rookie season, he tore up the contract and gave me a new one for twelve thousand dollars a year. After that I went up in increments of one, two, and three thousand a year. In 1955, my last year, my tenth in the league, I was the highest paid player in pro football at twenty-five thousand dollars. I suppose I could have gotten even more out of Paul by becoming a hold-

"It must have seemed comical," Unitas admitted, "for a six-dollar-a-game quarterback on the sandlots to be talking about playing with the Steelers or Browns."

Johnny Unitas

out, but it never really occurred to me. What he offered always seemed fair, so I signed.

"Of course, we played for the title every year for ten straight years. They were great years, carefree years. When you went in to talk contract with Paul, he always used the championship money as part of your salary. He would just add it on, like a grocery clerk figuring the tax. We always got it, and you could hardly negotiate against it.

"I suppose athletes then were more naive. Certainly, we still talked about things like sportsmanship, and we didn't question everything. We accepted some things simply because they were. There weren't many prima donnas in the league. They got weeded out early, because it just wasn't worth it to them to stick.

"We didn't put a price tag on everything. When we were dominating the old All-America Football Conference for four years, we burned, because those were the days when the NFL was still telling us to go get a football. Well, when we played that first game against the Eagles, in Philadelphia, in 1950, we had been looking forward to playing that game for *four years*. Paul Brown didn't have to do anything to get us up for that game. If anything, he had to tone us down. We'd have played those guys anywhere, anytime, for a barrel of beer or a milk shake, just to prove we were a good football team.

"We were, and we proved it. Paul Brown was just light years ahead of everybody. I'm grateful I got to play under him. I learned an awful lot about football, organization, life. There were times when I hated his guts, I could have killed him. Other times I felt something close to love. All I know is, when I got into coaching I found myself doing and saying the same things that used to make me so mad at him.

"One night, I ran out of the pocket a couple times, for what I considered a very valid reason. I didn't want to get my bones broken. He took me out, sent in George Ratterman, and walked over to one of his assistants, five, six feet away from me. Loud enough for me to hear him, he said, 'At least, now we have someone in there with the guts to stay in the pocket.'

"If I'd had a gun I would have shot him. I know, going into the game later, I told myself, 'I'll show the so-and-so.' And I played a helluva lot better football.

"Paul ran the game from the sideline like a computer, but at the oddest moments he would surprise you. During the championship game in 1950, I came out in the fourth quarter, two points behind, a minute and a half to go, after fumbling at the end of a good gain on a draw play. If I could have found a hole I'd have crawled in. As I crossed the sideline Paul came over to me, put his arm around my shoulder and said, 'Don't worry, Ots, we're going to get them anyway.' He was right. We did get the ball back and we beat them on a field goal by Groza with a few seconds left.

"When Paul began calling the plays from the bench, I disagreed, but the whole thing was exaggerated over the years. I didn't like it, but I didn't resent it. Calling a play is nothing more than a guess. You see those movies where the quarterback raises up from the huddle, looks at the defense, then ducks down and calls the play. Well, that's baloney. Paul could see as much or more from the sideline than I could from the huddle. My complaint was that he didn't want me to audible. He did let me check off now and then, but I had to be right. The rest of the time, Paul called the plays, and the record shows he called 'em pretty good.

50

5

Where We Stood Politically

There was apathy among the college students in the 1950s, although that wasn't the word anyone used. What did we call it? Actually, no one cared enough to give it a name.

Politics? Young people mostly ignored politics. They were too busy polishing their hub caps and playing the latest records (stax o' wax). With Dwight Eisenhower in the White House, and the Korean War over in 1952, and the good times beginning to roll, not even their parents could stay mad. When Ike was elected with a record 33 million votes, one Pennsylvania housewife said it for all: "It's like America has come home."

Few seemed to be asking any questions. And no one seemed to be listening.

The candidacy of Adlai Stevenson, who lost twice to Ike, confused a good many people. He was, well, different: literate, gentle, cerebral. The only ones who seemed to understand what he was saying were professors. He inspired a new synonym for intellectuals—eggheads.

Stevenson never had a chance against the universal army hero, but he brought a touch of humor to politics and, in time, the country came to like him for that. When he lost, in 1952, he quoted Lincoln: "It hurts too much to laugh, and I'm too old to cry."

Harry Truman was another man whose style the country was slow to appreciate. But in what he did and what he said, Truman was always consistent. And he was unsinkable.

When President Truman and General MacArthur had their historic meeting on Wake Island in 1950, MacArthur pulled out his corncob pipe—his trademark —and asked, "Do you mind if I smoke, Mr. President?"

"No," said Truman, a nonsmoker, "I suppose I have had more smoke blown at me than any other man alive."

Aside from any emotional judgment, there was one overriding impression of the Truman years: To the people they were real and human, sometimes too human, but not a drama acted out stiffly on a distant stage.

When Truman referred in a letter to the Marine Corps as "the Navy's police force," and credited them with "a propaganda machine that is almost equal to Stalin's," the country could not have been more outraged if he had personally given away the A-bomb secrets.

The next day Truman did what no other president in memory had done: He made a public apology. And he made it at a convention of the Marine Corps League. In that moment of tension before the President rose to speak, the convention's 70-year-old bugler began to blow "Hail to the Chief," only to have his dentures fall out.

Without fanfare, Truman made his regrets. The audience cheered, and he joined them in singing, "From the Halls of Montezuma."

In November, two Puerto Rican nationals, in a plot distinguished by its lack of planning, dropped by the Blair House—where the President lived while the White House was being remodeled—for the purpose of assassinating Truman.

Security guards and Secret Service men killed one of the attackers, wounded and captured the other. Within seconds after the shots rang out on the very doorstep of the house, an agent looked up and saw the President, awakened from an afternoon nap, peering curiously out of an upstairs window, in his underwear.

Later, Harry Truman said: "The only thing you have to worry about is bad luck. I never have bad luck."

In the fifties, the politics of assassination had not yet developed into a deadly art in this nation.

By 1956, television was changing the process by which we chose our national leaders, how we reacted to, perceived, and believed them. It was no longer possible for some of the people to be unaware that their President was crippled, as Franklin Delano Roosevelt had been.

In 1956, the Republicans re-nominated Ike and Richard Nixon, the vice president who had saved his place on the ticket in 1952 by going on network television to answer charges that he had accepted improper campaign contributions. Though his appeal to the national audience never actually dealt with the specific charges—he said the Nixons had received one gift, a black cocker spaniel named Checkers, "and we intend to keep him"—the country, and Ike, responded warmly to his speech. Television salvaged his career.

The Democrats, in 1956, nominated Stevenson and Tennessee Senator Estes Kefauver, after Adlai had taken the almost unprecedented step of leaving the choice of a vice presidential candidate to the convention. For a time, it appeared the delegates would go for a relative unknown, John F. Kennedy, whose candidacy Stevenson had seemed to encourage, hoping to win the friendship of Kennedy's Catholic constituents. But still, Stevenson was flabbergasted when young Kennedy quite nearly joined him on the ticket.

"It reminded me," JFK said later, "of the story about the Irish girl who worked so hard at converting her Jewish boyfriend to Catholicism that he became a priest."

In the spring of 1953, the junior senator from Massachusetts had other than political thoughts on his mind. "Do you think," he asked his friend, Dave Powers, "there is really much of a problem in getting married to a girl twelve years younger than you are?"

The Sunshine Boys

All of the players and the champions of the 1950s have an affection for the bygone decade, the sense of a great deal lost from "the way they were." But for one team, one group of men, this feeling is even more so. The old Rams are plainly overcome by a nostalgia that is almost painful.

"I just get warm all over when I think of those great years," linebacker Don Paul said, "the players, their attitudes and desires, their efforts—when the league was coming into its own."

"The players wanted to play football," said Tex Schramm, the club's general manager during the glory years. "Hell, they quibbled about salaries, but that wasn't a big deal. The football was the big deal. It had to be much more fun. We used to sit around and talk—we don't do that at all anymore. We had a succession of Bears coaches, and you'd hear them talk about [George] Halas and the early days, hilarious things that people like George Trafton did. There doesn't seem to be anything funny happening anymore. If they are, you don't hear about them."

"There was an awful lot of *esprit de corps* in all of the ball clubs of that era," said Hamp Pool, one of the club's head coaches. "A lot of loyalty to the clubs. You knew the players loved to play football. Heck, salary hardly ever came up. I guess there was still a holdover from the real old days, when I was a player and played the whole ten-game season for a hundred fifty dollars a game. I hardly had enough money left to get home on, but I was so determined to be a football coach, I would have paid them to let me play, for the experience. Like tuition money."

"What established the game in the fifties," Schramm said, "was that the public knew the players felt the game was the thing. So their heroes were heroes."

All the old Rams have another thing going for them, the memory of a fabulous series of teams—explosive, colorful, interesting.

"When you start talking about Van Brocklin and Waterfield at quarterback," Pool says, "running backs like Dick Hoerner, Tank Younger, Deacon Dan Towler, Vitamin T. Smith, and Glenn Davis, and receivers like Tom Fears, Elroy Hirsch, Bob Boyd—why, it sounds like you're listing an all-star team."

The Rams' all-star team of 1950 left an indelible imprint on the league by scoring 466 points, 38.8 per game, a pinnacle unmatched in the NFL before or since. These Rams would win games 45-28 and 43-35, and then lose one 56-20. Paul said, "The plan was, Van Brocklin would tell us, 'You guys hold 'em to three touchdowns and we'll win by two.' We spent most of our practices working on the home-run offense. We were more dangerous inside our fifteen-yard line than inside theirs. The record that still amazes me from 1950 was the forty-one points we scored in one quarter against a Detroit team with Bobby Layne that was going to win two straight titles a couple years later."

Hamp Pool

There was always time for laughter along the way. Tank Younger asked Bob Waterfield late in the season, "What do you want for Christmas, Cap?" Waterfield stopped Younger in his tracks with his quick reply. "I'd like a tank that runs," he said.

A year before, as a rookie, Younger had earned the name "Bass Eyes" from quarterback Van Brocklin, who had a flair for giving nicknames (Night Train Lane, for example). Younger had been tipping the defense by rolling his eyes in the direction the play would go.

Younger also was a symbol of the Rams' famed expertise in scouting collegians. He was the first player ever drafted from a black college into the NFL, in this case Grambling, which later would send hundreds more. "Some years," Schramm said, "we would put up a list of the twenty top players in the country, and by the end of the draft we would own ten of them. It was incredible. Later on, this may have spoiled us."

Younger was only one of three blacks in the league at the time, and Grambling head coach Eddie Robinson had armed him with a tip for making the squad: "He told me in dummy drills to run out the play twenty-five to thirty yards, don't turn and come back after ten like the others do. He said, 'The longer you have the ball under your arm, the longer the man is watching you.'"

The Rams had won the Western Conference in 1949 under head coach Clark Shaughnessy, then lost the title to Philadelphia on a quagmire field that nullified the lightning in the Los Angeles attack. Shaughnessy, a demanding genius who that year created the modern flanker back, converting a running wingback into a deadly receiver, was fired and replaced by Joe Stydahar. Stydahar hired as his top assistant a former Chicago teammate, Hamp Pool, and for two seasons they were a terrific combination. "Joe was a big happy guy, a nice guy," Paul says. "He was good with the press. Pool was the guy who worked his butt off and handled the offense and defense."

Pool stayed up nights devising new ways to get all of his talented, speedy pass catchers into play at one time. "We had all kinds of formations," Pool said. "We used quite a lot of the slot formation, with the halfback just outside the linemen and off the line of scrimmage. Then we'd put the other halfback in motion the other way. This would leave us with only one setback, the fullback, to block on pass protection. But we would get four men into deep patterns in a hurry and we would just eat them up. The defenses we were facing were exclusively man-to-man, and no one person could stay with Hirsch or Fears. One game we scored seventy points [70-27 over Baltimore]."

Waiting for the Rams in the 1950 title game were the Cleveland Browns, who were completing their first season in the NFL after four years as rulers of the All-America Football Conference. The two teams hadn't met during the regular season, and, though Cleveland had opened the year by beating NFL champion Philadelphia, the Rams were not convinced they were for real. And then they scored on the Browns on the first play.

"It was a play that was called two weeks before the game," said Paul.

Explained Pool: "We saw that their right linebacker would key on the halfback. If he stayed in place, as if to block, then the linebacker would go with the wide receiver. So we sent Fears across the middle, had Glenn Davis hold, then go into the empty area." Waterfield threw to Davis for an 82-yard touchdown.

But the Browns fought from behind to win in the last seconds on a 16-yard field goal by Lou Groza. It was a crushing defeat for the confident Rams. "To this day," Schramm said, "that one hurts more than any other game I've been involved in."

"Every time I think about that game," Paul said, "I have one visual image. Fred Naumetz [Rams linebacker] is in the end zone and Graham is hitting him in the hands. This is right before they got the field goal. I can still see Naumetz's hands—the fingers are curved instead of open, and the ball hits him on the knuckles. Oh, God, how it killed me to see that ball hit the ground."

The Rams' defense gave up 48 fewer points next season, while the offense "fell" to 32.6 per game. Tom Fears had caught 77 and 84 passes in consecutive seasons, and while he saw double coverage every step he took in 1951, Elroy (Crazylegs) Hirsch came to the fore. Hirsch tied Don Hutson's record for touchdown catches, with 17. The offense set a total offense record of 5,506 yards.

Once again the Browns were waiting in the title game, as they always would be whenever the Rams made it, but this time the big play did the job. Fears zoomed deep between the two Cleveland safeties and outreached one of them for the pass thrown by Van Brocklin—a decisive 73-yard touchdown in a 24-17 victory.

But there was trouble in paradise. Stydahar became convinced that Pool was after his job. Just before the 1952 season got underway, Stydahar came into Paul's room at training camp and said, "I've got to fire Pool." Paul said, "What the hell are you telling me for? You're the head coach. Fire him." Stydahar said, "Well, I have to get the defenses; you're the only one who has 'em."

One game into the league schedule Stydahar told owner Dan Reeves it was one or the other, him or Pool. Reeves opted for Pool, much to the latter's regret. "I couldn't convince Joe, haven't to this day," Pool said, "that I didn't want the job. I had everything just the way I wanted it. I could involve myself in the technical side of football, which I loved, and never had to talk to the press or fool with any other administrative duties."

Some of Pool's best ideas came to him at five o'clock in the morning, after he'd been up all night working. He couldn't understand others with less dedication. "Hamp was a gung-ho winner," Paul said, "whom you could learn to detest as you won the world championship. He is the greatest guy in the world on a social occasion, a witty, gentle, vivid conversationalist. But when the football season is on he doesn't want to be bothered by anybody or anything until he's won the title."

The Rams' offense continued to outscore the league, and the defense kept getting better (at one stretch in 1952, the defense scored touchdowns in eight straight games). But the Rams lost a playoff to Detroit for the conference title with a constant quarterback controversy over Waterfield and Van Brocklin. Waterfield retired after the season. The Rams fell to third place the next year, and to a 6-5-1 record in 1954.

"I realize now there are a lot of things I should have done differently," Pool said. "I should have spent less time on the field, held fewer meetings, kept everything simpler. I would change the offense every week to fit the opponent. I was a stickler for detail. Football should be a simple game, really, more the way Lombardi had it. My way, there was too much to learn and not enough time to learn any of it."

But a fellow came along in 1954 who makes Pool glow to remember, linebacker Les Richter. "Les Richter and Don Paul," Pool said, "were two men who could take more pain and punishment and still play, than any men I have ever known. They played with broken jaws, with a cheek smashed in. Broken bones just didn't seem to bother them at all. And they hit!"

Younger had earned the nickname "Bass Eyes" from quarterback Van Brocklin. Younger had been tipping the defense by rolling his eyes in the direction the play would go.

Sid Gillman

Paul remembers all of that well. "I broke my jaw on the third play of a game at Philadelphia in 1951 and I stayed in. Then I felt blood coming out of my ear and I had to leave. The next week I played without a protector because it wasn't ready yet! I put a rubber bit in my mouth and clamped on it. We went into Detroit and I played the piano in front of that damned Leon Hart for four quarters. That was when we first used the bird-cage, by the way, the protector they finally fixed to shield my jaw. That's what linemen and linebackers wear today. Les got his cheek smashed by Don Joyce—Joyce jerked his helmet off and hit him in the face with it. Oh, Les played with a broken wrist, I played five games with a broken ankle. Listen, any 'backer worth his salt enjoys inflicting and even being inflicted upon."

Pool was fired after a player-coach uprising following the 1954 season and Sid Gillman was brought in from Cincinnati University. Gillman made a tactical move at the beginning of training camp to counter his college image. He called in Paul and Fears and Van Brocklin and made them an ex-officio committee. "He asked us what we thought about curfews," Paul said, "what did we think about this, or that. And when we got into the league season we won our first five games. After that, you didn't hear anything about 'college coach.' We didn't care if he came from high school."

Paul had been voted, by the Detroit Lions, "the league's dirtiest player," as reported in *Time* magazine. It was a reputation that almost cost him a role on Gillman's team. "We played an exhibition in Portland that summer against Pittsburgh," Paul said, "and I kicked one of their guys right in the ass, as hard as I could. He'd been holding me. While I was teeing off, the ball carrier ran right by me. Gillman had a fit. He said he was going to cut me off the squad. And yet before the training season was over he named me defensive captain. That's the way Sid was, doing the psychological thing, showing the squad that here's a guy who was almost gone and now he's captain."

Gillman was astounded at the particular talents of the men he had, especially as throwers and catchers. The air game reigned supreme. "It wasn't a question of innovations," he said. "We had Dutch Van Brocklin, godawmighty what a passer he was. We had Fears and Bob Boyd, the sprinter, and Hirsch back out of retirement, and a great back, Ron Waller.

"The main thing was Fears. We were just beginning to understand how 'moves' are made by a receiver. Fears was one of the greatest 'move' men in the history of the game. He didn't have much speed, but he could turn 'em on their heads. We studied Fears and we began to coach what he was doing.

"Another thing was the success of the Giants' defense. The Giants preached that if you wanted to stop passing, the way to do it was man-to-man. As a consequence, everybody believed it—coaches are inclined to grab from the successful team, to this day. Well, perhaps the Giants could do it, but with us it was bombs away, and there was just no way the man-to-man was going to stop the bomb."

And the bombardier, the Dutchman, was nonpareil. "Every time Van Brocklin threw the ball," Gillman says, "you could hear a little 'zzt!' as it left his fingertips. We commented about it in practice. Zzt! Zzt! It was an oddity. Well, one week Van Brocklin hurt his hand and he could hardly throw in practice. You no longer heard that 'zzt!' And then one day, he started throwing better and better, and suddenly we could hear it again. Everybody started laughing and yelling, 'The zzt is back.'"

Gillman's Rams came into the final game of the season half a game ahead of Chicago and needing to defeat Green Bay to win the conference title. "We didn't know what kind of a crowd we were going to have, and we looked around the Coliseum and there's ninety thousand, just wall-to-wall people. The popularity of pro ball in L.A. then was not to be believed. We'd average ninety thousand people at home. The Brinks truck used to stop every fifteen minutes at the stadium to haul the money away."

The Rams disposed of the Packers easily in the Western Conference and met the Browns in a last title game. Los Angeles didn't play for an NFL championship again until 1979. "Otto Graham's running won the game for them," Gillman says. "I think he ran for two. And they came out in a Double Wing, a formation they hadn't shown before and we didn't cope with it very well. I think Otto was out to prove something. It was his last game." It ended 38-14, and Graham went out a winner—a champion.

Still, it was a great beginning for the rookie head coach. In the loser's locker room there was a certain amount of euphoria, and a word of caution from Schramm. "Sid," he said, "just remember it isn't always going to be this easy."

The Rams' record tumbled the next four seasons and Gillman was fired at the end of 1959. The Rams spent those years becoming famous for owner squabbles and massive trades. Schramm went to work for CBS television in New York and Pete Rozelle became general manager. A telegram dated February 28, 1959, addressed to commissioner Bert Bell belongs in the Rams' archives:

LOS ANGELES RAMS TRADE TO CHICAGO CARDINALS TACKLE KEN PANFIL, TACKLE FRANK FULLER, TACKLE ART HAUSER, TACKLE GLENN HOLTZMAN, END JOHN TRACEY, FULLBACK LARRY HICKMAN, HALF-BACK DON BROWN, THE RAMS' SECOND DRAFT CHOICE IN THE 1959 SE-LECTION MEETING, PLUS A PLAYER TO BE DELIVERED DURING THE 1959 TRAINING CAMP SEASON, IN EXCHANGE FOR FULLBACK OLLIE MATSON.

PETE ROZELLE LOS ANGELES FOOTBALL CLUB

That massive turnover turned out to be inconsequential, but it was a symbol of the Rams' troubles. They traded away three quarterbacks who later won NFL championships elsewhere (Van Brocklin, Billy Wade, and Frank Ryan) and kept discarding heroes as fast as they were grown—Red Phillips, Del Shofner, and Jon Arnett. The club's decided edge over the rest of the league at the draft table convinced them that draft choices were better than humans.

"That was after I left," Don Paul said. "Don't tell me about that. I just remember the good years."

"Every time Van Brocklin threw the ball," Gillman says, "you could hear a little `zzt!' as it left his fingertips. We commented about it in practice. Zzt! Zzt! It was an oddity."

7

The Game on the Line

When the decade rolled in, Ernie Stautner was in business with his brother-in-law, building a drive-in movie theater in Saranac Lake, New York. The heavy work (constructing 250 speaker stands) had to be done in the cellar of Ed Hoffman's house, and their arrangement was nothing if not equitable.

Hoffman would pour the concrete—into a mold the size of a small washtub—and Stautner would carry the thing up to the front porch. "We got half of them done," he said, "and the porch fell in." Thereafter, Stautner had to carry them into the front yard, then load them onto a pickup truck.

The New York Giants never fully realized it, but this exercise with concrete cost them a horrendous amount of trouble the next 14 years—and more. Perhaps the one incident that would best encapsulate Stautner's career in the NFL occurred the season after it ended, when he was a rookie defensive line coach for his old team, the Pittsburgh Steelers.

Coach Stautner had spent all summer teaching his replacement, first-year man Ben McGee, his tricks of the trade. These tricks were primarily physical, as even Stautner would gleefully admit. And all went well until the first game against New York, when McGee was matched against a gentle giant of the offensive line, Roosevelt Brown. In the first quarter, Brown suddenly began slugging McGee, and McGee began slugging back, and both were ejected from the game.

New York writers were astounded. Rosey Brown had never so much as drawn a 15-yard roughing penalty in all his life. What happened? Brown's reply was succinct: "I took that shit from Stautner for eight years, but I'll be goddamned if I'll take it from a rookie."

The thing was, back in 1950, Stautner's exercise with the drive-in stanchions had wasted him down to a svelte 215 pounds. You couldn't blame New York owner Wellington Mara and head coach Steve Owen for looking askance at a skinny Stautner when he applied for a job at their—untimely coincidence—Saranac Lake training camp. "Mara and Owen told me," Stautner said, "that they had guys like Arnie Weinmeister, Al DeRogatis, Jim White—nobody at tackle who was smaller than six-three or weighed less than two-forty-five. I told them I didn't care how much anybody weighed, or how tall they were, I could make their team and I would *start* at tackle on offense or on defense."

As Stautner learned, Mara and Owen didn't believe him, and so was launched a career in the 1950s that seemed to symbolize all those championship players who never had a chance to play on a championship team.

It even may have been more than that. Alexander Solzhenitsyn spent the fifties in Siberia, but not by choice. Stautner knew what he was doing when he signed with the Pittsburgh Steelers—oh, brother, did he know. But he accepted it, welcomed it, fought it, and, in the end, conquered it. Stautner survives in pro football history as a member of the Hall of Fame; and, yet, who were the great ones of the Philadelphia Eagles, the Chicago Cardinals, the Washington Redskins...the men in the pits who slogged out a career and never saw their names in the deathless line-up of a championship game? Stautner stands for them all. In his decade, no team had less of a look-in on the glory days than Pittsburgh. Not that he'll concede such a point. "Whaddya mean?" he said, loud in indignation. "I never thought we didn't have a chance to win until we were *mathematically* eliminated!"

Roosevelt Brown

It could be that Stautner symbolizes more than all of the above; it could be that he stands for a certain steeliness, a quantity of sacrifice, which emptied out of the American condition as sand pours through an hourglass.

Stautner was born in Kalm, Bavaria, and emigrated to Albany, New York, at age 3. By the time Stautner's father began farming at East Greenbush, six miles outside of Albany, his son's heart had been captured forever—by the sandlot football games at Our Lady of Angels grade school. There was a Columbia High School in East Greenbush, but it didn't have a football team. Pleading parochial devotion, Stautner won his parents' approval to attend Vincentian's Institute in Albany. "This cost money," Stautner said, "and we didn't have any money. So I worked in the Woolworth's to make it back and forth. I was a stock clerk. From three to five I'd play football, and from six to nine—the store was open until nine twice a week—I'd work at the store. I got fifty cents an hour and all the candy and popcorn I could eat. That was part of the deal."

Stautner's high school career was a subterfuge until the very last. His parents, most importantly his old-school father, mustn't know. He tore up his ankle, and never limped when Papa assigned him chores. He broke a collarbone and let it mend itself, because a doctor's bill would have ended his football. He forged his father's name to school documents absolving responsibility for injury. Mama and Papa never read the sports pages because they were printed in English.

"My senior year," Stautner said, "I made All-Albany and my picture was in the paper and some friends showed it to my father. What could he do then, but be proud? I was already through it, anyway."

Later, when someone suggested to Stautner that his father may have discovered the deception earlier, Stautner shuddered. Ernie Stautner thought he was tougher than any man in the world, but he was not so sure about that in relation to his father. "He would have killed me," he said.

In quite another way, Stautner was a perfect manchild of the fifties—a fellow who could sit at the bar and trade war stories with you.

"You were off Okinawa? In the big blow?"

"Yeah. Five days, my ass over my head."

Stautner meant the Okinawa typhoon that sank 26 navy ships and claimed uncountable lives. His credentials: Marine task force on the Black Island CVE (converted aircraft carrier). He had graduated from high school just in time to join in World War II.

For a couple of years, at least, it was more educational than testing. In 1943 he played for the Cherry Point, North Carolina, Marines, in company with Leo Nomellini. In 1944, on the West Coast, he was with the El Toro Marines, tearing it up against fellows such as Joe Stydahar, Indian Jack Jacobs, Wee Willie Wilkins, Cliff Battles—all ex-NFL stars—for the Fleet City Navy team out of California.

Ernie Stautner

This "ship's company" was fast company, indeed, and it led him to apply at war's end to the finest of all football factories, Notre Dame. "I went to South Bend and saw Frank Leahy," Stautner said. "He had everybody in the world coming out of the service to make those great teams he had right through 1949. I told him I needed help to get through college. He said I was too small and too slow to deserve help. So I said to hell with college ball, then, I will play pro."

One of Stautner's Marine buddies, guard Don Papaleo, went with him to see Herb Kopf, head coach of the Boston Yanks in the National Football League. There was a slight misunderstanding. "You fellows can't play pro football," Kopf said.

Stautner and Papaleo were ready to punch him, until they realized he meant they had to put in four years at college to be eligible. Kupf steered them to Danny Meyers at Boston College and Meyers said, hiding amazement at his good fortune, "Yeah, we'll take you on."

It is four years later and Stautner begins to get inquiries from National Football League teams about his future. "Everything I got from Pittsburgh," he said, "I wrote out, 'No, I don't want to be drafted by the Steelers,' and mailed it back. I'd heard about the Steelers, even in college. They had an undertaker [Ray Byrne] in Pittsburgh sending out the questionnaires—a guy we called Digger O'Dell. He was their scouting department. I told Digger I didn't want any."

Whereupon he was drafted in the second round by the Steelers, who couldn't care less about his sentiments because there were only 12 teams in the league, only one league, and let him go make a living out of a drive-in movie if he could.

The New York Yankees of the All-America Football Conference also had drafted Stautner, and he received their contract in the mail and glowed. They had met his price. And then he picked up the morning paper and read about the merger of the two leagues. The Steelers offered him a $4,000 salary. "I countered with an equally ridiculous demand, twelve thousand," Stautner said.

The Steelers sent business manager Earl Holloran to negotiate. Stautner came down, Holloran came up—finally to an agreed figure of $7,000. "Holloran went into the bathroom and came out with the contract all folded up," Stautner said. "'Sign here,' he said. I said, 'Hey, let me see what's on top.' We had quite an argument and finally I made him show the upper part of the contract and it said $6,000. I threw him out of the house. I told him that's it with the Steelers, I'd never play for 'em after that. I wired Bert Bell, the commissioner of the league, and said I was going to sue Pittsburgh, and the NFL and *him*, and I'll never forget, Bell called me long distance and he said, 'Stautner, who in the hell are *you*?'"

Out of this contretemps, Stautner asked and received permission to "make a deal for himself" with the New York Giants. He had arrived on the scene as innocent as a newborn babe, if not more so. But he was learning fast. "I was naive," he said. "I thought the league was open. Hell, the Steelers just called the Giants and said, 'Don't pay attention to this nut.'" Cerebrally, Stautner could accept that. But, physically, he was to play his greatest games against the Giants who rejected him, a dedication he did not reveal until years later when he had become the defensive coach of the Dallas Cowboys.

"I screwed it up a notch anytime I went against the Giants," Stautner admitted. "One time when there had just been a book out about the Giants' 'Umbrella Defense,' they came into town and they didn't have a quarterback so Tom Landry had to play quarterback. In the first quarter I broke his nose, and we won something like forty-nine to fourteen and I remember walking off the field, yelling at the Giants where they could stick their umbrella."

Of course, when Stautner became an assistant on Landry's Dallas staff in 1966, he hoped no one would remind the coach of that game.

Looking back, even the broken nose was worth it. Stautner would forever be collecting for that moment of turndown in Saranac Lake. "I told Steve Owen, 'You'll be sorry,'" he said. But Stautner knew he'd be sorry first, and he was prepared for it. "I got back home and got on the phone to the Steelers. I told them to send me the damned contract for six thousand dollars, I would sign it. The only way I had to get to the Giants was through Pittsburgh—and, besides, if I wanted to go on playing football, it was the Steelers or nothing."

The coach of the 1950 Steelers was John Michelosen, who had gained his fame at the University of Pittsburgh. "Michelosen," Stautner said, "thought he was Jock Sutherland. He was no Jock Sutherland."

The point of this opinion is that Sutherland had kept the Steelers in a Single Wing offense in defiance of the new fad in pro football, the T-formation. Michelosen persisted in the Single Wing. "There is no way to practice the Single Wing," Stautner said, "unless you go all out—and hit. It is slam, bang, thank-you-ma'am. Or it's no good. So in training camp we scrimmaged and we scrimmaged—four hours a day. I didn't think anything of it.

Stautner gradually became aware that other pro football teams did things differently. "The veterans who came to us from other clubs," he said, "they couldn't believe this was happening. I remember from those days the sounds of squeaking shoes, moving down the hall. I'd crack open the door and see a veteran, a suitcase in each hand, tiptoeing out the door. Dan Rooney, the owner's son, he and another guy had a regular morning assignment—drive out on the highway to talk the guys into coming back. We were training at Cambridge Springs, Pennsylvania, and there was no railroad, not even a bus line, so the only way the guys could get out was to hitchhike. Rooney and the other guy would tail 'em back. When other clubs were worrying about cutting down the roster limit, the Steelers were worrying about keeping enough guys in camp to play exhibition games."

Michelosen's practice sessions developed some on-the-spot dramatics. "We had a big defensive tackle—he was six-five and two-sixty-five—and he was a veteran, named Carl Samuelson, from Nebraska," Stautner said. "One day in the middle of practice he drops and starts writhing in pain. 'Oh, my knee!' he says. The trainer runs up and says, 'Which knee?' Samuelson wasn't taking any chances. '*Both* of 'em,' he says.

"A few days later we're having a run-through of plays, and when the Steelers ran through plays the running backs had to *go*—like thirty yards downfield. We had a rookie halfback named Horn. I don't remember what else about him, but he only ran about ten yards and pulled up. This is after we'd gone into our fourth hour of workouts that day. The backfield coach was Mike Nixon and he yelled, 'All the way, Horn! You gotta go all the way!' Horn never looked back. He slammed the ball on the ground and kept running. He yelled, 'Look, you son-of-a-bitch, I'm *going* all the way,' and he ran to the locker room and out of the stadium. We never saw him again. To this day, I don't know what became of Horn."

This kind of preparation resulted in the special personality for Steelers teams. "After a whole week of workouts like that," Stautner said, "playing a game was like having a day off, like having a party. I guess we took it out on the other guys." The

Buddy Parker

"other guys" got the message. Tom Landry said of his days with the Giants, "We would much rather play Cleveland twice than the Steelers once. The Browns would beat you on the scoreboard, but the Steelers would make you ache all week."

Stautner bristled at such putdowns. "You look it up," he said, "and with all those great Giants teams we got our share of wins. We played physical, all right, but we had it on the scoreboard, too." Indeed, while the Steelers were finishing fourth—except for two years in third—in the NFL's Eastern Conference, they played the Giants dead-even. In the 1950s, Stautner's team went 45-54 against the rest of the league, but 9-9 against the successful Giants.

There was more to inspire the Steelers to meanness than the rugged workouts they were put through. In fact, practice sessions became relatively tame under Joe Bach and then Walt Kiesling. The Steelers were motivated in other ways. Buddy Parker, the championship coach from Detroit, moved to Pittsburgh in 1957. "I finally got an idea why the Steelers were the way they were," Parker said. "A player reacts to his surroundings, and the way he's treated. The Steelers had a horrible little office off the lobby of the Roosevelt Hotel downtown. It was a mess. Even Art Rooney's office wasn't respectable. And they played and worked out at Forbes Field, the baseball park. Rats ran around the dressing room. The field itself was terrible, and I don't mean just the skinned part of the infield, which nobody ever dreamed of sodding. They didn't even have a tarp until I got there, and when they had one you couldn't get anybody to put it down. When it rained we practiced in the mud all week. I don't believe we ever lost a bad-weather game there. The Giants would come in, or the 49ers, and they would slip and slide and curse the mud. And we were just slopping around in it with no mind. Now, you take all these things, including how you travel your players and how you take care of them at hotels, and if you're not treating them like champions they are not going to play like champions."

"No," Stautner said. "They are going to play mean. We knew everybody had it better than us. But they were going to have to take us on man-to-man every Sunday. A lot of times when we went somewhere close to training camp for an exhibition game, we never even got into a hotel—I mean, not into the rooms. We flew into Hershey one time to play Philadelphia and they took us down to the Schenley Hotel and said, 'Okay, fellows, sit around the lobby until game time.' There were games where we had a four-and-a-half hour bus ride from our Cambridge Springs camp and back."

Stautner's style of retribution became his own patent on the field. "My move," he said, "was to slap one hand to the side of the helmet and then come up with the other forearm—right and left, left and right, it doesn't make any difference, though I think it worked better with the left-hand slap and the right forearm."

Stautner had learned at Boston College that this kind of work was hard on the forearms. One Saturday he had forgotten to tape his arms, and then had to spend a night in the hospital letting the broken blood vessels drain.

In the NFL, his arms always were taped, and some opponents complained to officials that there were other things inside the tape than muscle and bone. The accusation brought a joyous laughter from Stautner. "It was all me," he said, proudly.

His toughness became legend around the league, so his teammates were astounded one summer evening in 1957 when a Pittsburgh rookie invited Stautner to "step outside." They were in the lobby of the Roosevelt Hotel after an exhibition game. "This kid, a big defensive tackle from the farm country, had been needling me about something," Stautner said, "and I just told him to go away, go play with his toys, and he said he wanted to fight. We went out to the alley alongside the hotel and it wasn't much of a fight, except we knocked over some garbage cans and people in the hotel were hanging out windows. I picked him up and walked him back into the lobby, and I asked him what the hell was this all about? He said, 'My college coach told me if I wanted to make it in the pros, I had to pick out the toughest guy on the team and whip his ass.' Can you imagine that? Not a bad idea, but he wasn't much of a player, and they sent him back to the farm."

Stautner's physical condition and his amazing constitution were tested to the utmost later that season, when a team doctor blundered in giving him pregame medication. Buddy Parker recalled, "This was a society doctor, a friend of a friend of Rooney's. He was a very dandy dresser. Ernie had a muscle spasm in his shoulder, so the doctor said he'd give him a relaxant while we were in pregame warmup and then he'd be ready to go. When I came back Ernie was out cold. I said, 'I thought he'd be ready. What's wrong with him?' The doctor said, 'I don't know.' Then Ernie went into convulsions and they had to rush him to the hospital. Now isn't that something to happen to a coach, losing one of his top players just before the kickoff?"

The doctor had mixed ampules and given Stautner a lethal dose of demarol. At the hospital, interns sent for a priest to administer the last rites. "When I saw the father," Stautner said, "I knew things were bad. He leaned down and said, 'I have come to hear your confession, my son.' I said, 'Okay, father, but I don't have much time, so if it's all the same to you I'll only hit the highlights.'"

The arrival of Parker in 1957, and Parker's acquisition of quarterback Bobby Layne the next season, gave Stautner renewed hope. He had never enjoyed a winning season in eight years until Layne came along. "It was a thrill to get Parker and Layne," Stautner said. "Now I knew we'd be a winner."

The combination produced a 7-4-1 record in 1958, when the Steelers went undefeated in their last six games. There were more changes than that. "Parker had us going first class from the day he got there," Stautner said. "And Layne...there was just no way you could tell Layne he was going to lose. He was like me, or I was like him."

The two became roommates and close friends off the field as well. Layne introduced Stautner to a lifestyle he had never known. "I never bounced around much before Layne got there," he said, "mainly because you would run into fans who would knock the ball club all night. But Bobby changed that. Oh, we had some times. But it never interfered with football. I remember once we stayed out all night and came right to practice without sleep. We'd work out for a while, then go over to the sidelines and throw up. Parker was watching, but he didn't say anything. But—we would stay after practice and work extra. That's because we owed it to the club. We had our fun, but we were making it up. Then we left practice and went bouncing around again."

The elusive championship was to elude Stautner forever, and Pittsburgh ended the careers of all three: first Layne and then Parker and finally Stautner. "Sure, I'd do it all over again—if I had to," Stautner said. "But I don't mind telling you, it might have been more fun with the Giants."

Of course, as matters developed, Ernie had no choice. He was not only supporting himself and his family, but the drive-in movie, which for 15 years was a drain on his pocketbook. "My brother-in-law wanted to keep it going." Stautner said,

Parker: "Forbes Field didn't even have a tarp until I got there, and when they had one you couldn't get anybody to put it down. When it rained we practiced in mud all week."

Art Donovan

sadly. "He just refused to admit that it was too damned cold in Saranac Lake to go to an outdoor movie."

There was a touch of irony in that. Elsewhere, the drive-in theater flourished in the fifties, a sign of the times. They were called passion-pits, and a generation of teenagers did their serious courting there.

Cheap entertainment still was in vogue. Bowling. Cards. The beach. Picnics. People played parlor games called Monopoly and Parcheesi. The real boom in leisure time, bringing with it boats, stereos, motor homes and sports cars, was a few years away.

Pro football players, with their limited freedom and less money to enjoy it, found many creative ways to agitate each other. Such as eating contests.

The extroverted Baltimore tackle, Art Donovan, promoted an eat-off during one training camp, matching his man, Gino Marchetti, against Don Joyce, an offseason wrestler known to his teammates as "The Champ." The Colts ponied up close to $500 in bets, the issue being which contestant could put away the most chicken.

Marchetti devoured 26 pieces of chicken, but was simply outclassed by Joyce, who out-ate himself. "Joyce was eating it all," said Donovan. "Thirty-six pieces of chicken, plus peas and mashed potatoes. You know, the full Maryland dinner. I think he even ate the bones. When the match was over he poured himself a glass of iced tea. Then he reached into his pocket and put two packets of saccharin in the tea. He looked up and explained, 'I got to watch my weight.'"

Donovan was one of the symbolic players of the fifties, a lovable rogue, with an Irish zest for life and cold drink. On the bus to a game he would mentally fix the temperature outside and determine how much beer he would need, after the game, to resupply his body fluids. Then he would turn to his seat-mate, usually Bill Pellington, and announce, "Well, Bill, it looks like a six-canner today."

Pro football was a smaller world then, in some respects almost parochial. It was the way high school football still is in rural Texas, where no one is a stranger, and they know what is going on in the next town and they read each other's writeups.

Donovan came to Baltimore in 1950 as a rookie out of Boston College, where he had been known as "The Other Tackle," opposite the more publicized Ernie Stautner. When Ernie was elected to the Professional Football Hall of Fame in 1969—a year after Donovan's enshrinement—it represented a unique sweep for Boston College. No college ever had qualified both positions—in this case, both defensive tackles—off the same team.

Donovan—they called him "Little Arthur," for family reasons—was the inheritor of a colorful sports tradition. His grandfather Mike was the world middleweight boxing champion, after serving as a teenage soldier in the Civil War. His father Big Arthur was one of the most famous boxing referees of his time, the third man in the ring for 18 world heavyweight title fights, including the historic rematch when Joe Louis knocked out Max Schmeling.

Young Arthur served with the Marines in World War II aboard the aircraft carrier San Jacinto. His father volunteered, though he then was in his 60s, to work with USO sports tours, an assignment that brought him one day to a dirt road on an island called Guam. He turned to a companion, pointed, and said with some excitement, "That Marine coming down the road...I know him."

The Marine was his son Little Arthur, now grown to a brute of a fellow at 250, casually bumping into his old man halfway across the world from their home in the Bronx.

Art was a strong, gutsy tackle with an instinct for which direction a play was going. He had a round, almost cherubic face that contradicted his toughness; a face hardened not at all by the 39 stitches needed to mend it after two 1951 accidents—a slash across the cheek from the spikes of an unidentified shoe, and a cut over one eye (nine stitches) from a Deacon Dan Towler elbow.

Donovan's weakness was food. He could gain weight by breathing in the fumes from a distant bakery. In 1954, he ballooned to 309 pounds, after which the Colts inserted in his contract a clause providing that he would be fined $50 for every five pounds he weighed over 265. Never again did the Colts have to weigh him on a freight scale. Obediently, Art held his weight at 265 or below.

He was the team's dispenser of sunshine, and in his view all the players were great, all the brothers valiant. On the day of his most meaningful honor, when the skill and courage of his long career were recognized, Art Donovan remembered a player he couldn't whip.

"I know one fellow who has to be laughing," Artie said, "when he reads that I made the Hall of Fame. That was a guard by the name of Bruno Banducci, who played for the San Francisco 49ers and blocked me all over the field. What a great lineman."

Unfailingly, they respected each other. It seemed as if there was always someone playing out there who could eat your lunch, chicken bones and all.

It was no coincidence that so many of the enduring linemen of the fifties were Irish, Italian, or Polish, who had fought a war and made it to college on football grants and G.I. subsidies, who came from the farms and mines of America, born of European parents who saw no purpose in games where people hurt each other.

When Gino Marchetti's father agreed, reluctantly, to allow his son to play football, he warned him: "Gino, whatever you do, stay out of the other boys' way so they no hurt you."

Over the years, many an offensive lineman and running back had reason to wish that Gino had listened to his good Italian papa.

His father was so opposed to the sport, that he never watched his son play in high school or college. He did not relent until the 1958 sudden-death title game, the Colts against the Giants, and he tuned in on television. "And in that one," Gino pointed out, "I broke my leg."

That play, and its immediate aftermath, may have been the best remembered moments of Marchetti's career. With the Colts trailing by three, and a little more than a minute to play, the Giants needed a yard for the first down that would have enabled them to run out the clock. But a Baltimore charge led by Marchetti met Frank Gifford at the line of scrimmage, and the yard might as well have been a mile. As the Colts wrestled Gifford down, Big Daddy Lipscomb fell across Gino's ankle, breaking it in two places.

From deep in their own end of the field, the Giants had to punt, and Unitas began the drive that brought the Colts back and sent the game into overtime, and into legend.

Marchetti, of course, had been carried off the field. But he had the stretcher bearers pause at the mouth of the stadium tunnel, and from there he saw Steve Myhra kick the field goal that tied the score. Later, flat on his back, Gino received the game ball.

From his childhood in Antioch, in northern California, there seemed to be an extra dimension to the way Marchetti lived and played. His Italian parents were in-

When Gino Marchetti's father agreed, reluctantly, to allow his son to play football, he warned him: "Gino, whatever you do, stay out of the other boys' way so they no hurt you."

65

Gino Marchetti

terned, along with the town's Japanese families, at the outset of the war. On his eighteenth birthday, he quit school and enlisted in the army. His parents were released when the news reached the local papers that Gino Marchetti was winning medals, fighting with the Sixty-ninth Infantry on the Siegfried Line.

After the war, he finished high school, tended bar, and resumed his football career at Modesto Junior College. He was recruited for the University of San Francisco by an assistant coach, Brad Lynn, who found him at a racetrack, dressed in grimy overalls and smoking a cigar. He was not exactly the picture of a young man you would want to bring home to the Jesuit priests.

But Lynn hauled him to the campus, where head coach Joe Kuharich saw them coming out of his office window. He took one look and whispered to Lynn: "Get that Okie out of here—fast."

"But Joe," protested Lynn, "this kid picks up the interference and throws them at the ball carrier."

"Does, eh?" said Kuharich, quickly reconsidering his position on "Okies."

In his early years as a pro, Marchetti, 6-4 and 245, was a self-avowed hatchet man. He had a reputation, not undeserved, for seldom missing a chance to get in a few extra rough licks. He did not exactly get religion, but an incident involving Detroit's Doak Walker led him to clean up his game.

Walker had swept end for good yardage, when Marchetti caught him from an angle in time to keep Doak from going all the way. Pleased with himself, proud of his speed, feeling salty, Gino couldn't resist rubbing his hand across Walker's pleasant features as they disengaged. He dug the heel of his palm into Doak's nose the way you would grind out a cigarette butt with your shoe. Then he waited for Walker to complain.

But Doak didn't. He just looked at Marchetti, a long, slow, penetrating, unforgettable look. "I could see it in his eyes. I knew exactly what he was thinking. A big guy like me, with probably eighty pounds and six inches on him, having to resort to a mean, low-down trick like that. That look of disgust reformed me."

After that, Gino became a law and order man, functioning as the Baltimore "cop," the guy who dishes out the justice when an opposing player has been caught taking cheap or dirty shots. "I became the hunter, instead of the hunted," he said.

Marchetti retired at 37, after the 1964 Pro Bowl, with his place in pro football assured. Sid Gillman, once with the Rams, then coaching in San Diego, called him "the most valuable man ever to play his position."

An admiring rival, San Francisco's Leo Nomellini, said, "He was just the best defensive end there ever was. He had the look of death in his eyes [on the field]. It's a good thing his parents brought him up right."

Gino believed that the pros of his generation were tougher than modern players. Certainly they were less indulged. "We carried only thirty-three guys on a roster," he said. "Often you had to play hurt. In 1955, I played the last four games with a dislocated shoulder. I was all taped up on one side and I could use only one arm. It hurt like hell, but they had no replacement for me. Today, if a player gets a bruise or a cold, he takes Sunday off. He doesn't have to play because they have the subs now."

Marchetti was to make a lot of money in the fast food business ("Gino's"), an opportunity made possible for him by Colts owner Carroll Rosenbloom, who underwrote his first investment and advised him shrewdly.

Gino understands a contract, and the value of a buck, and he doesn't resent today's high salaries. "I don't if they produce," he said. "Me, I signed for a five-hundred dollar bonus, and it thrilled me to death. Imagine getting all that money for doing something I loved to do! My first pro contract was for sixty-five hundred."

In the fifties, it wasn't simply a matter of money. Football was still one of the ways out, an escape hatch for those born to poverty. An escape to what? Not just fame or fortune. Respectability. It offered them a chance to be respectable, in a short time, without the hours and the hardship their fathers had suffered.

One of those who made it was Robert Lee Huff, called Sam for reasons long since forgotten. Sam Huff, from Jamison Number 9, a tiny company town in West Virginia where people lived in five-room houses, all in a row, painted red to hide the coal dust, a town where the sons grew up to work in the mines with their fathers.

When West Virginia sent a scout to watch Sam's high school team play, their interest was really in one of his teammates. "Rudy Banick was his name," Huff said. "But the guy saw me and the next thing I knew I was talking to Pappy Lewis [the head coach]. Rudy didn't make it and he wound up working in the mines. It's that close. If they don't like you, there's nothing to do but go get a shovel."

Sam Huff never owned a suit until he went to college. They called the football team at West Virginia the Mountaineers, but it was Park Avenue compared to the life he knew. On his first day on campus, Pappy Lewis and one of his coaches climbed on a blocking sled and told him to hit it. "I had never seen one before," Sam said. "In high school we used each other for those drills. I hit the sled and it flattened me. As I lay on my back, I heard Pappy say, 'There goes another scholarship wasted.' And I hadn't even enrolled yet."

Huff played on the team that lifted West Virginia to national prominence. He flew to New York, after the 1955 season, as a member of the *Look* magazine All-America team, and there he met Wellington Mara of the Giants, who had drafted him. Huff agreed to sign for $7,000 when Mara offered $500 in cash to pay his bills. It was irresistible. He did not know, until he found the deduction in his first paycheck, that it wasn't a bonus.

He came along when pro football was still considered seasonal work, like picking berries. "It carried you for six months," he said. "If you tried to live on it all year, you had nothing left. The trick was to get a good job in the offseason, and you wound up in good shape."

For Huff, as with the other bright and ambitious men, pro football became his yellow brick road. It led him to that special kind of celebrity reserved for New York sports heroes; and to corporate success, on jobs that required a public relations touch; and into politics, as a favorite of the Kennedy family.

He lasted 13 seasons, including a comeback year under Vince Lombardi at Washington, where he had retired after the 1967 season. That was roughly five years more than Huff ever had intended to play. "Most guys who stay in this business over eight years," he said, "make a mistake. Pretty soon, all they wind up being able to talk about is football. They don't know anything else.

"There is a bad psychological problem with the game. From the minute practice starts in July, until the season ends, you make yourself mean. You get mad. You say, 'To hell with them all. Look out for Ole Sam Huff. He's mean today.'"

Huff was feeling especially testy on a day in 1959 when he flattened the gentle Ray Berry on a play near the sideline. That brought Weeb Ewbank charging over

Huff agreed to sign for $7,000 when Mara offered $500 in cash to pay his bills. He did not know, until he found the deduction in his first paycheck, that it wasn't a bonus.

67

Huff: "The next day, Howell told us the bit about winning and getting a day off did not apply to rooks. We decided to quit. We figured we could make almost as much money teaching school."

from the Baltimore bench, screaming at Huff and shaking a pudgy fist, accusing him of playing dirty. "He hit me right in the neck," Huff said. "So I popped him on the chin with a punch. I would've hit him again, too, because I didn't like the way I got him the first time. I wanted to cream him. I was wild."

In 1956, Huff reported to the Giants of head coach Jim Lee Howell, whose staff included Vince Lombardi as offensive coach and Tom Landry as defensive coach. Huff was one of a group of five rookies arriving late from the All-Star game to the Giants' training camp in Vermont. Don Chandler, the punter, was another one.

"We were tired, hungry, and pretty well beaten up by the Browns," Huff said, "but after we got a snack—in place of supper—Howell told us to be ready to scrimmage the next day. He said the winning team in the scrimmage would get the following day off. I played middle guard, on the head of the center, and I will never forget—Chandler attempted to punt and I actually caught the ball as it came off his foot and ran about fifty-five yards for a score, and our Blue team won over the White.

"The next day, Howell told us the bit about winning and getting a day off did not apply to rooks and we had to work out against the White team. We decided to quit, Chandler and me. We figured we could make almost as much money teaching school. We were homesick, too. I was a hillbilly from West Virginia, and Don was a country boy from Oklahoma. I had a sore knee, too.

"We went down to turn in our playbooks to Howell, who roomed with Lombardi. Howell wasn't there, and Lombardi was taking a nap. I raised my voice and said, 'Coach,' and he woke up. I'll never forget that, either. It was the first time I ran into Lombardi because he only worked with the offense. Chandler was standing behind me. When I said, 'Coach, we've decided to quit,' Lombardi flew into a rage. Chandler ran out of the room. I couldn't turn quick enough, because of my bad knee. Lombardi scared me to death. Chandler kept going, all the way to the airport, and Lombardi went after him. He talked us into staying. Don finished up his career playing for him in Green Bay and so did I, in Washington."

Huff and Detroit's Joe Schmidt were the model linebackers of their time: quick enough to get back to cover pass receivers, big enough to drag down backs barreling through the line. Huff was poison to running backs with big reputations. In 1957, when the Chicago Bears visited New York, they were led by Rick Casares, who was ripping the league apart. The Giants put Huff on him, one on one, and the big fullback wound up gaining only nine yards all day. That game established Sam as a New York hero.

In 1958, his duels with Cleveland's Jim Brown were treated as a kind of *mano a mano*. The day after one of their confrontations, the two were reintroduced by a mutual friend. Brown was sporting a swollen nose, a mouse under one eye, and assorted bruises. "Sam Huff," the guy said, "I would like you to meet Jim Brown."

"I don't want to meet him," Huff said. "I met him yesterday." And the evidence seemed to bear him out.

As the defenses of the fifties matured and grew more demanding, Sam Huff came to symbolize that side of the game. "The Violent World of Sam Huff" was first the title of a magazine story, and, later, the title of a television special. The science of playing defense totally absorbed him. In 1958, the Giants struggled past Cleveland 13-10 in the final regular-season game. In the process, Huff reduced the entire mystique of playing defense to one stop-action moment:

"We got Robustelli, Katcavage, Grier, and Modzelewski on the line. We're in

Portfolio:
DEFENDERS

Philadelphia's Chuck Bednarik (60) was "the last of the 60-minute men," a Pro Football Hall of Fame center and linebacker who was tougher than a leather helmet.

The NFL of the 1950s was rife with bullies, none of whom was nastier than Hardy Brown (opposite), whose shoulder dizzied many a ball carrier. Other headhunters included, clockwise from top left, Ed Meadows, who fell out of favor after breaking Bobby Layne's ankle; Ed Sprinkle, nicknamed "Pattycake" for his impolite late hits; Bud McFadin, whose career briefly was interrupted when he was shot in the stomach in a barroom brawl; and Charley Powell, who made an attempt at professional boxing.

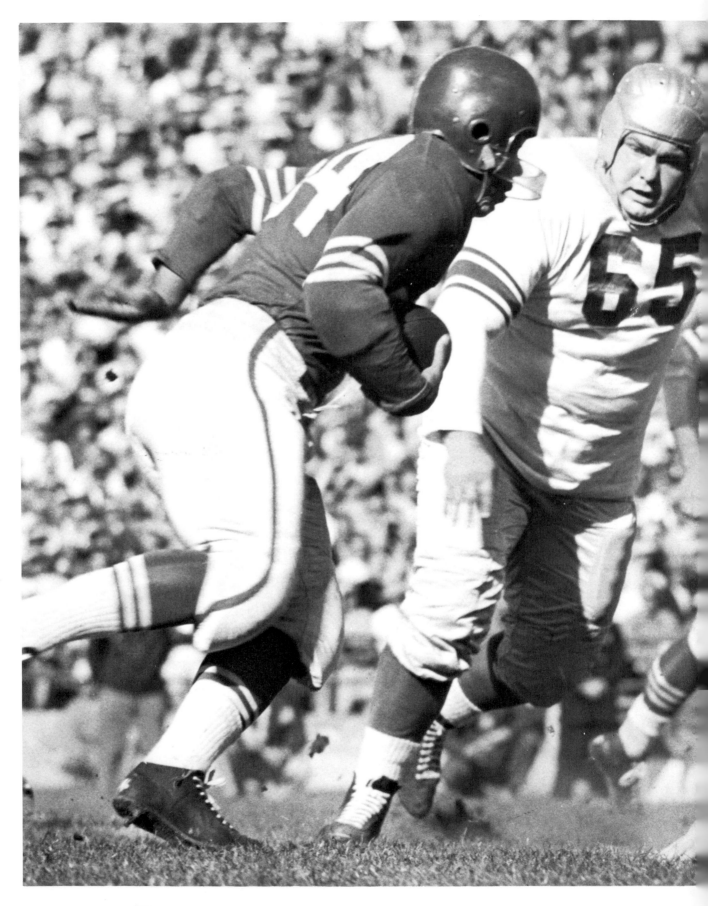

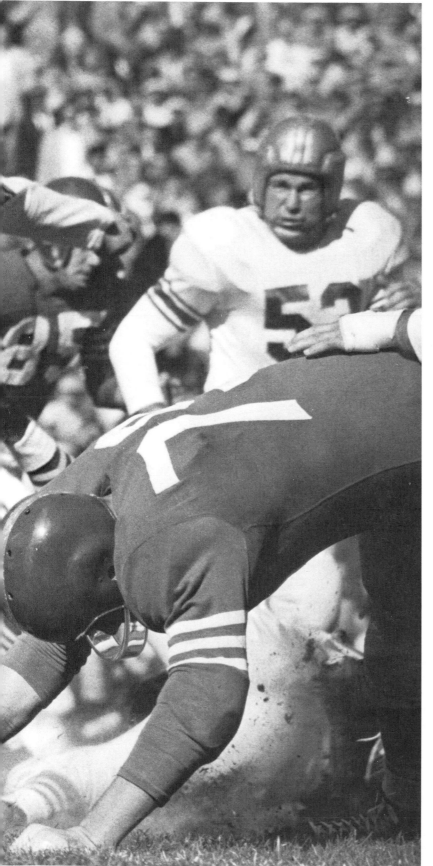

Les, but not least: Les Bingaman (left) was teased about his girth, but the big guy was a dominant defender. The Rams' Les Richter (above) didn't get as much attention as Sam Huff or Joe Schmidt, but he might have been the best and toughest linebacker of his era.

Even the defensive backs seemed to be tougher in the Eisenhower decade. One-eyed Bobby Dillon (opposite) was voted to four Pro Bowls, despite playing for the Packers, the NFL's losingest team. Detroit's Jim David (left), a six-time Pro Bowl choice, broke Y.A. Tittle's cheek and jaw, and Tom Fears's back—in the same season. Don (Blade) Burroughs (below) was a fiery, underpublicized player.

Ernie Stautner was an all-pro defensive tackle who would give up anything short of his life for a Steelers' victory.

what we call an outside four-three. My job is to cover the center and the two guards. They got Art Hunter over the ball. Milt Plum is the quarterback. Jim Ray Smith and Chuck Noll are the guards. Jimmy Brown is at fullback. I key off him. We figure him to run about twenty-eight out of their fifty-six offensive plays, so I get ready to step right into the line the minute the ball is snapped.

Joe Schmidt

"I key myself off Brown—and Hunter, too. I'm watching how Hunter gets over the ball. If his rear end starts sagging, I figure he's gettin' ready to drop back and protect the passer. If he's pushing over that ball, I figure he's ready to block ahead for a run. He's pushing this time. I'm ready to come in. Then we catch it.

"I step into the line, but Cleveland is blocking down. Their linemen are going for the man inside them. They got good angles. They pull Smith and he gets our end, Katcavage, coming in. Everywhere else they angle-block us. I come in and Noll gets me from the blind side. Smith pushes Katcavage out. Brown goes through tackle. I see him going but I can't do a thing. Sixty-five yards he goes, and we're a touchdown behind before most of the people get to their seats. "But here's the thing. As I was going down, *I knew what Cleveland had done to us*. The minute we got off the ground, we told Katcavage not to charge in if he sees the Cleveland tackle blocking down. We told him to close up the hole. You know, drift down the line. He did that for the rest of the game and we came out a winner.

"Now that's professional football to me."

It also was the sight of Joe Schmidt backing up the line, neck pulled in like a killer turtle, pep-talking the Lions. He was the middle linebacker to whom Huff was most often compared, the first of the great ones to make the Hall of Fame at a position he helped create. (The middle linebacker didn't exist until the four-man front came in.)

The professional *attitude* was seldom more honestly represented than by Schmidt. He shared temmate Bobby Layne's contempt for failure, for dumbness, for not bearing down. Schmidt was enraged when Milt Plum threw a pass interception in the final two minutes of a game against the Packers, losing one the defense had fought mightily to win. As Joe saw it, he could have kept the ball on the ground, used up the clock, then let the defense stop them.

For weeks after that, each time the ball went over and they passed each other on the field, Schmidt would say to him: "Run three times Milt, and then punt."

Schmidt was as subtle as a punch in the mouth. In 1952, he captained an ordinary University of Pittsburgh team that found itself a large underdog to Notre Dame. Before the game, the Pitt head coach, Red Dawson, left the locker room, while Captain Schmidt delivered the pregame inspirational. It consisted almost entirely of a promise to whip the ass of every man in the room if Pitt did not defeat Notre Dame, which it proceeded to do, by a score of 22-19.

Schmidt was a fiery presence on the Lions for 13 years, joining the team in 1953, on the heels of that championship season. Buddy Parker, hoping to doctor the team before age could overtake it, began trading away some of his regulars to make room for the young Lions. When Parker dealt off Dick Flanagan, the middle guard, in favor of Schmidt, some of the veterans complained. "They wouldn't have anything to do with me," Schmidt said. "I went through six league games as a regular and no one talked to me. I played the game, dressed, and then I went home to my apartment and looked at the wall."

The veterans did not tolerate rookies gladly. But Joe Schmidt paid his dues with pride and talent, coin they all understand. He was their surest tackler. He loved to

Frank Gifford

blitz. And he had the kind of dedication that made him, always, the last man off the practice field.

Near the end of his career, when the Lions were trying to tame the wildly erratic halfback, Joe Don Looney, they commissioned Schmidt to call on him, on a day when Looney failed to show up for practice. He simply had decided that he needed a day off. The Lions were hoping desperately that Looney would turn out to be the big halfback they had been needing for so many years, but he was not what you would call reliable.

Schmidt walked into the room to find Looney sitting cross-legged on his bed, his hi-fi set turned up full blast. "Joe," Schmidt began, gently, "we sure missed you out there today."

Looney said, "Well, I'm kinda glad you did, Joe."

Schmidt said, "I'd just like to say one thing: I've been with this club twelve years and I've never missed a practice or been late for a meeting in all those twelve years."

Looney's eyes widened and he looked at Schmidt quizzically. "You mean to tell me you never missed *one* practice in twelve years?"

"That's right," Schmidt said.

"Goddam, Joe," said Looney, "pull up a chair. If there was ever a guy who needed a day off it's you."

If there was one other guy his name would be Chuck Bednarik, the last of the two-way linemen, the last of pro football's 60-minute men. *Bednarik.* Just the sound of it was like a character reading: tough, mean, hard as an anvil. And something else. Absolutely unforgiving.

He was born hard-nosed. He was another of those products of a lean childhood, this one in Bethlehem, Pennsylvania, where his father worked at the open hearth in the steel mills. The first footballs he owned were those he made himself, stockings stuffed with leaves or cloth. His first authentic football was one his father picked up as a merchandise premium, in exchange for 25 coffee bags.

At 18, he flew the first of his 30 missions over Germany, as the waist gunner on a bomber.

In the post-war years, when Glenn Davis, Doc Blanchard, Johnny Lujack, and Doak Walker were the golden boys of amateur football, Chuck Bednarik was the best of the college linemen. He was twice an All-America at Penn, the winner of the Maxwell Trophy his senior year. He did the team's punting, when he wasn't blocking or tackling.

He joined the Eagles in 1949 and for the rest of the decade was hailed as the Spirit of Philadelphia. But by the end of the 1959 season, despairing of ever playing on a championship team, Bednarik announced his retirement. The Eagles rewarded him with a color television set and a $1,000 bonus, and the fans reacted as though they had retired the Liberty Bell.

So he changed his mind and, at 36, agreed to return for the 1960 season, explaining that his wife was pregnant, again, and he needed the money to build a bigger house. Early in the season, injuries forced coach Buck Shaw to play Bednarik both at center and linebacker, promising to rest him when he got tired. He never did, or at least he never told Shaw, and week after week he held his ground, a 60-minute man in a part-time world.

Several times a game Bednarik experienced a sensation that set him apart, 42 players (both offenses and defenses) trotting on and off the field, "and there I would be, alone, waiting. It's hard to describe, staying out there with only the officials."

What happened in 1960 was enough to make an Eagles' fan believe in Kismet. With Chuck Bednarik doing double service, and playing beyond himself, the Eagles finally grabbed the brass ring. They won 10 games, carried the Eastern Conference, and then, in the climax to a fairy tale season, stopped Green Bay 17-13 to win the NFL championship. "When you win," Bednarik said, "you're on Cloud Nine. It's mostly mind over matter. You get high, you get hepped up by winning, and you keep going."

When the season telescoped down to one last play, it was Chuck Bednarik, naturally, who rose up to drop Green Bay's Jimmy Taylor at the 10-yard line. He literally pinned Taylor to the grass as time ran out. When the gun coughed, he said, his voice imperious, "You can get up now."

The home fans at Franklin Field, 67,000 of them, would have wanted it that way.

Center Bednarik had no equal in the NFL. But linebacker Bednarik always felt overshadowed by Sam Huff and Joe Schmidt. In what may have been a dig at Huff, or the New York publicity mill, or what those in sport call the "Hudson River Syndrome," Norm Van Brocklin said of his Philadelphia soul-mate: "If Chuck had played for the Giants, they would have erected a statue of him in Yankee Stadium."

Actually, what the Giants' fans really wanted to erect in his honor was a scaffold. This was in November, and the teams met with the Eastern Division title still at issue. Bednarik blindsided Frank Gifford in an open field at the Philadelphia 30, with a tackle so ferocious it knocked the popular halfback out of football for a year. Bednarik tunes in the instant replay:

"We were leading 17-10 with about 1:35 left and the Giants driving. Charlie Conerly threw Gifford a pass and he zig-zagged around. He finally headed toward me. I'm ugly. He's handsome. I'm two-forty. He's one-ninety. He never made a bigger mistake. He took his eye off me and I ran right through him. He went five feet up in the air and then landed hard. He didn't move and it didn't look like he was breathing. Giff fumbled, Chuck Weber recovered, and I knew we had the game won. I jumped up and down, because I was happy. Their team doctor ran out to work on Giff, and as he went past me made some snide remarks. He was a little guy. I was so happy I told him he was next."

Gifford did not regain consciousness for 36 hours, and the doctors forced him to retire. A year later, he returned to play three seasons as a flanker.

Bednarik didn't enjoy the sight of a motionless Gifford on the cold, hard earth, no matter how it seemed to the Giants and their fans. But he was unable to apologize, to express regret, and not only because Gifford went into television and struck it rich. It simply was against his gladiator's code to feel guilty for doing what he perceived to be his job. Sam Huff understood.

The incident could have led to a long blood-letting between the Giants and the Eagles, but it didn't, partly because Huff came forward as a witness for the defense. "By damn," he said, slapping a fist into the palm of his other hand, "we linebackers dream about making that kind of tackle...a good, clean whack that knocks the other team's big gun out of the game."

Sam Huff hated to lose, hated to see his friend Gifford hurt. But, aesthetically, he admired that tackle. An artist knows the Mona Lisa when he sees it.

Bednarik: "He [Gifford] zig-zagged around. He finally headed toward me. I'm ugly. He's handsome. I'm two-forty. He's one-ninety. He never made a bigger mistake."

What We Watched

In the second week of May, 1950, Baltimore had the distinction of becoming the first American city in which more people watched evening television than listened to radio.

It was truly the end of an era. Up to that time, hardly a home in America did not have in its living room a radio set shaped like a small cathedral. "Glued-to-their-radios" was an expression that conveyed, instantly, the import of a certain piece of news.

Creative sound effects and our own imaginations made radio more real than life. Daily, four million housewives listened to dramas such as Helen Trent, queen of the soap operas, whose message was "what so many women long to prove—that because a woman is thirty-five or more, romance in life need not be over."

But television would soon seduce us all, becoming not only a major industry but a cultural force more powerful than anything the nation had ever seen. Television turned the old western folk hero, Davy Crockett, into a multi-million dollar industry, featuring coonskin caps, T-shirts, guitars, and a record, "The Ballad of Davy Crockett," that sold four million copies.

Some tend to forget, but between Watergate and the Black Sox scandals of 1919, the severest blow to American innocence was the disclosure that the richest of television quiz shows, *The $64,000 Question*, had been rigged.

The shocking news broke in August, 1958. It developed that Charles Van Doren, a handsome English teacher at Columbia and member of a prominent literary family, had been fed the answers that enabled him to win $129,000. Such practices on other quiz shows were quickly exposed. It was a bad time for public confidence.

Despite its weaknesses and its critics, television found an outlet in the fifties for its unique capacity to entertain, inform, and educate—all at the same time. Two separate political forums provided the ideal theater.

The first, in May, 1950, was known as the Senate Crime Committee Hearings, and it catapulted the committee chairman, Estes Kefauver, to national prominence. It afforded the first real glimpse at what television could accomplish, its scope, its power, its access.

The hearings were held in six major cities, with a parade of characters out of Damon Runyon testifying while millions watched, spellbound. In New York, the star witness was gangland's elder statesman, Frank Costello. Forbidden to show his face during his testimony, the cameras dwelled on Costello's writhing hands, which frequently cradled an English Oval cigarette. The grateful manufacturers, ecstatic over such a windfall of publicity, shipped him large quantities of their product each month, which Costello forwarded to Veterans Administration hospitals.

In one of the most dramatic confrontations ever seen outside of a courtroom, television—and a courtly old Boston lawyer named Joseph Welch—broke forever the power of Senator Joe McCarthy, the famed hunter of Reds, Pinks, fellow travelers, and all those who opposed him.

Welch had been appointed special counsel to defend the Army against McCarthy's charges that it was: (a) coddling Communists at Fort Monmouth, and, (b) holding one of his ex-staff members, a draftee named G. David Schine, as a hostage to thwart his investigation.

When Welch learned that a young lawyer in his own firm had been a member of a legal guild once listed as pro-Communist, he advised the McCarthy side that he was sending the young man home, rather than make him an issue in the case.

But in the last week of the televised hearings, McCarthy could not resist using the information. Although totally irrelevant to the point then under debate, he rose to accuse Welch of harboring in his firm a "young man named Fisher who has been...serving the Communist cause..."

As McCarthy droned on, the rumpled Bostonian cried out, "Let us not assassinate this lad further, Senator. You have done enough. Have you no decency, sir, at long last? Have you left no sense of decency?"

The galleries applauded the honest indignation of Joseph Welch. And to millions looking on across the land, Joe McCarthy, smirking, whispering behind his hand to his counsel, Roy Cohn, seemed coarse and irresponsible. At that moment, the McCarthy spell was over.

He had achieved a position in government where the State Department had agreed to clear its appointments with him. President Eisenhower had not disagreed with him when McCarthy called George Marshall, Ike's great friend, "an instrument of the Soviet conspiracy," or even when he implied that the Eisenhower administration itself was ridden with subversives.

But when McCarthy took on the Army, Ike's Army, he overreached himself. After the Army-McCarthy hearings had ended, and the Wisconsin senator had been censured, Ike gleefully asked friends if they had heard about McCarthyism: Now it was called McCarthywasm.

Life in the Fast Layne

It was the kind of scene a good Hollywood director would have used for the climax of a film. Honest emotion juxtaposed with phony cliche. It was a fans' banquet, fathers and sons coming to glory in and admire their heroes. It was a preseason banquet, when even the worst are undefeated and the hope that springs eternal is never dashed. Certainly not by the master of ceremonies.

One man on the dais is red-necked. He is from Texas. And furthermore, a man familiar with the breed can discern even then that the neck in time will be marked by those cross-thatched wrinkles that denote a dirt farmer, an old rancher, a man in the sun. In this case, a pro football veteran and a championship coach. But now the particular redness of his neck stems from anger. When the unsuspecting master of ceremonies introduces this paragon of leaders, this font from which all victories flow, the honoree comes to the microphone and says:

"I'm through with this team. I'm getting out. This is the worst team I've ever seen—I've seen enough in training camp—and I like winning too much to go through a losing season." There were a few more words in that vein, but not many more, and then Raymond (Buddy) Parker stalked out of the banquet hall.

No other moment of Parker's career so epitomized the saga of the Detroit Lions of the fifties as his manner of leaving it. What makes the vignette perfect, exquisite in its preservation, is the fact that the team he left, his team that he publicly denounced as losers, went on to win the 1957 NFL championship.

Because Detroit didn't win another championship—division, conference, or any other kind—until 1983, and had indeed won only one in all the years before 1950, this decade marked the hours of greatness of the franchise. All the hours of greatness rightfully belong to Buddy Parker, farmboy and halfback, who ran his way up from nothing and then walked away from a championship team. It was a matter of principle, and the principle was this: When management and the coach do not operate on the same wavelength toward the players, then you do not have a champion, you have an also-ran. Parker's principle has remained true through all the ensuing years of the NFL—but he had a mighty good ride before the horse gave in.

Parker's blessing was that his personality fitted the times, and his players fitted his personality; in particular, one player, who, with Parker, set the tone and flavor of the Detroit team, Bobby Layne. Layne had grown up to maturity, or what passed for maturity in that era, in Dallas. And Dallas was just 60 miles from Kemp, Texas, where Parker had grown up years before, a harder way. They spoke the same language, Texian. This is a language where one man says to another, "How about a drink?" and the answer is, "I don't mind if I have one or two." And the signal is silently exchanged that neither really gives a damn if he wakes up about two weeks later in Hong Kong or some exotic place like that.

Parker introduced the "two-minute offense" to the NFL. First came the notion: "I had noticed how so many teams let down the two minutes before the half, and the last two minutes of a game. It seemed you could get things done then that you couldn't in the other fifty-six minutes of play. So we drilled on it. Every day." Well, that was the idea, but Parker acknowledged that any theory is not worth much without execution. "What made it work," he said "is I had The Big Guy." The Big Guy was Layne.

Bo McMillin

Parker took over the Lions in 1951, grasping the baton from the old guard of Bo McMillin, slamming the door on one era and opening up the new one. McMillin was the storied quarterback of the Praying Colonels of little Centre College who upset Harvard in 1919, and he had made his living out of football ever since. But when Parker joined McMillin's Detroit staff in 1950, he chafed under the old-time regime. Parker had had a taste of head-coaching responsibility in 1949, when he and Phil Handler had begun the season as "co-head coaches" of the Chicago Cardinals. The reins had been handed solely to Parker before midseason, and the Cards went 4-1-1 the rest of the way. "I kept asking Walter Wolfner what he was going to do about next season," Parker said. "When he wouldn't say anything by February, I took the job with Detroit."

As Parker was to leave a legacy of quarterback Tobin Rote to successor George Wilson six years later, McMillin was the instigator of a trade that brought Layne from the New York Bulldogs. Parker and fellow assistants Wilson and Aldo Forte suggested to McMillin that the Lions' system be modernized a bit, suggested that he modify a few of his old-time ways. "McMillin knew football backwards and forwards," Parker said, "but he had play numbers that nobody could get straight except him. Hell, the coaches never could remember what the plays were, much less the quarterback. He had a 'ninety-eight' where the left halfback went into right guard, then he had an 'eighty-seven' where the quarterback threw a pass. Nothing had anything to do with anything. Bo also believed in long practices. He'd have the whole squad out on the field for three or four hours, but half the time he had them standing around him while he told them about football. There were a lot of things I wanted to do some day when I got to be head coach, and short practices was at the top of the list." Parker's on-field regimen was limited to 90 minutes, a time frame that began to gain favor simultaneously around the league and has become standard.

Parker and his fellow assistants suffered in silence during the 1950 season, McMillin's last hurrah, but when it was all over the players suffered aloud. Bobby Layne, rookie Doak Walker (in Layne's tow), and fellow-Texan Cloyce Box were invited by a Detroit owner to tell him why the Lions had gone 6-6 that season. The three players later denied a knifing job, but admitted they had said, "We can win with Parker."

McMillin, also a Texan, had been coach of the year at Indiana in 1945, coaching his "po' little boys" to the Big Ten title, and his recruitment into the pro coaching ranks in 1948 had been regarded—by the Detroit ownership at least—as a coup. He was signed to a five-year contract, and the payoff on the last two noncoaching years left a sour taste that was to affect Parker's tenure. McMillin moved to the Philadelphia Eagles, but he was a dying man. He died in March, 1952.

McMillin, perhaps inevitably in handing over one squad to another coach, had provided some basis for a winning team. He had purchased a running back, Box, from the Washington Redskins for $250, and had sense enough to convert the

Pat Harder

slender fellow into a great receiver. He picked running back Bob Hoernschemeyer and offensive tackle Lou Creekmur out of the collapse of the All-America Football Conference. When he couldn't salvage a quarterback out of that league's demise, he gave the New York Bulldogs $50,000 and a player (Bob Mann) for Layne. He was nominally responsible, captain of the ship, when the Lions drafted Doak Walker from SMU, Leon Hart from Notre Dame, and Thurman (Fum) McGraw from Colorado A&M. These names would be carved on stone in Detroit lore.

Parker himself emerged as a wheeler-dealer whose like would not be seen again in the league until the emergence of George Allen. Parker traded a first-round choice for defensive end Jim Martin of the Cleveland Browns (and Parker didn't know Martin could placekick), then dealt a player, a number-two draft choice for fullback Pat Harder of the Chicago Cardinals. "The club needs a hard-nosed guy up the middle, and a pass blocker who knows how to use his elbows," Parker said.

"I have very sharp elbows," Harder said. In fact, Harder's elbows led to an incident that nearly marred his later life. In 1950, when the champion Cleveland Browns were included into the NFL, they had a defensive end of great mayhem named Lenny Ford. Harder, in blocking for the Chicago quarterback, had occasion to warn Ford about his zeal. "I'm going to knock your ass off," was the way he put it. Ford laughed. So Harder advised the Cardinals' offensive tackle to let Ford come in unmolested on the next pass play. Ford was overjoyed and rushed with great abandon—until Harder delivered an elbow to Ford's face that broke his jaw, knocked out several teeth, and indeed knocked Ford out of action for five weeks.

The old earth took a couple of whirls, Cleveland head coach Paul Brown was fired from his job and spent endless seasons in idleness in La Jolla, California, then came back as head coach and owner of the Cincinnati Bengals. At the first league meeting Brown attended—this was nearly two decades later—he tried to have Pat Harder barred from officiating NFL games "because a man of that character does not belong in pro football." Brown's motion was ignored, but it showed a long memory.

It also showed why Buddy Parker desired Harder. Parker also drafted defensive back Jack Christiansen, end Dorne Dibble, and linebacker LaVern Torgeson.

These were the men around whom Parker built a challenge for the NFL championship, and it is significant that his teams were not eliminated from title contention until the last game of the schedule in six of the next seven years.

Parker and Layne and the Lions captured the city of Detroit, the city of the working man, in 1951. The club attendance increased a whopping 103,000. The Lions did it partly by sending the scoreboard whirling—winning, among other victories in a 7-4-1 season, a 52-35 extravaganza over Green Bay in the suddenly traditional Thanksgiving morning battle. Only twice in 12 games did Detroit score less than 21 points. "We are getting killed on pass defense," Parker said. So he took as his first choice in the next draft, after having traded away his top two, Yale Lary from Texas A&M. With incredible luck, Parker was to draft in the twenty-second round another defensive back, Jim David of Colorado A&M. They teamed with Jack Christiansen to form what became known as "Chris's Crew," a deadly secondary that led the NFL in pass interceptions.

Because Doak Walker had cut his arm in an accident at Dallas, Parker traded for defensive back Earl (Jug) Girard from Green Bay. Parker knew that Girard wanted to play offense, he admired his toughness, and he wanted to give him the chance.

Parker's great career as the leader of the Lions almost never got off the ground.

"Bert Bell, the commissioner," Parker said, "always had a hand in the schedule. He believed in matching strength against strength. That's why we played Cleveland damned near every year. He also believed we should start out against San Francisco and Los Angeles. We had to go out there and play them back-to-back, and then they came into Detroit and played back-to-back. These are the teams you had to beat for the conference title and your whole season may be over after four weeks. I don't know how in the hell Bell ever got that idea."

In Parker's second year, he opened by losing to the 49ers, beating the Rams, then losing ingloriously to San Francisco again, 28-0. The following Sunday, when Los Angeles took a 13-0 lead in the first quarter, then hit a long touchdown pass at the beginning of the second period, the debacle seemed complete. But the latter touchdown was called back because of a holding penalty, and Layne rallied the Lions to a 14-13 halftime lead and Detroit eventually won 24-16. The Rams team had been through somewhat of a trauma, too, exchanging head coach Joe Stydahar for Hamp Pool after the first league game. Thus it was Pool whom Parker greeted in midfield after the fateful victory. "Don't feel bad, Hamp," Parker said. "You only lost a game. I could have lost my job." A holding penalty may have been the historic point in Detroit's success the next six years. Later, surveying the scene from the top, as an NFL championship coach, Parker termed the penalty the pivot of his team's drive to the title.

There were other things going on to power the Lions to championship level. Parker installed his team in a hotel the nights before home games, a procedure that was becoming common around the league, notably with the Giants and the Browns. He was using the double-digit signals for offensive plays, in which "twenty-eight" designated a left end sweep by the halfback. Pass formations were called by color, and the pass route of the primary receiver—"Green left, eight sideline"—and the other receivers' routes were designed to get "eight," the left end, into the open. Blocking was simplified. "We went into a number of games with only one formation," Parker said, "and Layne would call most of the plays at the line of scrimmage."

With Parker's tacit approval, Layne was meanwhile molding the Lions into something that transcends statistics and won-lost records, a flair that endures in the memory. Layne believed that a team that played together had a better chance of winning together, and his idea of playing included—demanded—off-field togetherness as well. Layne was the quarterback there, too, calling signals. At Kelly's Bar he would announce that the game of the day was "Cardinal Puff." You play Cardinal Puff in increments of one, and the honors go around the table clockwise. "Cardinal Puff," the honoree would say, then tap the table with the bottom of his glass once, take one sip, touch right forefinger to table once, stomp his right foot once, and his left foot once. The man to his left would do the same. And when it came around again, it advanced to Cardinal Puff-Puff, and everything had to be done in twos. When you fouled up the sequence, the table roared, "Drink to Cardinal Puff!" and the flummoxed one would have to chug-alug his beer. (Layne drank whiskey, and was a Cardinal Puff champion.) This is a difficult routine when sober, and it has its own geometric progression—which resulted in a lot of Lions being delivered senseless to their doorsteps.

"I didn't care what they did with their Sunday and Monday nights," Parker said. "But when we started game preparation on Tuesday I expected them to keep themselves in shape. We had a great group of players, but it wasn't only the play-

"The club needs a hard-nosed guy up the middle, and a pass blocker who knows how to use his elbows," Parker said. "I have very sharp elbows," Harder said.

Jim Doran

ers—there were a great bunch of wives with those teams. At some part in the middle of the season, we'd have a team party where the wives would put on a show—do skits, sing songs, dance. They were all pretty girls and it'd surprise you how talented they were. We'd have a great time."

Parker followed his own line of positive thinking. "I didn't want to tell them what not to do," he said. "I wanted to stress what they had to do, and that was win. Some teams, you know, are always looking to get beat, especially when they're ahead. They just expect to get beat, and so they do. The only way to defeat this defeatism is to win—so you have to talk 'up' all the time. I had discipline, but it had nothing to do with rules and fines. I didn't believe in a system of fines. If you've got to ride herd on players, then you've got the wrong kind of players and you won't win with them. I dealt with them as adults. If a player wasn't taking care of himself, I wouldn't fine him. I'd walk up to him and say, 'What the hell are you doing?' I remember one time Hoernschemeyer cleaned out a bar in Ann Arbor and I had to go up and get him out of jail. He didn't say a word to me, or I to him. He thought I was going to fine the hell out of him, chew him out. I didn't do either one. Hoernschemeyer was all right. He may have been the toughest runner I ever had."

That championship year of 1952 was one of personal triumph for split end Cloyce Box—returning from a tour of army duty during the Korean War. He caught 15 touchdown passes to lead the league, nine in the last three league games as Detroit and Los Angeles tied for the National (Western) Conference title with 9-3 records. So the Rams double-covered Box in the playoff game. They also put double coverage on Doak Walker, operating as a flanker-running back. It was Walker's first action in 10 games, because of an injured leg, but the Rams remembered he had led the league in scoring the season before. Layne thus threw to Leon Hart to win the game 31-21.

The preoccupation with Box, and the talents of Walker, would combine the following week to bring Detroit its first title in 17 years. Walker, barely 6 feet and variously listed at 170 to 180 pounds according to the whim of reporters, made a storybook partner for quarterback Layne. They had been teammates in high school at Dallas, college rivals at SMU and Texas, and now they were championship teammates again. "Walker wasn't at all like Layne," Parker said. "Walker wouldn't play unless he was a hundred percent. His daddy taught him that 'If you can't play a hundred percent, don't go out on that field.' He instilled that in him early. And he wouldn't. He later missed most of the 1955 season because of that, and that first championship game, he hadn't scored a touchdown all year, until we needed it most. That was the thing about Walker. He was a big play guy. Under pressure he would jump over the moon for you. And he wasn't little. He was the strongest one-hundred eighty-five-pounder you'd ever see—legs, chest, arms like rock."

But in 1952 the opponent was Cleveland, in the first game of the great Cleveland-Detroit series that was to color the decade. The Browns were appearing in their seventh consecutive championship game, including their solid domination of the defunct All-America Football Conference. The Lions were loaded with rookies, including two in the offensive line—guards Dick Stanfel and Bob Miller. But Detroit was a three-point favorite because Cleveland was without its two great receivers, Dub Jones and Mac Speedie.

The game turned on one play. From the Lions' 33-yard line, Cloyce Box lined up wide to the left and ran a deep pattern down the middle. Layne faked a handoff to Harder into left guard and gave the ball to Walker, heading between the right tackle and end. Walker then cut back to the middle, and the slender Box made "the block" that took out both the cornerback and safety who were downfield trying to cover him. The 67-yard touchdown gave Detroit a 14-0 lead and set up the ultimate 17-7 victory.

The defense had completely throttled "the greatest quarterback in pro football," Otto Graham. In the finest series of downs a Detroit team was ever to know, Graham and the Browns were wrecked at the 5-yard line. Trailing only 14-7, the Browns got there on a 42-yard end run by Marion Motley. Defensive back Don Doll threw Motley for a 5-yard loss when he tried another sweep on first down, linemen Fum McGraw and Jim Doran sacked Graham for a 13-yard loss on the next play, swarmed him again on a one-yard gain, and then batted away a fourth-down pass to Motley.

The Lions were suddenly greater than General Motors. Attendance increased another 45,000.

In Texas, the winner in a poker game frequently will call for a shuffle of the cards, a symptom of a Texan's nature, and now so did Buddy Parker. Seven rookies made the 1953 squad—including top draft choice Harley Sewell of Texas and Charley Ane of USC and Hawaii, both offensive linemen. It later became pro football dogma that an offensive line never reached championship form until it was bolstered by 50 years of cumulative experience, and now Parker was fielding a front five that had only one man with more than a year in the NFL. And still he won. Among the other rookies were a halfback named Lew Carpenter and a linebacker named Joe Schmidt from the University of Pittsburgh.

In Detroit, a rookie retained his status for a full year. It was not until the first league game of his second season that he was accepted as an equal by the veterans. Schmidt beat this tradition by half a year. At midseason, one of the Lions' starters said to him, "Why don't you drop by Kelly's after the game?" Two years later Schmidt was the prototypical middle linebacker, when Parker acknowledged the re-tirement of 350-pound middle guard Les Bingaman by converting from a five-man line to a 4-3 defense.

The 1953 Lions lost twice to the Rams, but didn't lose another game. Jack Christiansen led the Detroit backfield to a record 38 interceptions, stealing 12 himself. Cleveland again was a runaway winner in the East. Graham had complet-ed 64.7 percent of his passes that season, compared to Layne's 45.8, but Layne typically had concentrated on the bomb, throwing 16 touchdowns to Otto's 11.

The Detroit media guide lists an annual alphabetical roster of the all-time Lions, and under "D" there is a notation for "Doran, James, E, Iowa State, 1951-59." Doran was the most valuable player of the 1952 title game, and a year later he was scheduled for backup duty behind tight end Leon Hart, if Hart's injuries proved disabling. They did, and Doran became a receiver. He thus figured in the one great plays of the championship game, designed by Parker and executed by Layne. Cleveland led 16-10 with barely four minutes remaining, when Layne began his act. On a fourth down he had hit Doran for 18 yards on a pattern of Hart's. Now the ball was on Cleveland's 33, and Parker and Layne huddled during a time out. The decision was now or never, and Doran was spaced wide, with Cloyce Box lined up in Doran's usual role close to the line. "We figured," said Parker, "they would key on Box, and we also figured their cornerback, Warren Lahr I think he was [he was], would come up to try to pick off the pass to Box."

Parker: "Under pressure he [Walker] would jump over the moon for you. And he wasn't little. He was the strongest one-hundred eighty-five-pounder you'd ever see—legs, chest, arms like rock."

Doak Walker

Box ran an out-route toward the right sideline, and Doran took off downfield. "Layne gave Box a real look to fool Lahr," Parker said, "then he just lofted the ball to Doran."

It was the kind of dramatic, perfect, inside-reasoned play that typified the decade's championship games.

"From there," Parker said, "we went to a four-man line and Carl Karilivacz intercepted one of Graham's passes, when they could have won with a field goal."

It was the third consecutive victory for Detroit over Cleveland. Parker kept his explanation simple: "We'd change up our defense for the Browns—instead of an odd-man line with the middle guard we'd use an even-man setup, six men. But sometimes the outside men would drop off and sometimes they wouldn't. I remember a game when we had Hart as one of the outside guys and he dropped back and took one of Graham's passes and ran it for a touchdown. The thing was to give them something on defense they hadn't been seeing us doing."

Buddy Parker never forgot that he did not complete a triple-play championship by beating the Browns in the 1954 title game. The Cleveland Indians had won the American League pennant that season and pre-empted the Browns' ball park for a World Series. Detroit offered the home-town share of the gate if Cleveland would switch the site to the Briggs Stadium, but Paul Brown would have none of it. There was a one-week hiatus between the end of the season and the title game—to allow for playoffs—and Brown held out for the Lions game to be made up after the season. The Lions won that one, all right, 14-10, but then got clobbered 56-10 when it counted. Bobby Layne had an excuse: "We were pressing for three in a row, and everybody went to bed at ten o'clock. I woke up at four like an owl."

Cleveland led 21-3 early in the second quarter and never looked back. Parker's dream had turned to ashes. Since the beginning of the playoff system, in 1932, only Philadelphia and Chicago ever had put championships back-to-back as Detroit had done—and in another decade Vince Lombardi would be the next coach to lead his team into three championship games.

The one loss in a championship turned Parker's life sour, though it was not apparent at the time. "When we won the second title," Parker said, "a real good artist had done a portrait of me and I put it in my basement room, where I had a bar, and the movie projector set up on the bar to focus on a wall. When we lost to the Browns that third title game, I came home with a few drinks in me and I went downstairs. My wife knew enough to let me alone. And I looked at the painting. I always carry a pocket-knife, so I took it out and I cut a pretty good cut through Buddy Parker."

In 1955, with a new defense built around Schmidt, the Lions aimed at a fourth straight conference title. But Layne's knee was torn up, and Walker limped onto the bench for the duration. Detroit finished 3-9, in last place. "The Doak," playing only when 100 percent, had set a club scoring record of 534 points.

In retrospect, Parker said, "We had as great a player in the 1950s as they have today." But it was a different league, a different kind of game, sometimes labeled "basketball on the green" by college coaches who were using one-platoon football. Parker's words of that era show the difference: "As for size, because of the more rugged type of play in pro ball, I like offensive linemen who weigh from two-hundred-ten pounds up, with ideal weight around two-hundred-thirty pounds. And I like my linemen tall—six feet or over."

Some 12 years later, a prospective Dallas offensive lineman who weighed 230 would be hiding a 20-pound weight in his jock to make the weight requirement of the Cowboys' team.

There also is something quaint about Parker's strict admonishment in a 1955 coaching book: "I make sure that our placekickers work at least ten minutes every time we practice. In this way we keep their eyes sharp and have them ready to kick in a game when we need them." But Parker never believed a kicker should be less than a player. His field goal "specialists" were fullback Pat Harder, halfback Doak Walker, defensive end Jim Martin. His punter was ace defensive back Yale Lary.

The 1956 Detroit season ended in rhubarb and violence, a source of dark suspicions to this day.

The intrigue began at the Edgewater Beach Hotel, home of Guy Lombardo, Coleman Hawkins, and the Mickey Finn, if we are to believe the Lions. "We all ate together and stayed together the night before the game," Parker said, "and Layne was the only guy who got sick. He vomited all night. What are you going to think? Somebody at the hotel must have slipped something to him. Layne's never been sick in his life."

In this twelfth and final game of the season, with the title hanging on the line either way, Layne made a handoff in the second quarter and bemusedly watched the runner hit the hole. At the same time, he was blindsided by Bears end Ed Meadows, and knocked from the game. Various Lions spent the rest of the game taking shots at Meadows, and offensive tackle Lou Creekmur was to remember later that he smashed Meadows's jaw. But what shows in the record book is that the Lions lost the conference title by half a game, 38-21.

This bitter tea was Parker's draft as he entered the 1957 season. His bitterness, however, had been building for a long time. "There were twelve owners of the club," he said, "and a big deal with me coaching was I had to get with them every Tuesday of the season at a downtown hotel for a head-on meeting. They wanted to know what was what with the team, with the game we just played. That is all right. But I got in a crossfire. There were two factions in there. Lyle Fife had been president of the club, but this was a close-knit group—they partied together, socialized together, wives and all. So when Fife got divorced, the rest of the directors' wives didn't want to have anything to do with the new girl he married. That's the way things were in those days. Edwin Anderson became president. Anderson was my guy. But Fife had an anti-Anderson faction. So every Tuesday there'd be this polite war between Fife's minority and Anderson's people, and I was in the middle.

"I'll give you an example: Fife and his friends had an apartment near the club office. One Tuesday they asked me how come one of my players kept coming to the apartment when he was supposed to be in training. The sons-a-bitches had given the guy a key to the apartment, and they knew I knew it.

"Another time, we had a game in Los Angeles, and I mean all those fellows took pride in following the team, so a bunch were in the hotel we stayed in. We played the Rams, and the next Tuesday I was asked why six of our players didn't come in until two o'clock the night before the game. They named the players. Seems they were waiting in the lobby, taking roll call. Well, I called the players in and they told me this was a bunch of baloney. Anyway, we won that game."

Still, it was an electric field that surrounded Buddy Parker when he went to the Boosters Banquet that summer of 1957. "I got off the elevator at the banquet level and a guy told me Lyle Fife left word I should see him before anything. Fife had a suite. So I went up. And who is the first person I see but the quarterback I traded

The Lions got clobbered 56-10 when it counted. Bobby Layne had an excuse: "We were pressing for three in a row, and everybody went to bed at ten o'clock. I woke up at four like an owl."

89

Bobby Layne and Buddy Parker

three players to get, Tobin Rote. He is having a drink. The next night we play our first exhibition game."

Parker abdicated with a great deal more attention than he had gotten when he ascended to the job. And he could pick and choose his next station.

"Carroll Rosenbloom had been after me the year before and I should have gone. Offered me a house and every damn thing in the world up there in Baltimore. When I quit he called me up and said he wanted me to come out—he had a place there in New Jersey on the ocean. Wanted me and my wife Jane to come up. So I flew to Philadelphia, and he had somebody meet me in a limousine and drive me out to his ocean home. Spent the weekend out there. This was before they'd won the pennant, of course. He said he'd put a $35,000 salary in the Chase Manhattan bank that I could draw on the next year, then I'd take over as head coach from Weeb Ewbank. It sounded good, but when I thought it over it sounded too devious to me, and something I didn't want to do."

Parker eventually succumbed to George Halas, he said, with a stop in Pittsburgh. "I know Halas would have denied this," Parker said, "but I would never have gone to Pittsburgh any other way. I knew what the Steelers had and how they had no money. I went to Chicago and had lunch with Halas and Art Rooney, who owned the Steelers. The deal was I would coach the Steelers for two years and Halas would bring me over to the Bears. That's why I traded so many draft choices away at Pittsburgh. I wasn't building for the future—I had to win right then."

In the 1950s, there were two threats to make a recalcitrant player agree to salary terms. One was Green Bay and the other was Pittsburgh. "If you don't like it here," went the line, "we can trade you there."

It's ironic, then, that two of the great champions of the decade ended their careers on the wasted shores of the Monongahela. Layne broke a leg in 1957, and joined Parker on the 1958 Pittsburgh team. Rudyard Kipling wrote, "The sin they do two by two they must pay for one by one," and he was inevitably speaking of Parker and Layne in Pittsburgh.

Five years later, just before the season of Parker's greatest chance in Pittsburgh to win the Eastern title, he ordered Layne to retire, and Layne retired.

"I didn't think he was physically able to be a starter all the time," Parker said. "I knew he wouldn't want to be a backup man. He'd had a helluva career, see? I don't believe in a ballplayer that's been great to finish up as nothing. I like to see him go out on top. For example, Unitas. He shouldn't have played the last couple of years of his career. He didn't need the money. I wanted everybody to remember Layne as a great player, instead of a half-ass player. But I would have won the conference with him the year I made him retire. All we had to do was beat the Giants in the last game, and Ed Brown couldn't hit the ground with his hat."

The Lions spurted in 1957 without Parker, without Layne, enlivened by one of the wildest games in NFL history. San Francisco led, at home, 24-7 at halftime, in the playoff for the Western title, and had to handle queues of fans demanding tickets for the following week's title game. Then Tobin Rote put three touchdowns on the scoreboard within less than five minutes in the second half, and Detroit salvaged the game 31-27. One more time the Cleveland Browns awaited at the end of the rainbow, the Browns who had won 56-10 last time in the classic series. This time Rote threw four touchdowns, scored another, and Detroit won 59-14.

10

Up Front, and Personal

The late George Halas, who was called venerable when the game itself was still young, remembered the play as though it had happened a week ago Sunday. And, in the full, enriched sweep of his own lifespan, 1951 was a week ago Sunday.

Halas still could see Bob Waterfield of the Rams retreating to his own goal line with those quick, bird-like steps that seem, well, almost dainty for men of size.

He saw Waterfield release the ball, arching it against a cloudless blue sky, deep to the sideline. And he hardly could miss seeing Elroy Hirsch catch it, again, because that happened smack in front of the Chicago bench, right under Papa Bear's sensitive nose. Without breaking stride, Hirsch went 91 yards for the touchdown that sent the Rams away to a 42-17 gallop over the Bears (en route to a National Football League title).

"That play," Halas said, "demonstrated the big change that had come about in T-formation football. Almost without realizing it, we had reached the point where the pass-catching end had replaced the running back as a long-distance threat. There wasn't a back in the league who could have run ninety-one yards against us."

There it is again: only one play, one pass, one catch, out of a long autumn of passes and catches, thousands of them. But it became a moment embedded in memory, a collector's item, so that years later old George Halas could hold it to the light and say, there, that's when it happened.

In the 1950s, every team had a receiver or two who could catch passes and score touchdowns and break a game apart: Cloyce Box, Billy Wilson, Bill Howton, Bobby Walston...the list was unending. But there were three who, by virtue of a theory or a technique or just pure style, improved the craft and thereby left an imprint on the sport of professional football.

They were Elroy Hirsch, Tom Fears, and Raymond Berry.

Hirsch was a special case, known as "Crazylegs" to his fans, a glamour figure whose life story was made into a movie—starring himself—before his thirtieth birthday. He was a product of the odd but enduring union between the performing and the perspiring arts.

It had always existed, of course. Jim Thorpe and Red Grange made movies, and leathery Sammy Baugh did a turn in westerns. But the fifties seemed to speed up the chemical process by which sports and show biz were fused. Waterfield (Jane Russell) and Glenn Davis (Terry Moore) were among the first football heroes to marry actresses, while Hirsch cleared the way for thespians to come such as Frank Gifford, Jim Brown, Joe Namath, O.J. Simpson, and Lyle Alzado.

Elroy appeared in the Marine Corps epic, *Battle Cry*, and had the male lead in a motion picture called *Unchained*, which was distinguished primarily by its back-

Tom Fears

ground music, "Unchained Melody." The song was a hit, Hirsch a little less so.

For several years the annual question in Los Angeles was whether Crazylegs would retire to the cinema, or wind up in a jar at the Harvard Medical School.

Few players ever came back, so often, from so many severe injuries. He quite probably suffered more blows to the head than any player in history, one of those records-we-could-live-without-if-not-for-the-honor.

Hirsch joined the Rams in 1949 after three seasons with the hapless Chicago Rockets of the All-America Football Conference, where as a wingback he had suffered a fractured skull, a back injury, a torn ligament in his right knee, and other assorted bumps and bruises.

Clark Shaughnessy, then the head coach of the Rams, could demonstrate great patience where talent was involved. He ordered a daily five-mile running program to strengthen Elroy's right leg, and designed a special headguard to protect him from another skull injury. The headguard was molded from a light, extra strong plastic used in the construction of fighter plane fuel tanks. The helmet weighed only 11 ounces, about one-third the weight of the leather models then in vogue. It soon would be widely copied.

Partly to lessen the risk of injury, he thought, Shaughnessy positioned Hirsch as a flanker—probably the league's first true flanker. Hirsch lined up in the flat, close to the sidelines, rather than in motion. By 1951, he was in full flower as a pass receiver, leading the league with 66 catches, 1,495 yards, and 17 touchdowns. As George Halas had seen, pro football had a new ultimate weapon: the bomb. Few executed it more boldly than Hirsch, whose average per touchdown catch was 48 yards. In effect, every time Crazylegs scored he went virtually half the length of the field.

Joe Stydahar, who succeeded Shaughnessy, explained the secret of Elroy Hirsch: "He knows how to run with a football under his arm. Lots of players could run faster in a straightaway race. But when you put a football under their arm they would lose balance and slow down. Not Elroy. Put a football under his arm and he speeded up."

The Rams deployed him at both end and flanker, but he still was classified as a halfback in 1952, when he went the entire season without carrying the ball from scrimmage. It was the first time in his career that had happened. Some thought it was the first time in anyone's career that a halfback in the NFL had failed to carry the ball at least once.

That represented quite a switch for the elastic-legged runner who had thrilled them so at Wausau High and the University of Wisconsin. But if the idea, in part, was to limit his exposure, the strategy overlooked Elroy's tendency to confuse himself, on occasion, with Bronko Nagurski. Even as a full-time receiver, he never hesitated to dive into traffic. As a blocker he was surprisingly effective, often cutting in low and hard.

Unfortunately, that instinct brought him into contact one day, in 1953, with Hardy Brown, the famed hatchet-man of the 49ers. When Elroy drove in from his flanker position to block the San Francisco linebacker, Brown raised his knee and caught him on the top of the head. His helmet jammed into his neck. He saw white flashes, then passed out.

He was revived during a time out, and even returned later in the game, but his health was to become a public issue in Los Angeles. The next week, against the Chicago Cardinals, he was injured in exactly the same way—a knee to the top of the head while throwing a block. The next day's headline in the Los Angeles Mirror bannered the news: MEDICS SAY HIRSCH NEAR END OF CAREER; HEAD BLOWS AGAIN STUN RAM ACE.

Between injuries he had complained about having a problem focusing his left eye. His teammates revealed that he had been glassy-eyed after at least three games. In the idiom of sport, his bell had been rung more times than Quasimodo.

Crazylegs argued, with some logic, that a state of temporary light-headedness was not an uncommon condition in the NFL. But the Rams' offices were swamped with letters, telegrams, and calls urging that Hirsch retire.

He had the distinction of being the first player ever ordered by the Commissioner to be examined by a neurosurgeon.

But Elroy had the last word, which was the record book. For all his thumps, and his blackouts, he appeared in every game that year and caught 61 passes.

Hirsch also played in the Pro Bowl game in January, 1954, in the Los Angeles Coliseum. And again he was knocked goofy, gang tackled by Tommy James of the Browns and Emlen Tunnell of the Giants. His head struck the turf hard. He got up, staggered, and was grabbed by an official, who asked if he knew where he was. Hirsch didn't. They led him off the field. While he was down, his 5-year-old son, Win, turned to Ruth Hirsch and asked, calmly, "Is my daddy dead?"

His head cleared on the bench. After the game he collected his wife and son, drove to their ranch home in the San Fernando Valley, and fixed himself a highball, one more demonstration of his uncanny recuperative powers.

Hirsch lasted 12 seasons, a remarkable tenure considering the pounding he took. He became a national favorite with his movie looks, his Ipana smile, and his blond hair coiffed back in a fifties pompadour. But if Elroy established one thing, it was that the professional football of the fifties was hardly a movie.

The Rams of those years frustrated many an opposing coach, who yearned to concoct a special defense to contain Elroy Hirsch. They were dissuaded largely for one reason: the presence of Tom Fears.

It was once the proud boast in Los Angeles that Tom Fears caught more third-down passes, and more passes in the last five minutes, than any receiver in history—the kind of statistics that sports fans thrive on, because they have the advantage of being largely unprovable. But, beyond a doubt, Fears was a money player.

When the Rams defeated the Browns for the title in 1951, it was Fears, the precise pattern runner, who pulled in a pass from Dutch Van Brocklin and went 73 yards for the winning, fourth-quarter touchdown. He caught them big, and he caught them in bunches, and he caught some that could only be explained as an optical illusion, the way a magician pulls a watch out of your ear.

Mostly he was a master at running a pass route, gaining a step on the halfback covering him, getting to the ball and getting there alone. It was accepted in the fifties that before Fears, most teams still were in their everybody-out-for-a-long-one phase. His success at running patterns helped make pass receiving the science it now is.

Fears insisted on staying neutral, and friendly with both, when the rest of the team began to divide behind Waterfield and Van Brocklin. But the Dutchman, the great calculator, wasn't above using a little psychology of his own. If Fears made a spectacular catch, Van Brocklin would turn to him in the huddle and let him call the next play. But if he dropped one, Dutch would curl his lip, make a point of turning to Hirsch and say, "What do you want, Elroy?"

Stydahar: "Lots of players...when you put a football under their arm they would lose balance and slow down. Not Elroy [Hirsch]. Put a football under his arm and he speeded up."

Raymond Berry

Fears was a placid, unflappable fellow who did not needle easily. He was not a showman, but few players ever reached pro football out of a more exotic background. He was born near Guadalajara, Mexico, the son of a gold mining engineer. He still has vague recollections of hiding under the bed when bandits swooped down from the hills.

He was 7 when his family returned to California, where sports had become a major industry, the new mother lode for football and baseball scouts. Like many of his generation, Fears had a split education, playing his college football at both Santa Clara and UCLA. In between, he served three years as an Air Force pilot in World War II, where he had his first experience with running exact patterns.

He was drafted by the Rams in 1948 as a defensive back. Switched to end, he became the first rookie ever to win the pass receiving championship. By 1950, rival teams were telling themselves that they had nothing to fear but Fears himself. That season he caught 84 passes, breaking a record he had taken earlier from the immortal Don Hutson. It was against Hutson's old club, the Packers, that he established the single-game record of 18 catches.

A big fellow for the times, 6-2 and 220, Fears found that he lacked the speed and shiftiness to get clear consistently. Thus he began to concentrate on his moves and patterns, orchestrating every step until it became pure reflex.

He soon became the model for talented young ends breaking into the league such as Bill Howton of Rice, who was hailed in Green Bay as "the new Hutson." In 1952, his rookie year, Howton was startled to discover that his team had no end coach. "I was lost," he said. "I couldn't believe there could be so much difference between college and pro ball. I realized I knew nothing about end play, at least, not the way the pros did it. I had always admired Fears, so I got all the films the club had on the Rams and studied Fears.

"He was the all-time great for maneuvering and getting loose. Hutson was superb at grabbing the ball, and Elroy Hirsch was faster, but Fears had the finesse."

Howton was no peanut himself when it came to catching a football. Appearing in the Pro Bowl in 1953, in Los Angeles, he welcomed the chance to team with Tom Fears's batterymate, Van Brocklin.

"We were stalled at our own twenty," he remembered. "In the huddle Van Brocklin told me to get out and down the sideline faster than I'd ever run in my life. And to keep going.

"After going out about forty yards I looked back, couldn't see him, and decided he had been swarmed under. But I kept going, just in case. I glanced at Em Tunnell, the safetyman, and he wasn't paying any attention to me. So now I figured the play must be over. But I kept going. After sixty yards I looked back again.

"There was the ball, coming right into my lap. I pulled it in and just pranced across for the touchdown."

It was, as George Halas had suggested, the hour of the pass-catching end. And at mid-decade, onto the scene came a young fellow who looked so unlike a pro football player that he turned a popular joke into reality. His name was Raymond Berry and he actually did something that sounded like a comic's one-liner.

He went on "What's My Line," the television quiz show, and stumped the panel.

He was gangling, a spindly 185-pounder (at 6-2), who, without glasses or contact lenses, could read nothing larger than the "E" on an eye chart. He was a twentieth-round draft choice who became the foremost pass receiver of his time, an artist without temperament.

Berry came along on the heels of half a dozen great receivers: Hirsch, Fears, Howton, Box, *et al*. But he accomplished something that endeared him to a new generation of fans. He proved that endless work and sheer strength of will could lead to greatness, to machine-like near perfection, and that God-given talent wasn't always an absolute requirement.

He was so human, so conventional looking, not at all your popular stereotype of the athlete-god; he was, in fact, every man's Walter Mitty. And it was always Raymond, among his teammates and friends, never the more casual Ray.

One year, a fan of the Colts rented him a room on the third floor of an old abandoned mansion in an aging Baltimore suburb. Alex Hawkins drove by it one night and spotted a light in Berry's window. "Here we are living it up in the outside world," Hawkins told the teammate with him in the car, "and there's old Raymond in his haunted house, drawing pass routes and running his projector. What scares me is, maybe he's right."

Even Johnny Unitas, who was no hell raiser, marveled at the self discipline of this scholarly citizen from Paris, Texas. Unitas took careful note of Berry's habits: "He went to bed at half past eight, to make sure he got enough sleep, and when he got a pair of uniform pants that fit just the way they should, he insisted on hand washing them himself, so they wouldn't be given out to some other player after the laundry was done. He carried a football with him every place he walked around the camp grounds so he would get the feel of the ball and keep his fingers supple enough to catch any passes that might be thrown to him. It wasn't long before his name was a by-word on the club for dedication and hard work."

Berry arrived in Baltimore in 1955, a year ahead of Unitas. Curiously, he was convinced in the summer of 1956 that his chances of keeping his job, after a fair rookie season, were slender: "I got the drift right away—my neck was on the log all the time. I put pressure on myself and lost every bit of confidence I ever had. I was afraid for anybody to throw me the ball. I still remember that feeling. That fear is very real. I kept thinking I was gonna mess up. I remember a pass that was thrown to me in one of the early exhibition games. I kept thinking, 'I hope I don't miss it...hope I don't miss it.'"

He missed it.

Quite simply, Berry trained the fear of failing right out of his system. And when the rookie Unitas moved in as the team's starting quarterback, Berry sensed that they would be good chemistry. "I had an understanding with John," he said. "I told him I'd keep giving him information if I had something, and if he wanted to use it or not was his business. When an end has nothing, that's the time to keep his mouth shut. But I hated to come back silent. It's an end's job to go out and do reconnaissance."

Berry and Unitas were to become a combination, as attuned to each other's moves as a pair of cat burglars.

Other than Unitas, the only quarterback Berry spent any appreciable time with was his wife Sally. A pretty, shapely brunette, she had married Raymond for richer or for poorer, but no one had said anything about sideline patterns.

Raymond enlisted her as his practice-field thrower in the offseason. She became proficient at 10- and 15-yarders, corner patterns and slants and square-outs. Wherever the Berrys worked out, strangers would gape when they heard a receiver, streaking down the field, cry out to his passer: "Lead me, honey, lead me."

For hours they would go through this routine with Sally aiming the ball over his

His name was Raymond Berry and he actually did something that sounded like a comic's one-liner. He went on What's My Line? and stumped the panel.

Berry complained for three days that "something is wrong with this field." Finally, Berry borrowed a highway engineering tape, and found the field was one-and-a-half yards too narrow.

head, at his feet, to his right, to his left, in what is now recognized as: The Bad Ball Drill.

In 1957, Berry persuaded the Baltimore Orioles to part with an old batting cage, which he hung over the goal post to contain the passes he couldn't reach. He imposed on anyone he could find to throw him passes from all angles. Unitas worked with him until the exercises, all that wild throwing, began to affect his own aim.

Later, a Dallas firm agreed to publish Berry's scholarly conclusions about the bad-ball drill on an illustrated instruction chart, and to manufacture a 25-by-12-foot practice net. Chart and net sold for $50. Berry made no profit on it, an act of altruism not exactly common in pro sports today. "I didn't do it to make money," he said. "I did it to help boys who wanted to play end."

Throughout his career he received a steady flow of letters from kids wanting his wisdom on how to catch passes. He would write each of them long, handwritten replies. Finally, he prepared a 12-page text on the subject, single spaced, and the Colts had it mimeographed and mailed to those requesting information. At the end of the essay, the solicitous Berry could not resist adding a postscript: "If you have any questions on anything, just let me know."

When Berry retired, no one doubted his discipline had been worthwhile. He had caught, to that time, more passes for more yards than any other player who ever lived. Yet he could look back on his career and say, without conceit: "I'm a pro football player, but there are parts of the game I'm glad I had nothing to do with. I'm in awe of what goes on in the line, tackle to tackle, what we call 'the pit.' I wandered into 'the pit' three times in my career, chasing tipped passes, and all three times they carried me off, unconscious."

In all its facets, the sport fascinated Berry the way a laboratory fascinates a scientist. His instincts were sometimes uncanny. Years after his playing career, when Berry had joined Tom Landry's staff as receivers coach and settled in at Thousand Oaks, California, where the Cowboys trained then, Berry complained for three days that "something is wrong with this field." Finally, Berry borrowed a highway engineering tape, measured the width himself, and found the field, which the Cowboys had used every summer for six years, was one-and-a-half yards too narrow. Later, Berry brought that science to New England as head coach of the Patriots.

·Nowhere in sport is the concept of Team Play more effectively illustrated than in the execution of a forward pass. For Graham or Layne or Waterfield to throw, and Fears or Hirsch or Berry to catch, a number of other people must do their jobs. They are called offensive linemen.

Because football is geared that way—so many links in the chain—great players often are unrecognized on weak teams. This goes to the very bottom of what separates football from, say, baseball. We can picture Ernie Banks or Babe Ruth or Orel Hershiser performing just as nobly, just as productively, with a championship team or an ordinary one. But O.J. Simpson didn't really begin to run until the Buffalo Bills hired some blockers to smooth his way.

Football teams depend on timing and harmony and the right rhythms, in the way that a team of mountain climbers, connected by ropes, sense each other's shifts of weight. One misstep can sink them all.

From tackle to tackle, the men in the offensive line traditionally receive about as much credit as a pack burro (a job with which they could identify). But if they did

96

LINEMEN AND ENDS

Elroy (Crazylegs) Hirsch was the era's most famous halfback-turned-flanker. He was moved to receiver after fracturing his skull while playing for Chicago of the AAFC.

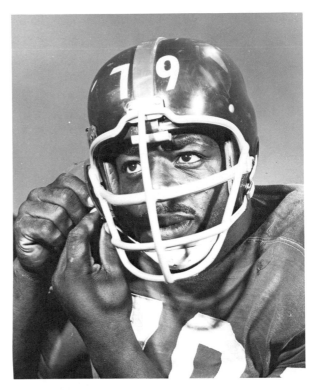

Roosevelt Brown (right) made the Pro Football Hall of Fame after a brilliant career with the Giants. Duane Putnam (61, below—blocking for Rams fullback Tank Younger) was a relatively small guard who relied on outstanding technique. Detroit's Lou Creekmur (opposite) was a dominating big man who played in eight Pro Bowls. Many people think Creekmur should join Brown in the Hall of Fame.

San Francisco's fans in the 1950s thought of Billy Wilson *(opposite) much the way their progeny think of Jerry Rice. Detroit's Leon Hart (right), big for a skill player, was all-pro on* offense **and** *defense in 1951. Billy Howton (below, trying to turn the corner against future Hall of Fame safety Jack Christiansen) was the best end on a losing Green Bay team.*

Harlon Hill of the Bears (above), from tiny North Alabama College, terrified 1950s defenses with his big-play capability. Raymond Berry (doing his thing, right) was small and slow, and one of his legs was a little longer than the other, but he was an incredibly disciplined receiver who was at his best when Johnny Unitas was leading the Colts in a two-minute drill.

The San Francisco 49ers hit a publicity jackpot when they invented
the Alley Oop play (named for the syndicated comic-strip caveman).
Fans loved the play, on which R.C. Owens (above) would set himself
under a high, arching Y.A. Tittle pass, and outleap the mere mortals on
the field for a reception.

not act as a unit, if any one player failed, the quarterback couldn't function. It was that basic. Oh, he could put up a "Hail Mary" pass and maybe hit it. Or he could scramble. But as Van Brocklin once put it, you had better have an offense designed for third-down-and-50.

Robert Bruce St. Clair of the San Francisco 49ers was an offensive lineman in an era in which the cheers were for everybody else except. Yet St. Clair is the most remembered of that faceless band of the period, precisely because he could not be overlooked. That is, he was no more conspicuous than any 6-foot, 9-inch behemoth who ate raw meat.

Bob St. Clair

At a time when pro football was trying to impress itself on the public consciousness—and succeeding—St. Clair was a delightfully mythic figure. Great copy. One of the most powerful men in the league, he credited his strength to eating raw meat. Not rare. Raw. *Uncooked.*

When a waitress would ask him how he wanted his steak, he would tell her: "Raw."

The reply was always the same, too. "You do mean, rare?" she would suggest.

"Raw," St. Clair would repeat himself. "Take it out of the icebox and put it on a plate."

St. Clair had learned from childhood to eat his meat uncooked: steak, hamburger, unroast beef. He also enjoyed a slab of raw liver, the idea of which has been known to frighten children of all ages. He was hooked on the high-protein, energy-producing properties of raw meat, plus his belief that it tasted better than when it was cooked. His diet also included raw eggs.

Such a charming custom, of course, would have gone unremarked if St. Clair had not been an exceptional football player. He was good, and, more to the point, he was mean. It was St. Clair, you may recall, who gave it to Sam Huff, no sissy himself: "I saw Huff standing there, is all. Standing by a pileup is a typical rookie thing. You can hit them so hard they'll think their head was on a swivel."

He was, as the saying goes, head and shoulders above most of the linemen of the day. He was so tall, in fact, that in 1956 he blocked 10 field-goal attempts, surely a record in a category no one ever thought to tabulate. He caught a few of them in the mouth, which he didn't like, but which he accepted as part of the job.

There was a kind of caveman aura to St. Clair. On the road he simply threw the hotel mattress on the floor, added a couple of pillows to its length and went to sleep. Yet as a high school sophomore he was judged too small, at 5-9 and 150, for varsity football. On his raw meat and health-food diet, he bloomed to 6-4 and 210 as a junior and he was on his way. As a pro, he acquired a taste for wheat germ oil, raw honey and beer, vodka screwdrivers, and chewing tobacco, and filled out to 260.

But this was no brainless brute. He had run the relays in high school, and played some offensive end at the University of San Francisco, where his teammates included Gino Marchetti and Ollie Matson. He had legs like the redwoods of his Northern California, but his speed, for such a giant of a man, was surprising.

When St. Clair reported to the 49ers as a rookie, in 1953, he immediately was matched one-on-one against Leo Nomellini, then an all-pro defensive tackle on his way to one of the great durability records in sport—266 consecutive football games—including preseason. Leo weighed 265, and was counted on to give the rookie his initiation.

Their confrontation was described later "like a couple of bull elephants trying to

Lou Creekmur

get out of a phone booth." They tore up divots large enough for a small bomb shelter. St. Clair hadn't had so much fun since he was running with street gangs, as a kid in the Mission district of San Francisco. He made the team.

Later, he saved that kind of effort, and passion, for his private combat with old college chum Marchetti. That was one of the two great personal duels of the decade, the other being the love matches between Jim Brown and Sam Huff.

Stories of pain are rampant in the NFL. But in 1957 St. Clair set something of a record by playing eight minutes with a severely separated shoulder. He didn't come out until a Los Angeles Ram blasted right into it. St. Clair nearly fainted. A few days later he underwent surgery.

In brief, Bob St. Clair, the 49er who ate raw meat, is the player who substantiates the argument that football players were tougher 35 years ago. In 1990, St. Clair finally got his just reward: He joined Nomellini and Marchetti in the Pro Football Hall of Fame.

One of the things you had to understand about any offensive linemen was this: They had a continuing chip on their shoulder. For everybody. They were always mad, either at the guy across the line, or at the backs behind them who got the glory when things went well and who could make them feel so guilty when things went wrong. It was a funny job, all right. No one knew how important you were until you failed.

Bobby Layne, for one, had a parent-child relationship with his offensive line (I-wouldn't-punish-you-if-I-didn't-love-you). Lou Creekmur, the offensive tackle who was an all-pro for the Lions every year between 1951 and 1957, remembered the way it was:

"If you ever missed a block, Layne made sure everybody knew about it, guys on the field, guys on the bench, everybody in the stadium. Layne would get the guy's number who creamed him, figure out who was at fault and call you right out of the huddle. He'd stand there, raving at you and shaking a finger in your face, and you wanted to punch him. A couple of times we had to grab people to keep 'em from hitting Bobby. But off the field there's nothing he wouldn't do for us. He showed us respect, that was the main thing. He bought us steaks. We would have killed for him."

Even the best of them—Rosey Brown of the Giants, Dick Stanfel of the Lions and Redskins, and, later in the decade, Jim Parker of the Colts and Jerry Kramer of the Packers—went largely unsung. But they had their way of getting even.

Creekmur was an artist of the flying elbow and the leg whip—in which a lineman thought he had gone past him, and Creekmur would whip his legs around and rack his shins. Creekmur had a device to avoid fights in the fourth quarter, which was the danger zone, when an opponent would be fed up with his treatment and preparing to settle his debts.

"I'd tell the ref to watch so-and-so, he's been punching me all game. Then I'd go say something to the guy just before the ball was snapped, he'd haul off at me, and the ref would penalize him fifteen yards. I did that to Charley Powell of the 49ers in the fourth quarter, and the penalty set up a field goal and we won by two points. Another time, after Ed Meadows of the Bears had knocked out Layne, I broke Meadows's nose and his jaw a few plays later and when he swung at me, on the next play, the ref kicked him out of the game."

It was like that in "the pit," where angels—and wide receivers—feared to tread.

11

What We Read

For those who wanted their prurient interest aroused in the 1950s, who were not offended by a little healthy violence and sex, books were about the only place one could turn. Unless, of course, you were willing to do your own research.

Radio was beginning to vanish from the American scene, along with the American scene itself. Television was new and nervous, going through a stage in which it was still attaching lace doilies to low-cut necklines. Broadway offered a continuing series of hit musicals, on the theory that it can't be dirty if people do it to music. Movie-goers had not yet recovered from the shock of hearing Rhett Butler, in 1939, tell Scarlet: "Frankly, my dear, I don't give a damn."

So that left it to books which, curiously enough, received a bit of a lift from, of all places, television. By the time people turned off their favorite shows, theorized one publisher, it was too late to go out and too early to go to bed. Up went the demand for books, and the publishing industry boomed.

The mystery writings of Mickey Spillane were broadly—no pun intended—condemned as trash, but his hero, private detective Mike Hammer, became the new god of the paperbacks. Spillane's works sold more than 27 million copies, and were widely found inside the history notebooks of high school students.

No book in the entire decade provided a better measure of the country's shock threshold than *Peyton Place*, the story of a small New Hampshire town, written by a previously unpublished school principal's wife named Grace Metalious. *Peyton Place* became a synonym for complicated sexual situations. The book enjoyed such popularity that anyone from a small New England town was automatically treated with envy or suspicion.

Time magazine warned the public, in 1956, that "her love scenes are as explicit as love scenes can get without the use of diagrams and tape recorder." A sample:

Her fingertips traced a pattern down the side of his face, and with her mouth almost against his she whispered, "I didn't know it could be like this..."

She could not lie still under his hands.

"Anything," she said. "Anything, anything."

"I love this fire in you. I love it when you have to move."

"Don't stop."

"Here? And here? And here?"

"Yes. Oh, yes. Yes."

On the whole, there was an infinite variety to the range of books the public bought most in the fifties. The readers indicated a strong taste for nonfiction that revealed their world and themselves: *The Exurbanites, The Status Seekers, Please Don't Eat the Daisies.*

Jack Kerouac

And there were novels of importance, as moving and truthful today as they were 20 years ago: *From Here to Eternity*, *The Caine Mutiny*, *Exodus*, and a Russian novel filled with names that hurt your teeth, *Doctor Zhivago*.

The Beat movement—some said it stood for beatitude, others said beatdown—produced a different gender of books: personal, painful, earthy, often obscure.

Jack Kerouac, the son of French-Canadian parents, a former Columbia football player and ex-sailor, seemed to speak for those who drifted through the decade. A sample from *On the Road*:

"What do you want out of life?" I asked, and I used to ask that all the time of girls.

"I don't know," she said. "Just wait on tables and try to get along." She yawned . I put my hand over her mouth and told her not to yawn. I tried to tell her how excited I was about life and the things we could do together; saying that, and planning to leave Denver in two days. She turned away wearily. We lay on our backs, looking at the ceiling and wondering what God had wrought when He made life so sad. We made vague plans to meet in Frisco.

The Decade's Best Sellers

1950—The Cardinal, *Henry Morton Robinson*
1951—From Here To Eternity, *James Jones*
1952—The Silver Chalice, *Thomas B. Costain*
1953—The Robe, *Lloyd C. Douglas*
1954—Not as a Stranger, *Morton Thompson*
1955—Marjorie Morningstar, *Herman Wouk*
1956—Don't Go Near the Water, *William Brinkley*
1957—By Love Possessed, *James Gould Cozzens*
1958—Doctor Zhivago, *Boris Pasternak*
1959—Exodus, *Leon Uris*

Start Spreading the News...

The pace was serene, the atmosphere almost pastoral, the relationships personal. In the late summer after a couple of weeks of working out, the team would travel about the countryside in 10 rented cars, meeting a team of semipros here, a squad of homegrown all-stars there. Another time they would play a Canadian team, half the game by NFL rules and the other half with a 12-man offense. An assistant coach might even substitute at quarterback. These were not called preseason games then, or even for that matter "exhibition" games. Practice games is what they were, and no admission was charged.

The giant of the Giants, portly Steve Owen, was the head coach, and had been for more than 20 years. Owen would preside over three-hour practice sessions, leisurely affairs that allowed him time to take an athlete aside, throw a meaty arm across the student's shoulder, and explain how football should be played.

Tim Mara was the owner, a "gentleman bookmaker" at New York tracks before they had pari-mutuel machines, and as late as 1950 the years had not dimmed Mara's essentially paternalistic view of life. He promised, offhand, to buy a defensive back a new suit if he would intercept two of Otto Graham's passes. The back picked off one, and that Monday Mara gave him the pants. The following game, when the fellow intercepted another, Mara gave him the coat to match.

It was a happy situation. The crowds weren't all that great at the Polo Grounds, but the living was easy. Then there appeared on the scene the Young Organization Man, Paul Brown and his Cleveland Browns, and the old, relaxed order of ways in the NFL would be forced to quicken the pace to match him. For a while it seemed that only Steve Owen and the Giants could match the Browns. In the breakup of the All-America Football Conference, the club got its greatest input of talent in history—taking tackle Arnie Weinmeister and defensive backs Tom Landry, Otto Schnellbacher, and Harmon Rowe, all from the defunct New York Yankees.

The Browns had been devastating the NFL in the early weeks of the 1950 season, with Graham passing to four deep receivers—his two ends, plus both his halfbacks. Steve Owen sat down and doodled a defense in the shape of an umbrella. "Boys," he said, "this is how I want you to line up."

Young cornerback Landry was even then "a coach on the field." He later explained: "I was really too slow to play cornerback, so to stay in the league, to keep my job, I had to figure out what the other team was going to do before they did it." This meant endless hours with a film projector, and charts that showed down-and-distance play selections. Landry knew that the Umbrella defense was an evolution of the Eagle defense originated by Greasy Neale's Philadelphia champions of the late forties. "Until then, you only had three defensive backs, two men on the corner and the single safety," Landry said. "So you could isolate a halfback like

Kyle Rote

George McAfee of the Bears on a linebacker. Greasy was the first to say, 'Heck, let's get another defensive back in there—get rid of the middle linebacker—and put him on that fast halfback.' He had a 5-2-4.

"Steve Owen had an excellent mind, but he was never a detail man. Detail to Steve was something you 'do' on the field. I learned most of my coaching under Steve by just playing, working out the details of what Steve came up with. He was very good at springing defenses on teams, like he did in that first game with the Browns with the Umbrella.

"We lined up against the Browns with a six-man front and a middle linebacker and the four deep backs fanned in a semicircle, an umbrella. The middle linebacker was the stem—that's how it looked in the press box, where they came up with the name. We played the 6-1 with those two ends dropping off. Sometimes they'd be down and going, other times standing up and dropping off. They never knew what we were doing, and Graham didn't complete a pass the first half."

The ends were Ray Poole and Jim Duncan, and when they dropped off, the outside rush was the responsibility of Weinmeister and Al DeRogatis, the tackles. The deep backs were Emlen Tunnell, Rowe, Schnellbacher, and Landry. The Giants won 6-0, the first shutout loss in Cleveland's history. For the rematch, Owen put in another twist, a five-man rush and five defensive backs in the Umbrella, and the Giants won again 17-13. This forced a playoff for the Eastern Conference title. The defense was again magnificent, but Cleveland won 8-3, on two field goals and an end-of-game safety.

The Browns would shut the championship door in the Giants' faces six consecutive years, and they forced the end of Owen's 22-year reign with a colossal 62-14 whipping in 1953. The six-year drought was not as hard to take as one might expect. "The thing I remember about the fifties," Landry said, "was that television wasn't a dominant force at all. And newspaper publicity across the nation was very slim. When I would come back home [to Texas], nobody ever asked me about pro football. They didn't know we kept finishing behind the Browns."

Jim Lee Howell—"a tremendous gentleman, a top-notch guy, soft-spoken," according to Landry—succeeded Owen. Howell believed in delegating authority to his assistants, and it was a good move. Landry was given charge of the defense as player-coach, and the offense was turned over to Vince Lombardi, who came to the Giants from Red Blaik's staff at West Point. "It just so happened he had a fairly dominant pair of people in Lombardi and myself," Landry said. "Jim Lee took the position, 'Well, they're doing a good job, so I'll just coordinate everything else.' He let Vince do his job and me do my job. The day of the game we ran our own units."

Kyle Rote, the running back and flanker who became a mainstay of the Giants' greatest years, put it differently. "Jim Lee Howell had enough sense to realize he had a couple of geniuses working with him. I can remember walking down our dormitory at training camp in St. Michael's, Vermont, and I'd look to the left and see Lombardi in a room running the projector for his plays, and I'd look to the right and I'd see Landry running his plays, and then on down the hall I'd look in Jim Lee's room and see him reading the newspaper."

While Landry was working out the 4-3, Lombardi was working just as diligently on the power sweep and his run-to-daylight philosophy. "Lombardi perfected the power sweep," Landry said, "with the two guards pulling and the fullback blocking. And he had the guy to make it go, Frank Gifford, because of the run-pass option—the same as he had a guy later on to work it at Green Bay, Paul Hornung."

In 1956, the season after Landry quit his playing role, he found a guy to make his 4-3 go, a rookie middle linebacker out of West Virginia, Robert Lee (Sam) Huff. Other first-year men were defensive end Jim Katcavage and punter Don Chandler. That was the year Tim Mara's son Wellington, a masterful trader in those days, acquired defensive end Andy Robustelli from Los Angeles, and defensive tackle Dick Modzelewski from Pittsburgh. It also was the year the Giants moved from the Polo Grounds to Yankee Stadium, increasing the potential seating from 50,000 to 62,000.

Most of the players and some of the coaches were now living at the Concourse Plaza on 161st Street, near Yankee Stadium. It probably was not a coincidence that Landry had his middle linebacker under the same roof with him. "I'd be watching television," Huff said, "really caught up in a Playhouse Ninety, and the phone would ring. It was Tom. 'What are you doing?' he'd say, and I'd say, 'Oh, nothing,' and he'd say, 'Well, come on up and look at some football with me.' He had the projector in his apartment and we'd go over the other team's offense. I learned more football that one season in Tom's apartment than I'd learned all through high school and college."

The Browns were playing their first season without Otto Graham and tumbling badly to a 5-7 record, leaving a void the Giants happily filled. And CBS Television was sending out a national telecast of NFL games every Sunday for the first time. "Everything came together for the greatness of pro football," Rote said. "New York is the heartbeat of the media—including Madison Avenue, where the commercial dollar is. When we won it in 1956, we were winning it in Madison Avenue's own backyard. These ad men were young guys—bright and sharp—but they'd never had an NFL champion in their own backyard. Suddenly, they happened to tie into pro football just when television advertising was hitting its peak. This propelled football far beyond what it would have been had Green Bay or Cleveland won the title that year."

The 1956 Giants had a peculiar quirk that has never been repeated in quite the same way by any other championship team. Third-year quarterback Don Heinrich would start the games, then old pro Charlie Conerly would come in at the beginning of the second quarter and play the rest of the way. "The theory behind it," Landry said, "was you'd have Heinrich come in and probe the defense, see what they were doing, and you could discuss it with Conerly during the first quarter on the sidelines: 'This is what they're doing and this is what we planned, and here's what we ought to do.'"

Rote says it was the particular assets of Heinrich that made the system work, though it had never been tried before or since. "Heinrich wasn't the greatest passer in the world," Rote said, "but he had a great football mind, a real instinct for the game. And he wouldn't hurt you being in there a quarter."

There was another element in this ploy. Conerly, a great and early graying All-America quarterback out of Ole Miss, had been the Giants' gunner since 1949 and he never had led them to a title of any kind. "Conerly," Landry says, "was getting a lot of flak in the early part of his career, before he produced like he did in the latter part. Heinrich was the young guy. You always have the problem with quarterbacks when you've got one old one and one young one. But Conerly was always 'The Pro' and Vince was always a believer in him."

Lombardi could well believe in Conerly, who came in at the start of the second

"I'd be watching television," Huff said, "really caught up in a Playhouse Ninety and the phone would ring. It was Tom. 'What are you doing?' he'd say... 'Well, come on up and look at some football with me.'"

Frank Gifford

quarter in the title game against the Chicago Bears, threw only 10 passes, and presided over a 47-7 laugher. The game transpired just the way Landry and Lombardi wrote it, only more so. Rookie Gene Filipski ran the kickoff back to the Bears' 39 in tennis sneakers, as decreed by a pregame warmup. Heinrich hit Gifford for a 22-yard pass. The Bears put up a seven-man line to blitz a pass play, and Heinrich checked off to Mel Triplett on a draw. Triplett went for the touchdown. The rout was on, and the Giants had their first NFL championship since 1938 (and their last until 1986).

But there was something more ominous happening that championship week of 1956 in New York, a veritable cloud no larger than a man's hand. The NFL Players Association was formed. The issue that spurred its birth was not salaries, or pensions, or unlimited free agency. The players were aroused about their face-masks. A year before, the commissioner's office had sent out a ruling: All face-masks henceforth would be limited to a single bar, instead of the double-bar protection players had adopted. Team captains began exchanging letters of outrage. In the winter and spring of 1956, they got together, first at Cleveland, then at Philadelphia, to draw up a resolution. Finally, the week of the championship game in New York, they met with Commissioner Bert Bell and got the ruling rescinded.

Meanwhile, back on the field, the Giants were gearing up for consecutive Eastern Conference championships in 1958 and 1959, based on a foundation of great defense. These were the teams that popularized a new chant from the stands: "DEE-fense!" Robustelli and Katcavage were the ends, Modzelewski and Roosevelt Grier the tackles, Huff, Harland Svare, and Cliff Livingston the linebackers. A rotating cast of stars got the job done in the defensive backfield—Tunnell, Jim Patton, Dick Nolan, Lindon Crow, Dick Lynch, Carl Karilivacz, Ed Hughes. One Sunday the Giants held an opponent to zero passing yards. Under the low-keyed Landry they got the job done with teamwork and quickness. Jim Lee Howell kept exhorting them for more meanness, and he took on as a special project the instilling of a "killer instinct" in gentle Rosey Grier. "You've got to punish your man to make him respect you," Howell would say, and then he'd wince when Grier helped an opposing quarterback to his feet. Howell finally gave up on his Grier campaign after the incident of "The Published Scouting Report."

Unnoticed by Landry, two writers were present when the defense was given a belittling rundown of the next opponent, Philadelphia. This Eagle was "too slow to cover the sweep," another would "quit if you take him on physically." The comments made great reading in the next day's sports pages, and even better reading when picked up by the papers in Philadelphia. At a team meeting, Howell sought to turn the situation around. "Those guys have been reading this stuff all week," he said. "They're going to come in here Sunday with fire in their eyes, spoiling for blood. So what are you going to do about it?" Howell happened to be looking at Grier when he roared the question, and Grier jumped up and said, "Maybe it isn't too late—we could wire them an apology."

Gentle or not, the Giants' defense was smothering. It held opponents to an average of less than 16 points a game in 1958, and one stretch of three victories was accomplished without a New York touchdown.

But the Giants could not shake the Browns, and both teams finished with 9-3 records, forcing a playoff for the conference title. Sam Huff and Company shut down Jim Brown and all the Browns for a 10-0 victory. The New York touchdown came on a double reverse with a lateral from beyond the line of scrimmage back to Charlie Conerly. It was an amazing departure from the usual bread-and-butter attack directed by Lombardi. Years later, Landry couldn't recall how it happened. "It must have been a free-lance move," he said, "because I can't ever imagine us having a play that ended with Conerly running the ball." It was a free-lance, and a story goes with it.

"The play was supposed to end with Gifford going through right tackle," Rote said. "Conerly handed to Alex Webster, and Webster handed inside to Frank coming the other way. But all week in practice when he got through the line, the linebacker would grab him—you know how you do in practice, around the shoulders. And Conerly was just loping along out there behind the line, so Gifford would toss him the ball. We all laughed about it. I said, 'Maybe that's the way the play is supposed to go,' but it was a joke."

So, on Sunday at Yankee Stadium from the Cleveland 9-yard line, when Gifford slipped through right tackle and came face-to-face with a linebacker, he pitched out to Conerly and Conerly kept loping around right end for the touchdown. "Real heads-up play," a writer said in the postgame locker room. "Nope," Rote said. "Gifford was just like Pavlov's dog: He did it according to the book."

Seven days later the Giants were back in Yankee Stadium for their losing roles in "The Greatest Game Ever Played," the sudden-death overtime of Johnny U. and the Baltimore Colts. The image of the floodlit stadium, of fullback Alan Ameche smashing through from the 1-yard line, the clock that stopped forever at 8:15 of the extra period—all of this erased the fact that the Giants had made a great comeback of their own.

Baltimore led 14-3 at the half and had a first down at New York's 3-yard line in the third quarter. On fourth down, the Colts still had a yard to go, and they went for the touchdown with Ameche around end. He didn't make it, and three downs later Conerly hit Rote for an 86-yard play to the Colts' 1, the last 24 yards contributed by Alex Webster after Rote fumbled when hit. The Giants scored, and scored again, to lead 17-14.

Don Chandler punted down to the 12-yard line, and Unitas had only 2:25 to reach field goal position. Passing to Lenny Moore and Raymond Berry, both of whom were double-teamed, Unitas made it with 15 seconds to spare. Steve Myhra kicked a 20-yard field goal to tie the score. It was 17-17 at what should have been—normally would have been—the final gun. But this was no normal day.

New York won the toss to start sudden death, but couldn't make a first down when Gifford failed on a third-and-two. Chandler punted to the Baltimore 20. And Unitas brought the Colts downfield almost as if the Giants weren't there, mixing sweeps and draws and slant-in passes to Berry, finally lofting a sideline toss to Jim Mutscheller down to the 1. Then it was Ameche's turn. This time he scored, and Baltimore won 23-17, ending the first fifth period in pro football history. How could the Colts, great as they were, drive so inevitably against the greatest defense in the league?

The Giants would ring up an even better record in 1959 and win the conference by three full games, 10-2 to Cleveland's 7-5. Then they would be beaten, soundly this time, 31-16, by the same Baltimore team.

Vince Lombardi had departed for Green Bay that season, taking Emlen Tunnell with him. Tom Landry left at the end of the year to set up shop in Dallas. Tim Mara died in 1959. The Giants would play for the NFL championship three more

"You've got to punish your man to make him respect you," Howell would say, and then he'd wince when Grier helped an opposing quarterback to his feet.

113

13

Moving Experiences

"It's like when you walk down a dark alley. That's how I feel when I'm out in the open, all alone—as if I'm walking down a dark alley. And you see at the end of the alley a glimmer of light from the cross street—that's the goal line—and you're in a hurry to get there. But on the way, even though the alley is so dark you can't see a thing, you sense a telegraph pole to your right and you sheer away from it. A few steps farther, you know there's a doorway with a man in it, even though you can't see him. You just feel it. So you turn away from that, too. Haven't you had that experience many times? I have."

No, most of us never had that feeling, that free-as-the-wind feeling of slipping and weaving through a broken field, of dodging and ducking around people as though they were garbage cans. But we know what he means, we get the picture, from those 35-year-old words.

Our man with the sixth sense, with the kind of wide angle vision that told him at a glance where every tackler was staked out, was Hugh McElhenny. They called him "The King." He ran with the ball the way little boys do in their wildest dreams. He had speed and power and guts and the complete repertoire of moves: the pivot, the sidestep, the change of pace, the sudden bursts, the spinning, the faking, and an uncanny gift for breaking a tackle. Perhaps more than any other back who ever played the game he was blessed with instinct—the kind that tells you when a stranger is lurking in a doorway.

Those who were close to the San Francisco 49ers—including the bankers who held the team's notes—insist that Hugh McElhenny saved the franchise. He never was able to convert his immense talents into a title for San Francisco, not in nine seasons of trying, but he became the dominant running back of the 1950s. And the 49ers were fun to watch. It was an eternal contest to see if McElhenny, and quarterback Y. A. Tittle, and Co. could score touchdowns as fast as the 49ers' defense gave them away.

People used to argue about his touchdown runs the way two guys on a beach argue about girls. The last one to pass by is always the prettiest. Descriptions of McElhenny runs were like passages out of children's fiction, liberally sprinkled with opposing players bouncing off each other, getting stiff-armed, and diving helplessly at his vanishing heels. It was pure Ripley. Things like that don't really happen, do they?

Against the Bears, in his rookie season of 1952, he fielded a punt at his own 6 and rocked on his feet for a split-second or two—a McElhenny habit that enabled him to see how the field was spread. Two Chicago ends thought they had him trapped. As they closed in, McElhenny zipped straight ahead and the two ends collided, bumping heads, a moment of fine burlesque. He changed pace and a tackler appeared on his right. In two steps he was in overdrive again. He swerved to his left and the leaping Bear landed two yards behind him. He straightened up and went through the rest of the Bears as though it were some kind of barn dance. The run covered 94 yards, not including the mileage he traveled sideways. "That," said George Halas, never a man to mince words, "was the damndest run I've ever seen in football."

Later, McElhenny said, casually, "I thought I had caught the punt at about our twenty-six. If I had known it was the six-yard line, I would have let it go."

Of course, one never knew what McElhenny would do. He was impetuous and honest, qualities that tend to confuse people. Once, against the Giants in his rookie year, he grew annoyed as Tittle mounted his racehorse offense, calling his plays quickly and getting back to the line, trying to stampede the Giants. "Dammit, Y.A.," McElhenny complained, as they broke a huddle, "give us time to get out there and see how the secondary is lining up, what they're trying to do."

Tittle was stunned. "If you don't like it," he snapped, "get the hell out of here and get somebody else in."

Hugh McElhenny

McElhenny shrugged. Without a word he turned and jogged off the field.

His attitude most of his career, most of his life, really, was a bit on the languid side. He would not have been bearable otherwise, with his raw talent and a temper that boiled suddenly.

Between Red Grange and Joe Namath, no college player arrived with more acclaim, for reasons that were not all flattering. "The King" was the most celebrated recruiting case of his day. His story, in fact, may have been the first to alert the public that college athletes were sometimes rewarded with more than locomotive yells, free laundry, and a wrist watch for playing in the Rose Bowl.

Some 63 colleges competed for the right to educate Hugh McElhenny, courting him by phone, mail, and limousine even as he was doing wonderful things for Compton Junior College. His decision to enroll at the University of Washington led to an investigation of the school's recruiting practices. The popular line was that he had found his way to Seattle by following a trail of $20 bills.

His 49ers' teammates never tired of boasting that he was the first player ever to take a cut in salary to play pro football (for $7,000 his rookie season). Financial inducements aside, the pros had to wonder about his reputation for being spoiled and unreliable. As long as a team wins, a player with Bolshevik tendencies can be considered tolerable, if difficult. When you lose, they are merely difficult.

McElhenny was indifferent to discipline, chronically late for practice. He drank, and drove away his wife. He was involved in a series of publicized fights. In one of them he knocked a cop over his motorcycle, something Emily Post has never recommended.

They couldn't tame him on the field, either. He broke every rushing record at Washington and many of his marks—for example, most yards in a game and best career per-carry average—still are standing nearly four decades later.

Yet in the 1952 draft, seven players were picked ahead of him, half of the first round. Of course, they were not exactly tackling dummies: Ollie Matson, Babe Parilli, Ed Modzelewski, Les Richter, Larry Isbell, Jim Dooley, and Bill Wade.

Astonished to find him still at large, the 49ers claimed McElhenny as the eighth selection. If there had been any hesitation on the part of head coach Buck Shaw, it was dispelled by a frantic, 2 A.M. phone call from quarterback Frankie Albert, in Honolulu, where he had watched McElhenny tear apart the Hula Bowl. In his enthusiastic haste, Albert assured his coach, "This is the greatest running back I've

Bill Willis

ever seen, Buck...don't let this guy get away," and promptly forgot to reverse the charges.

On his first play as a professional, "The King " ran 60 yards for a touchdown. As Albert crossed the sideline, he headed directly for Shaw. "Hey, the club owes me six and a half bucks," he reminded him, "for that long distance call from Honolulu."

Albert collected. So did the 49ers.

You never could tell from his record that McElhenny played much of his career in pain. It was contrary to medical opinion that he played at all. At the age of 11 he stepped on a broken milk bottle, severing the tendons of his right foot. He missed a year of school, spent five months in bed and seven on crutches. His doctors doubted that he would walk normally again, which is why doctors make such lousy football coaches. In later years he would need a steel plate in his shoe, and pain-deadening shots in his foot. It was such a handicap he lasted only 13 seasons.

In 1957, rookie quarterback John Brodie, who lived nearby, asked if he could ride to practice with him. When Brodie mused aloud one day that it was nice to have "The King" for a pal, McElhenny winced. "Listen, rook," he said, "I never want to get too friendly with anybody on this team. That's because the day will come when you have to say goodby."

That day came in 1961 when Red Hickey, with whom he did not get along famously, dropped him into the expansion draft. The string took him to Minnesota, New York, and Detroit. At a retirement dinner, Frank Gifford, a friend and a foe since their college days, narrated a film of McElhenny highlights. One after another, long runs filled the screen: an 86-yard twister against the Packers, 81 versus the Bears, 71 through the Rams. "If there is a certain sameness to these pictures," observed Gifford, "well, there was a certain sameness to the way he ran."

He was 6-1 and 205, and looked like Charles Bronson, or vice versa. To the extent that he combined so many qualities—he was tough, casual, impulsive, and short-tempered—and viewed football, and life, as a romp, he is remembered as a symbol of the 1950s. In a practical sense, he left his mark on the era. He was the first of the quality running backs to rest when the other team had the ball, to play no defense, to concentrate on doing what he did best. He helped start the age of the specialist.

It was a muscle game they played at the onset of the fifties, the heyday of the big back. None was more feared than wide-track Marion Motley of the Cleveland Browns, who accomplished something that made him the envy of his teammates: He knocked down his head coach, Paul Brown.

It happened during the war when Motley was a swab playing under Brown at Great Lakes Naval. That day he was favoring a sprained toe, badly swollen, as the squad stood in a circle watching Brown demonstrate a move. At one point he stepped back and landed on Motley's foot. Without thinking, reacting out of pain, Motley clubbed him with a quick forearm across the back. Brown literally flew across the circle and fell, face down.

Picking himself up, Brown looked quizzically at Motley. "What did you do that for?" he demanded.

"You stepped on my toe," said Motley. "You stepped on my poor hurt foot." Brown just laughed. For years after that he would caution people, "Don't step on Marion's feet, or he'll hit you."

Motley's relationship with his coach was a kind of Tom and Jerry cartoon, with

Brown using his wits to inspire, arouse, and outrage his big, good-natured fullback. Motley always knew how far Paul would go, which was further than most. Their military experience was always a frame of reference.

"Paul was a stickler for details," Motley said, "and a disciplinarian. Paul was sitting on a train one Sunday afternoon at the same time me and another player, a young kid, were sitting in another train on the next track. We were going out on liberty. This kid I was with didn't see Paul. But Paul saw him. The kid had a cigarette in his hand. On Monday morning, Paul fired the kid. They sent him to Iwo Jima, I think."

Later, on the Browns, Motley assured his teammates that Brown could cut players without regard to conscience or sentiment. He had, after all, once cut one to Iwo Jima.

Pro football was a white sanctuary when the war ended. Motley, and teammate Bill Willis—there's a story in that—were two of four blacks who integrated the sport. The others were Kenny Washington and Woody Strode at Los Angeles.

Marion had written Paul in 1946 to ask for a tryout with the Cleveland team he then was assembling. Brown wrote back and said, sorry, but he thought he had enough backs. But other forces were at work.

Willis, an All-America guard from Ohio State, had reported to the Browns' training camp, the only black on the roster. Meanwhile, Blanton Collier, one of Brown's coaches who had followed him from Great Lakes, was agitating Paul to bring in Motley.

Brown thought it over. "One day," Willis remembered, "he asked me if I would like a roommate. I said, that would be nice. He said, 'Well, Marion Motley is going to be reporting.'"

That night Collier called to invite Motley to the Browns' camp at Bowling Green. He was under no illusions. "I've always believed," he said, "that they needed a roommate for Willis. I don't think they really felt I'd make the team."

On the field, the Browns were quick to rally to the support of the black players. After Willis had been worked over one day, Lou Rymkus, the lantern-jawed tackle from Notre Dame, assured him: "There's no use in you getting into fights and risk getting thrown out of the game. If anyone gives you a bad time, just tell us. We'll take care of it."

Long after a black presence was to command special notice, the old Browns remained fiercely loyal to Motley and his career. "There is no fair way Marion can be compared to Jim Brown," argued his old roomie, Willis. "Brown may have been the greatest running back in pro football. But, in my opinion, Motley was a better all-around player. He was a great runner. And a great blocker. He'd catch flare passes and turn them into long gains. And those famous goal-line stands we used to make, a lot of that was Motley, backing up the line."

Motley made the fullback trap famous in the fifties, and the records that Jim Brown would break later were his. A proud man, Motley was touchy about the inevitable comparisons. "I didn't have the running plays Jim had," he said. "I had one wide play, the end run, and that was it. Just an ordinary old end run. See, I didn't have the flips. I often said to Paul, 'Let me get them out there and scatter 'em. Let me take a few of them out there with me.' But he'd say, 'No, the flip wasn't designed for you.' I had to make my yardage up the middle."

Paul Brown could bring Motley to a fever with the twist of a phrase. "I'd come out of a game for a rest," he says, "after playing offense and defense, working hard

Picking himself up, Brown looked quizzically at Motley. "What did you do that for?" he demanded. "You stepped on my toe," said Motley. "You stepped on my poor hurt foot."

Jim Brown

as I could, but maybe I hadn't done something I was supposed to. When I came out of the game Paul would walk up to me and, in a low voice, almost like he was hissing at me, he'd say, 'Do you know that you are killing our football team?' Then he would walk away from me, like nothing had happened. I could have walked up behind him and choked him. I'd go back out there and the first jersey that got in front of me I'd try to kill the guy."

Ed Modzelewski was Cleveland's interim fullback, the fellow who bridged the years between Motley and his eminence, Jim Brown of Syracuse. James Nathaniel Brown came along late in the decade, 1957, when the game and the Browns and the country were all changing.

That fall America heard the eerie, electronic signals broadcast back to earth by a Russian satellite called Sputnik. It was a bad time for kids, who suddenly found a new classroom emphasis on science and math. The New York Giants and the Brooklyn Dodgers fled to California, and for the first time major league baseball was played on both coasts. Social quiet was ending. President Eisenhower sent paratroops to Central High School in Little Rock, where the integration of nine black students had been threatened with violence.

A new black awareness was coming and, in professional sports, Jim Brown would be in the forefront. But, in the summer of 1957, he was just a rookie trying to make a team, and an unhappy rookie at that, having spent the All-Star game returning kickoffs.

In his first appearance in a Cleveland uniform, Brown ran up against the loyalty ceiling that existed then on every pro team—that is, the protective feeling that the veterans felt for each other.

As Big Mo tells it: "We were playing an exhibition game against the Lions and he had just come in from the All-Star game at Chicago. He didn't know the plays very well and wasn't sure of himself. He didn't look too good so I figured 'Well, he's just another challenger.' There had been others. One kid—an All-America from Colorado [John Bayuk]—was supposed to be the greatest thing since penicillin, but they cut him and he went back to selling encyclopedias or something and I kept playing fullback. So my first reaction to Jim was just that—probably another encyclopedia salesman.

"Then there was another thing going against him. The law of the jungle. Let's face it. I had a lot of friends on the team. They'd try to hit Jim just a little harder than they'd normally hit in practice. But he'd bust out of their arms and gradually you could see him gaining respect. You could almost see them thinking, 'Maybe he'll help us to a championship.' The writing was on the wall for me, so I became his number-one rooter. You know, I doubt Jim ever knew the guys were hitting him extra hard."

There was a higher loyalty, of course, and that was to winning. You can picture the eyes of the Browns growing wide, and the wheels turning in their heads, and a chorus of "Sorry about that, Mo," for their old friend.

Jim Brown sent him to the bench and, three years later, into retirement, but Ed Modzelewski paid him the ultimate tribute: "I'll tell you, I feel like the guy who played behind Babe Ruth."

It is history now, in Cleveland, that Paul Brown took 45 minutes in the draft to decide between Jim Brown, Milt Plum, or Clarence Peaks. It was a curious draft, that one. The early rounds moved up to November, 1956, with the season still going on, because of competition from Canada. Some of the teams were still drafting out of *Look* magazine, but Paul Brown was prepared. The Cleveland table looked like headquarters for the invasion of Normandy.

The Browns drafted sixth—after Jon Arnett, John Brodie, Ron Kramer, and Len Dawson had been taken. Paul Hornung led it off as the bonus pick by the Packers. The Cleveland scouts wanted Peaks of Michigan State, feeling that the Big Ten was a better testing ground than the kind of opposition Syracuse had seen. But Brown disbelieved the school doctors, who said that Peaks would not be affected by recent knee surgery. Thus the delay. The scouts wanted Peaks. Paul wanted Jim Brown. And some of his coaches argued for Plum, the quarterback. They compromised, and drafted Jim Brown.

He was, as they say, a different breed of cat. In college he read Chaucer for pleasure and relaxed by listening to Bach. But there was a kind of controlled anger in him—some thought him arrogant. He never compromised his dignity. He insisted on being treated like a man, which, under the circumstances, was not unreasonable.

His father left home before he was 2. His mother worked as a domestic for a well-to-do family on Long Island, and he grew up there, not uncomfortably, but no stranger to the streets and the gangs that prowled them. But sports called him. He won 13 varsity letters in high school and, after a period of mutual suspicion, performed wondrous deeds for Syracuse in football, basketball, track, and lacrosse.

Brown would see pro football salaries escalate wildly before he retired—he helped drive them up, of course—but when he came into the league the players were still conspiring to find ways to save their meal money.

One of Brown's best runs came the night he and roommate Bobby Mitchell were trying to beat the curfew in Los Angeles. Failure to make the curfew on the Browns was an automatic $250 fine. They had bare seconds to go, and were sprinting down the hallway when they spotted Ed Ulinski, an assistant coach, in their path, making bedchecks. Ulinski pinned himself to the wall as Brown and Mitchell pounded past. They opened the door and fell into their rooms, grinning at each other while catching their breath. They had made it safely.

In the game the next day, Brown returned to the huddle after a short run. As he bent over, he whispered to Mitchell: "You know, if Ed hadn't got out of the way he would have gotten hurt. For $250, I'd have run right over him."

Of course, Brown did not need a reason to run over people. "Let's face it," said Sam Huff, his great adversary. "No linebacker in this league could stop Brown man-to-man." He was 6-2 and nearly 230 and he had a build that would make Charles Atlas gasp. In addition to his speed and power, he used his shoulders and his free arm as weapons. There was something about the way he ran, or the way he looked, that simply froze tacklers. He went through them like a blowtorch in a wax museum.

He was many things, Jim Brown of Cleveland, but mostly he was consistent. In eight of the nine seasons he played, he led the league in rushing. He also led six times in carries and five times in touchdowns. He was as close to the perfect running back as any coach ever craved. Against the Cardinals in 1959, Paul Brown ran him 37 times, which made a lot of people nervous. He had to be taking a beating. "If he keeps doing that," predicted Sid Gillman of the Rams, "he's going to end up either punch-drunk or a basket case."

More likely, the people who had to stop him were getting punch-drunk. "If you have a big gun," said Paul Brown, calmly, "you shoot it." Jim didn't belong to a

Modzelewski: "One kid was supposed to be the greatest thing since penicillin, but they cut him and he went back to selling encyclopedias. So my first reaction to Jim was just that—probably another encyclopedia salesman."

union. They could run him as often as they liked. It created a sensation the first time he carried more than 30 times in his rookie season. It was against the Rams, in Cleveland, before 65,000, largest home crowd of 1957. The Browns won 45-31. Jim Brown scored four touchdowns, set up two others, plus a field goal, and gained 237 yards on 31 carries. One first-quarter play seemed to tell the fans that, yes, Jim Brown was the guy they had waited for all their lives.

It was a fullback draw from the Cleveland 31. Two Rams linebackers, Dick Daugherty and Larry Morris, blitzed and hit Brown from either side as he took the handoff. Daugherty cracked him so hard his helmet flew off. Maybe a science professor could explain what happened next, based on the principle of actions and reactions. But the impact was such that both linebackers bounced off. They just flew apart, like some kind of trapeze act, and Brown gave his legs a little shake and sped 69 yards for a touchdown, carrying Alex Bravo the last five.

He played on an Eastern Division winner that rookie year, but it was the last hurrah for the Paul Brown Browns. Then began the long years of coming up empty. In the sixties, Jim Brown led a workers' revolt, and the new owners fired Paul Brown, who had invented the team. Under Blanton Collier, whose call had brought Marion Motley into pro football, they briefly revived the glory years, winning it all in 1964 and losing out to the Packers in 1965. Before the start of the next season, Jim Brown retired at 30.

He was not, as his critics kept pointing out, a complete player. The Cleveland quarterbacks sometimes grumbled, not always in private, about his failure to pass block. He did not always follow through on his fakes. He had a knack of absorbing a tackle, rather than struggling, digging maybe for an extra yard, a habit that annoyed some observers. But Brown was pragmatic: "You have to sense what's dangerous enough to put you out of business."

He struck some as selfish, unwilling to get down in the dirt for his team. One of those was Jim Taylor, of Green Bay, to whom Brown lost his rushing title in 1962. "Vince Lombardi taught me how to crab block, down on all fours," Taylor said. "That way you get every bit of yourself around your man. I bet Jim Brown doesn't know what a crab block is."

It did not sound like something Jim Brown would have enjoyed knowing. But from the moment he joined Cleveland in 1957—after driving all night from the College All-Star game—he commanded their attention. One of his admirers was Chuck Bednarik of the Eagles, who knew a man when he saw one. "You could kick him, scratch him, punch him in the mouth and he'd never say a word," said Bednarik. "He'd really tee guys off by never grumbling."

Of course, when the action got really overt—stopping, say, just short of hand grenades—grumbling wasn't the way the boys settled it. In Kurt Vonnegut's psychedelic novel, *Slaughterhouse Five*, one of the characters says: "Anybody ever asks you what the sweetest thing in life is, it's revenge." Sometimes pro football in the fifties gave that impression, too.

Take the case of Joe Perry, the San Francisco fullback who, in 1950, was blindsided by Chicago's George Connor, suffering two broken ribs in the process. Perry waited. Two years later, against the Bears, he broke loose on a trap up the middle, and suddenly had only George Connor between himself and the goal line. With the entire field to maneuver in, Perry gathered up a head of steam, lowered his helmet and barreled into Connor, laying him out. Perry stumbled on for a few yards and was dropped from behind. An old debt had been repaid.

Portfolio:
RUNNING BACKS

Small and black, Claude (Buddy) Young had to contend with twofold prejudice, but he was a scintillating tailback who played in the 1955 Pro Bowl while with the Baltimore Colts.

Bob (Hunchy) Hoernschemeyer (above) was one of the no-names who helped the Lions to the top of the heap in the early '50s. George Taliaferro (left), one of the early black stars, played in three Pro Bowls while on three bad teams—the Yanks, the Texans, and the fledgling Colts. Dan Towler (opposite) of the Rams, one of the game's best runners in his prime, was all-pro from 1951-53.

The 49ers' Hugh McElhenny (39) and Joe (The Jet) Perry (opposite), two future Hall of Fame members, were part of one of the era's greatest backfield combinations. Frank Gifford (above), Mr. Versatile, excelled at both halfback and, later, receiver. Ollie Matson (right) was a former Olympian whose athletic prowess was unmistakable on a football field.

*W*hether playing in the AFL, the NFL, or Canada, John Henry Johnson (opposite) dished out more punishment than he absorbed. (Touchdown) Tommy Wilson (right) is a somewhat-forgotten back who had some big years after leaving the Army. Alan Ameche (below), who scored the winning touchdown in the '58 title game, eludes Clay Matthews, father of 1980s stars Clay, Jr., and Bruce Matthews.

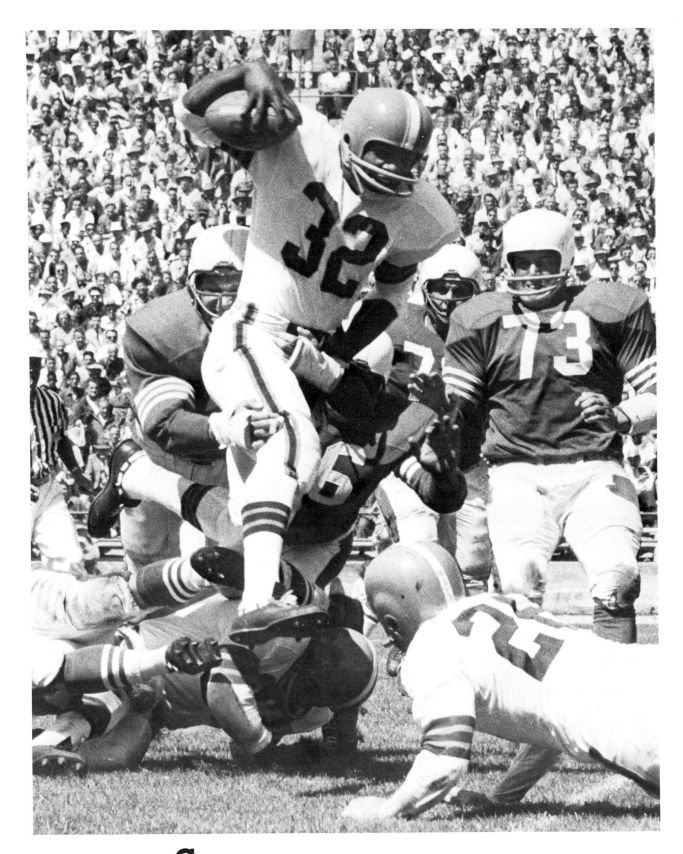

Cleveland's Jim Brown set a league rushing record as a rookie in 1957 (above), showing stunned NFL veterans an unheard-of blend of power, speed, and sheer grittiness.

One of the league's most famous accidents took place in 1955, when John Henry Johnson, then with the 49ers, threw a vicious blindside block into the Cardinals' Charley Trippi. The damage was amazing, when you consider that it did not involve the use of a car. Trippi suffered a fractured skull and required plastic surgery to repair his fine Italian profile. Doctors had to remove one of his ribs to obtain new cartilage for his nose.

John Henry Johnson

Later, the story went around Chicago that a fellow of sinister influence called Trippi, and offered to even the score by sending John Henry for a long swim. Trippi tactfully declined. "I didn't think it would be in the best interests of professional football," he said.

A rookie in 1954, John Henry quickly established himself as one of the league's resident ogres. He was a devastating blocker, a runner of unusual toughness, and he played the game only one way—mean. Once, he bloodied the mouth of Cleveland's Ed Modzelewski with a forearm, bringing Paul Brown raging onto the field. The Cleveland coach shook his fist and yelled at him, "You've hit everybody in the league, do you know that?"

"Then we got a tie game," Johnson retorted, "because everybody in the league has hit me."

Trippi returned after his surgery to appear in a few of Chicago's late games, but he wasn't the same. At the end of the 1955 season he retired, closing the book on one of pro football's most versatile careers. He was a creative ball carrier who ran to daylight long before Lombardi made the phrase popular. He could throw, catch, punt, return kicks, and play free safety. He was the kid from the Pennsylvania coal fields who became a college idol in Georgia. With the Cardinals, Trippi was a member of the original Dream Backfield, joining with Paul Christman, Marshall Goldberg, and Pat Harder.

Although the casualty toll was high, the supply of great backs in the fifties seemed inexhaustible. They kept coming out of college as though machine-stamped, like link sausages: Alan Ameche, Rick Casares, Frank Gifford, Lenny Moore, Ollie Matson. Most of them lasted longer, but they came along when a running back hoped to make five or six good years, if he was lucky, and then out.

It was that way for Ameche, who led the league in rushing as a Baltimore rookie, played on two championship teams and then, hobbled by injuries, called it quits after his sixth season.

It was a pity, of course, as it always is when an athlete leaves ahead of his time. Ameche had been one of those who gave flavor to the sport. To the public he was "The Horse," a nickname he carried since his undergraduate days at the University of Wisconsin, a tribute to his style and performance. When Ameche drove into the parking lot at the stadium in Baltimore one day, a new guard routinely asked for his identification. Ameche stepped out of the car, neighed mightily, pawed the ground with one foot, and snorted.

"That's a good one," the guard laughed, waving him through. "You're 'The Horse,' all right."

Frank Gifford claims that when he returned to California after his rookie season with the New York Giants in 1952, his friends were startled to see him. "Where have you been all winter?" they asked. That may be a slight exaggeration, but it makes a point. Pro football was not yet our new national hysteria. Coast to coast flights still took all day, and network television was years in the future. A fellow could come out of Southern California, as Gifford did, handsome and celebrated,

Jack Christiansen

go east, and still get lost. But not for long. Few backs ever did as much, with consistent skill, as Gifford. The Giants used him to carry the ball, to block, to receive, and, on occasional option plays, to throw. He had speed, and he had class, and he looked good just standing for the National Anthem.

He was another of the glamour players invited to dabble in motion pictures, with results that ranged from gruesome to hilarious. Gifford played a fullback named Stan Pomeroy in a Tony Curtis drama called *All-American*. He was part of a dream backfield, so to speak, that included three other actors who had never played football. Gifford had to coach them on a lot behind the studio for two or three hours a day in the afternoon. Janet Leigh, then Curtis's wife, used to drop around to cheer for them.   His looks and gentlemanly ways were mistaken by some as indications of softness, but Gifford could take it. He played both ways for the Giants in his early years and held his own, though it was never easy to defend against fresh receivers after you had been on the field for 50 minutes.

And so it came to pass that the coaches decided to liberate their running backs, and playing the secondary became a full-time job. A new breed slowly emerged in the National Football League, picked for their speed or quickness, some of them college runners, whose role was to cover the men who got the glory—and beat them.

It is an unending contest that goes on between a defensive back and the men behind the other line who are out to destroy him, his family, and his way of life. He must think with the quarterbacks, run with the wide receivers, and meet the ball carriers—all of whom have knees like bazookas—in an open field. In short, his mind and his body must be everywhere.

The job wasn't all that clearly defined when Jack Christiansen broke in with the Detroit Lions in 1951. "I was picked to play defense," he said. "They had just started to do that. The next year the Lions drafted Yale Lary. Up to then, they would try everybody on offense, and the ones who didn't make it would play defense.

"It was just getting popular, the defense was. It became important. The people started to cheer for the defense, to recognize us as a unit. When it came to techniques, we were on our own. When they told you to cover a guy man-for-man, you just did it, no one told you how. Under Buddy Parker, Buster Ramsey coached the defense. He was a former linebacker and offensive guard. He coached all of it, the whole defense. Today they have four guys."

If Christiansen did not invent the position of free safety, he at least helped make it an art form. "I never tried to psych anybody," he said. "With me it was just trying to be in the right place. It was like being a good hitter in baseball. You had to have the good swing, and the concentration, but you were guessing, too. You'd guess curve, guess slider. Well, we'd guess with the quarterback, where the ball was going, and with the receiver. You'd guess a guy was going to run a curl. You'd gamble.

"Pass defense was the fun part. But every team had a big running back who could just paralyze you. Steve Van Buren, I hit him once and my whole body went numb. Deacon Dan Towler, Tank Younger, Marion Motley...he was as close as anyone has ever come to being a human wave. I don't think I ever tackled Hugh McElhenny, but I tried a lot."

Once a nonscholarship player at Colorado A&M, the studious Christiansen was absorbed by the strategy of the sport, the match-ups, the X's and O's. He had the eye of a future coach, and the changing defenses excited him. "It was during this time," he said, "that the passing game began to explode. Teams had been using what we called the old Eagle defense, five linemen and two linebackers. Then we [the Lions] started going to the four-three to get one more man back on pass coverage. The Giants came along with their Umbrella defense, a semi-zone, in which they would invert into a four deep.

"What we were using as a prevent defense—the three-man rush with five men underneath and three deep—that's the defense that came into wide use in the sixties and seventies. You know, there is just nothing new in football. Anytime somebody brings up an idea, someone says, 'Hell, we did that forty years ago.'"

Christiansen was among the NFL leaders in pass interceptions most years, and he earned respect as a kick returner. He wryly remembers a time in 1951 when Norm Van Brocklin was punting for the Rams in a game against the Lions. Van Brocklin was summoned to the sideline twice by his head coach, Joe Stydahar, and warned not to kick to Doak Walker. "Kick to the tall, skinny kid," he said, referring to Christiansen, then a rookie.

And twice the tall, skinny kid returned them for touchdowns, 70 and 50 yards. "The second time," Stydahar said later, "I thought the odds were on our side."

"I can't forget that day," Christiansen said. "They were the only touchdowns we scored. We got beat, I think, fifty-six to fourteen."

In those years playing defense well depended in part on one's ability to improvise. Anything went. "I can remember picking up a handful of snow, or mud," Christiansen said, "and throwing it in the receiver's eyes. They'd holler and bitch, but we'd get away with it. You can't do that today. For one thing you can't pick up a handful of AstroTurf."

If you were to chart the career of Jack Christiansen it would be pretty much a high, level plane, uniformly brilliant, with an occasional squiggle to show the special heroics—the time he ran a kickoff back 103 yards in the Pro Bowl, and the '57 Cleveland game, in which he came up from free safety to drill Jim Brown on a third-and-three, forcing a fumble and saving a Lions' victory. He reveled in the give and take: "We had great contests. But those big offensive linemen, it was a matter of principle for them to hit us late, and give us a kick in the shins."

In 1951, for the first time, the wire services recognized the team that plays without the ball. They selected an all-pro defense. The safetyman was Emlen Tunnell of the Giants, a boulevardier who would help make pass defense a profession. When the other team had to kick, he was wound tight and loved to run.

In 1948, Tunnell had become the first black man to play football for the New York Giants. That summer the Giants, in the second year of a rebuilding program under Steve Owen, brought in 50 rookies. Tunnell was the only black among them.

On his first day in camp, he found himself in the dressing room, among a sea of white faces, in what amounted to a Caucasian social club. And one by one they started to come over and shake hands—Francis Xavier Reagan, out of Penn, whose photos Tunnell had seen so often in his hometown Philadelphia papers; Paul Governali, the Ivy Leaguer from Columbia; Jim White of Notre Dame; and Tex Coulter of Army. Years later, when Tunnell wrote a thoughtful autobiography (with Bill Gleason), he remembered that moment and he said: "When I tell you that I was proud to be in the presence of those men, I'm not just putting down words that will look good now. I'm trying to tell you exactly how I felt then."

One of the enduring friendships Tunnell made on the Giants was a white quarterback from Mississippi, Charlie Conerly. They partied together, and Conerly

"I can remember picking up a handful of snow, or mud," Christiansen said, "and throwing it in the receiver's eyes...You can't do that today. For one thing, you can't pick up a handful of AstroTurf."

Night Train Lane

spent many an hour on Em's turf, the night spots of Harlem. They were team-mates for 11 years and yes, they talked about race. Once, Conerly told him: "Time will heal everything, Em. Just like you came here to play. You were the first colored guy here and since then there have been more and more. That's how it will be in everything else."

Tunnell was a romanticist, the kind of guy, a friend once said, who cries at the grand opening of a tavern. He was also one of those rare people with an eye for the tempo of life around him. "This wasn't so long ago, by the calendars," he said, of his salad days, "but it was another age of pro football. In my rookie year we traveled around the Upper Midwest in ten big cars [for exhibition games], I mean with our playing gear piled on top in luggage racks. It reminded me of a movie I had seen, *The Grapes of Wrath*. Our opponents usually were the local 'all-stars,' a pickup team of college and high school players in Grand Rapids or Fargo or wher-ever. We took our competition where we could find it, and the games never were more than loosening-up exercises. Things were different then. If our football shoes were ripped in a game, we had to have them repaired at our own expense. The Giants had been losing money for years. So had most of the clubs."

Tunnell walked in off the streets to offer himself to the Giants in 1948. It could happen that way once. They discovered actresses sitting on a counter stool in Schwab's Drug Store, too.

But Tunnell had taken stock of his life—he was 22, out of the Coast Guard and his junior year at Iowa behind him—and he was tired of school books and being broke. He hitch-hiked from Philadelphia to New York, stayed at a hotel where his room cost 75 cents, and strolled into the Giants' offices the next morning to ask for a tryout.

The Giants got the permission of his coach at Iowa, Dr. Eddie Anderson, to sign him, and the ceremony took place in the Broad Street railroad station in Philadelphia. Timothy Mara's sons Jack and Wellington rode the train down, bear-ing a contract that would pay Tunnell $5,000, plus $500 as a bonus for signing and another $500 when he reached camp. He signed, and the Maras climbed back aboard the train and returned to New York.

He played both ways until halfway through his rookie season, when he intercept-ed four passes against the Packers, returning one of them for 43 yards and a touch-down. He was through forever as a running back. He talked of that later as though it were a religious experience. "I believe," he said, "that every man who plays pass defense, and plays it well, is a free spirit at heart or eventually becomes one."

In 1952, he gained 924 yards returning punts, kicks, and pass interceptions, the only time in NFL history a defensive back outgained the rushing leader, the Rams' Deacon Dan Towler (with 894). Tunnell claimed the unofficial ground-gaining championship.

During his career he returned 258 punts, 38 of them in 1953, both league records at the time. He was a cutback and change-of-pace runner, and he relished the chance to go in a scattered field. "You have to keep in mind," he said, "that al-most all techniques of punting and punt returning were vastly different in the ear-ly fifties. The punter then wasn't as far behind the line of scrimmage when he kicked; the punters tried to kick the ball away from the single safety instead of kicking it as high as possible; the punt coverage men didn't have as much time to get downfield; the safetyman often had a chance to catch the ball on the fly or on a bounce while he had momentum going for him."

Steve Owen, who was no debutante at 6-1 and some 300 pounds, became a kind of father figure to Tunnell. He went to some lengths to convince him that defense was more fun than running with the ball. "A little boy can carry a football," Owen told him, "cause it's real light." In time, Tunnell came to the same conclusion: "Tackling is football; running is track."

Tunnell made an even more lasting discovery in 1956, when the Giants ended 18 years of frustration by crushing the Bears 47-7 for the championship. "Losers," he concluded later, "assemble in little groups to share their misery and to bitch about the coaches and the guys in other groups. Winners assemble as a team."

The career of Emlen Tunnell served as a kind of beacon for Richard (Night Train) Lane, another walk-on who played his way into pro football legend. Dick Lane was out of the army in the spring of 1952 with a pregnant wife and a job in an aircraft factory in Los Angeles. At night, he played basketball for the company team.

"It wasn't what I thought it would be," he said. "The job, I mean. They said I'd be a file clerk and I thought I'd work in an office. I was a filer, all right. I filed big sheets of metal into bins. I'd take 'em out of tanks and they'd be dripping with oil and the oil would drip all over me when I raised them over my head. I ruined fifteen pair of khakis that way, fifteen pair. I used to go home at night and my wife would try to scrub the oil out of my hair. I was depressed."

He wanted to quit but he wasn't sure how one did it. He'd heard some of the guys on the job use the word "terminate." So he went to his boss and said, "I don't know what it means, but I'm terminated."

The next day, he was out looking for another job. He was on a bus that cruised down Beverly Boulevard in west Los Angeles, past a sign that said "Los Angeles Rams." When he had played service ball at Fort Ord, the San Francisco 49ers scouted one of his games. He decided to try the Rams, then the defending National Football League champions.

He walked into their offices and started to ask for the coach, except he couldn't remember his name. "It begins with an 'S'," he coaxed the girl at the reception desk. "Oh, you mean Joe Stydahar," she said. In a few moments, Dick Lane was being interviewed by the coach of the Rams and two of his assistants, Red Hickey and Hampton Pool, who could best be described as bemused.

Exactly what impressed them isn't clear. His earnestness, maybe. He claimed to weigh 185, but didn't look it. Maybe it started out as a gag. But Stydahar offered him $4,500 if he made the team, as an offensive end. All he had to do was beat out Elroy Hirsch or Tom Fears.

He had trouble learning the plays, and Hickey rode him hard. "He told me if I didn't learn the plays I'd be sent home. I'd study 'em and study 'em but they never looked the same on the field as they did in my book. I went downtown and bought myself one of those pocket flashlights. When the lights went out at eleven o'clock I'd stay up under the covers and go over the plays some more."

In the afternoon, he began to drop by Tom Fears's room for private counseling. Fears had a phonograph in his room, and he seldom tired of playing a Buddy Morrow record entitled "Night Train."

"Every day I'd go up there and he'd be playing it," said Lane. "He roomed with a guy named Ben Sheets. Whenever I'd walk into the room, Sheets would say, 'Hey, here comes Night Train.' Norm Van Brocklin was our official team nicknamer. He hung it on me and it stuck."

Tunnell: "In my rookie year we traveled around in ten big cars (for exhibition games), I mean with our playing gear piled on top in luggage racks. It reminded me of The Grapes of Wrath."

Yale Lary

Realizing that Lane was baffled by the intricacies of offense, the Rams switched him to defensive end for their annual intrasquad game. Stydahar had seen the quickness, the reactions, the bare bones of a player who might yet be. In the scrimmage he wound up at cornerback, and he made some spectacular plays. In a pile-up he reached out and grabbed an ankle. It belonged to the ball carrier. On another play he was blocked out, but he tried to spin away from the interference. As he did, he lost his balance completely and did a somersault in mid-air. He landed on both feet and ran smack into the runner, Deacon Dan Towler, and sent him sprawling.

That brought Stydahar racing onto the field. "Great work, kid," he shouted. "That's the kind of player I want."

So began the career of Night Train Lane, who as a cornerback expressed himself in wondrous ways. His career spanned 14 seasons with the Rams, Cardinals, and the team with which he did his last and some of his best work, the Lions. He was the midnight gambler who never hesitated to take the big risk, who so often made the big play and the key interception. He had superb reflexes, and what he modestly described as a "sense of recovery."

He avoided watching a receiver's eyes or head, as many did, because he felt that was to invite a fake. "I look at the belt buckle," he said, "at the waistline, which is always fixed no matter how much sashaying and fakin' is goin' on."

He was a snappy dresser, a buoyant character whose rich language delighted his teammates. But Night Train had a touch of steel in him. He was an expert at the clothesline, or necktie, tackle, and at yanking a ball carrier down by his face mask, until the NFL legislated against this little gesture. It was suggested, in fact, that Lane's head hunting had inspired the action. Night Train took the position that if a player couldn't take getting his neck wrung, he shouldn't be playing.

Even after law and order became the rule, Lane continued to tackle high. "My object," he said, "was to stop the guy before he gained another inch. I was usually dealing with ends who were trying to catch passes, and if I hit them in the legs they could fall forward for a first down. There was nothing I hated worse than a first down. It meant I had to stay out there for three more plays. I grabbed them around the neck so I could get back to the bench and sit down."

Sadly, Night Train retired after 14 seasons without ever playing on a team that reached the finals. Tragedy invaded his personal life in December, 1963, when his wife of six months, famed blues singer Dinah Washington, died of what was described as an accidental overdose of drugs. On the road, he had always carried her photographs with him. One was inscribed: "I keep my eye on all trains."

Yale Lary was a bulldog of a Texan, at 5 feet 11 inches and 186 pounds, who in 10 seasons in Detroit, doing double service in the secondary and as a punter, suffered only one injury. And that was more to his pride than anything else.

At the time, he was punting out of his own end zone, and a Green Bay lineman spun into him an instant after the ball had ridden away. Yale went down, his ankle twisted. He looked up, his eyes pleading slightly. The official at the scene shook his head. "Won't do, Lary," he said. "You won't get away with that little acting job."

"I pulled myself up," he said, "and limped off the field. I couldn't punt the rest of the day."

When Lary arrived in 1952, the kicking game still was a rather casual science. It was regarded roughly in the same way as the yo-yo: If you couldn't do it the first time you tried, you couldn't be taught. Lary averaged 44.3 yards a punt, in the years before kickers were given the extra 20 yards on punts into the end zone. He could hang them high enough to serve as weather balloons, and allow the Lions to get full coverage. Six consecutive teams failed to return Lary's punts a single yard, a total of 32 punts.

"Back in 1958," he said, "Buster Ramsey came to me and said, 'Say, do you know you're leading the league in punting?' I said, 'Hell, I didn't even know they kept stats in it.'"

He was the first to retreat 14 yards from the center—"I'd gauge off fifteen and take a step up"—and he posed a running threat, even from there, that made many a team nervous. He faked and ran 10 times in his career, for 150 yards, and only once failed to make a first down.

His fame as a punter (and nonpunter) tended to overshadow the fact that Lary, as the other safety, played tenacious defense. He had been a superior athlete at Texas A&M, the kind of fellow who, in basketball, would be assigned to guard the other team's top scorer. The Lions did that once, in effect, when they told Lary to bird-dog Harlon Hill, then in his heyday with the Bears. Lary clung to him like Saran Wrap. "They told me to go wherever he went," he said. "Right, left, straight up, or back. He caught a few, but I don't remember him breaking a big one."

More and more, the pressure was on the secondary. "When I came up in 1952," he said, "the game was in transition. They were a little typed then. But it opened up. And by the end of the decade it was wide open. I think we saw the whole parade."

The Detroit trinity of Christiansen, Lary, and Jim David worked together so long, and so closely, they developed that special communion that required no words—just a nod or a glance or a shrug. "After a time," he said, "we did things automatically, maybe switch off or double up or help out. I remember when the 49ers sprang the Alley Oop on us. The pass always went to R. C. Owens, who was a foot taller than Jim David and could jump two feet higher. If it hadn't hurt so much, you'd have laughed...that silly thing, just hanging up there. Poor Jim. You could see it in his eyes, he was in trouble. But that time, we had no help to give him."

Bobby Layne, his leader, divided people into stayers and leavers. "I was a stayer," said Lary, proudly, meaning at the bar as well as on the field. He was also at his coolest under pressure, such as the 1957 NFL Championship Game that was played in the rain and mud of Briggs Stadium, when Charley Ane centered the ball back to him on two bounces. Lary picked it off the ground and got away a 74-yard punt, a playoff record. The Lions routed the Browns 59-14.

Under pressure, of course, is not the way to remember Yale Lary or the 1950s. A better way is through a scene from an NFL highlights film, in which the view from the camera is directly behind the punter.

The punter is Yale Lary. You see the ball spiraling back to him. He steps into it. He booms it out of there. The camera ignores the ball as it sails out of the frame. The camera stays on Lary. While the action goes on somewhere down the field, and people unseen are beating and tugging at each other, Lary goes skipping—yes, skipping—down the field like a kid on his way home from school, just full of himself and the sun and the smell of autumn. It is so light-hearted and carefree that, in this one, timeless moment, it seems to trap the whole atmosphere of the game, and the decade. People in the park, on a Sunday, having fun.

"You've heard it said many times, I'm sure," Lary said, summing up the times,

The camera stays on Lary. While people unseen are beating and tugging at each other, Lary goes skipping—yes, skipping—down the field like a kid on his way home from school.

135

What We Went Crazy Over

To catalogue the fads and foibles of the 1950s is to create the effect of a carnival funhouse, with a skeleton rising up to rattle itself at you one moment and hysterical laughter echoing in your ear the next.

It was a madcap time, made even more remarkable by the fact that in the original running so much of it was played straight. The country was in a mood to accept almost anything.

If one catch phrase were needed to instantly identify the times, if there was one memory to flip our national switch, you would have to choose *The Search for Bridey Murphy.*

That was the title of a best-selling book, as well as the description of a massive public effort that had our collective eyes growing heavy, our thoughts turning back...back...back...

It developed, in 1952, that a 33-year-old housewife in Pueblo, Colorado, had recalled, under hypnosis, in weird and astonishing detail, a previous life as a red-headed Irish lass named Bridey Murphy, born in County Cork in the nineteenth century. What made the story so chillingly persuasive was the mass of circumstantial detail about people, places, and customs that the lady recounted in a rich brogue, and in words that seemed utterly foreign to her.

To this day there are people who steadfastly believe the story of Bridey Murphy. It was told and retold in the newspapers, in two books, and eventually led to a Broadway play and a movie based on the same theme and entitled, *On a Clear Day You Can See Forever.* A long-playing record, enabling the purchasers to hear Bridey herself recorded on tape, sold 30,000 copies.

Hypnosis, reincarnation, the occult all became new national rages. Around the country hostesses gave "come as you were" parties, and bartenders featured the reincarnation cocktail, guaranteed to make you wish you were someone else. Ordinary Americans began turning up in earlier lifetimes as German leather merchants, French peasants, and, in at least one reported case, a horse.

As the search for Bridey reached an emotional crest, a Chicago newspaper discovered what it suspected was the source for the authentic detail that lay in the subconscious mind of the Colorado housewife. As a child, it developed, she had lived across the street from a 59-year-old matron whose family had moved to this country from Cork.

Burying their disappointment, Bridey Murphy fans took comfort in the words of comedian Joe E. Lewis: "You only live once, and if you work it right once is enough."

Meanwhile, fathers were wondering why they wasted their money trying to educate their children, which is what fathers always wonder.

In 1952, the favorite outdoor sport at colleges across the country was a harmless form of rioting called "panty raids." The ground rules called for male students to storm or barricade girls' dormitories, demanding as a token of submission some articles of feminine underclothing, which were, as a rule, freely distributed. This led to many warm friendships.

A less interesting campus activity was called cramming (or stuffing), in which the object—as if there were one—was to wedge as many people or things as possible into a single confined space. At one time, records were claimed by 40 students in, on, and clinging to a Volkswagen; by 22 who sardined themselves into a phone booth, and—in a feat of true machismo—by seven Fresno State fraternity men who jammed into a phone booth at the bottom of a swimming pool.

Those were transitory items, of course, amusements of the moment. For an entire decade, America was confounded by strange luminous disks that whirled like giant hula hoops across the evening skies. The Air Force called them Unidentified Flying Objects, and spent $60,000 a year, mostly in photography, trying to prove or disprove that something was up there. We still don't know.

They came to be called Flying Saucers, and sightings were reported all over the nation by people in varying stages of hysteria. A cigar-shaped object here, a formation of flying bananas there. Government officials repeatedly denied that they were emissaries from outer space, offering instead a variety of bewildering theories. The net result was to convince a good many people that Mars was calling.

Speking of hula hoops, no fad toy ever burst upon the scene with more impact. Was there an American family that didn't have one?

For adventurers of both sexes, the fifties produced its own hair-raising controversy. The poodle cut enjoyed a brief popularity among sophisticated ladies, who seemed almost naked in their short, scalp-tight curls. Teenage girls favored ponytails.

Male coiffeurs ranged from flat-tops to the artistic duck-tail, molded into a Vaseline aspic, intricate, swooping, gleaming like brown porcelain. There was something, well, obscene, or at least, carnal, about it. In 1957, a school in Massachusetts won the respect of the PTA by banning the duck-tail.

On careful reflection, it is possible to conclude that the hair styles of the fifties may have contributed to the oil shortages of the seventies.

15

Colts on a Fast Track

It is a matter of record that the Baltimore Colts serviced four cities in a span of five years—a distinction that must inspire envy in the hearts of sports promoters who race through towns like the old medicine shows, selling snake oil from the back of a wagon.

In their various disguises, the Colts bounced around a little—in Boston, New York, Dallas—before surfacing in the mother city in 1953. Until that time, the Colts—and many teams like them—simply found it necessary to chase a buck very hard to remain in business.

How the Colts were transformed into a championship team before the end of the decade qualifies as one of pro football's great bedtime stories. It is, in a sense, the story of three men—Carroll Rosenbloom, who had the money and a theory; Weeb Ewbank, the coach who crafted his team with the pride of a master watchmaker; and Johnny Unitas, a living legend, even then.

It isn't true that Rosenbloom woke up one morning and found the Baltimore franchise on his doorstep, in a wicker basket. But it's not far from the truth. More than any other owner in the sport, he made himself essential to his team's success, a kind of checkbook twelfth man. He did this simply by getting involved in their lives, by creating a relationship that was symbiotic. Certain other owners, who held the position that they took a player to play, not to raise, were horrified by Rosenbloom's methods. But they seemed to work: Eventually, he won four NFL titles with three coaches—Ewbank (2), Don Shula, and Don McCafferty—although Shula's Colts lost in Super Bowl III (before the AFL-NFL merger).

With patience and a fine instinct for what Norman Mailer called "the talent in the room," Ewbank recreated the Colts. He did not strike people as an exciting presence. He scolded players, never bullied them. With his clipboard and whistle and portly shape, he often reminded them of a kindly counselor at Camp Runamuck. Yet no coach ever won two more Olympian games than Weeb Ewbank: with the Colts, in 1958, The Game for the Ages; and against them in 1969, the victory Joe Namath *guaranteed*, the one that closed pro football's generation gap.

Ewbank coached the winning side both times, a trick that could have gotten most coaches elected Caesar. But Weeb was never one to put on airs. His nature was benign, although on the sideline he could get owlish when angry.

By the end of the decade, from their ragamuffin beginnings, the Colts were the class of the NFL. After a narrow miss in 1957, they won titles back-to-back. Together, Rosenbloom and Ewbank gave the Colts something beyond pride and even beyond victory—they gave them tradition. Even after Rosenbloom found it necessary to fire him, they remained friends—divorce, American style—although they differ slightly on how much prior security Weeb enjoyed.

This is the story of the Colts, in the fifties, in their words. It begins with a letter from a fan in Pittsburgh, addressed to Ewbank, about a sandlot quarterback he thought the Colts should hire.

Ewbank told the story.

"I've always read every letter I ever got, for that reason, because of that one-in-a-thousand shot that comes in. I always accused John of writing it himself. I called Frank Camp, his college coach from Louisville, and I asked Herman Ball about him—he was on our staff then but had been with the Steelers the year before when they had Unitas in camp. A lot of people gave Pittsburgh hell for letting him go, but the fact is they had two good quarterbacks there at the time and, according to Herman, the kid hadn't played that well.

Weeb Ewbank

"But I needed one bad, so I had Don Kellett, our general manager, call John and ask if he'd come to a tryout camp we were having. He said he would. That's where the story started that we got him for a seventy-five cent phone call. He came in and we took pictures of him in practice. Not movies. *Still* pictures. In those days, back in 1956, we didn't have any film equipment. The only good the stills did was, when you had a bunch of kids at a tryout, you could keep the pictures in front of you and it helped you remember which ones they were.

"We took pictures of John under center, and again when he set up and right at the last, when he followed through. That was the thing we noticed right away, the way he followed through. It was exceptional. The pictures showed it clearly. His arm went through so far that he turned his hand over like a pitcher. I often wondered how he kept from injuring his arm because it was like throwing a screwball, and all those guys would end up with crooked arms. When he followed through, his fingers turned over and you could see the back of his hand. And when he used to throw a lot of times, with this tremendous follow-through, he'd snag his fingernails on the back of a guy's shirt and jam his fingers, like one of his own linemen. He had to be careful of that. I worried that he might get what they call a tennis elbow, but, boy, I saw the way he could throw and I never bothered him about it. You knew right away. He was in camp no time at all and we knew that as soon as he learned the offense he would be our quarterback.

"Usually a coach can't afford a first impression. Look at Raymond Berry. He had one leg shorter than the other, he wore contact lenses, he needed a back support, he had to build his shoes up, and he came to us at a hundred seventy-five or a hundred seventy-eight pounds, a skinny-assed kid. For him to come through, with the great dedication he had, why, he made coaching a joy. He'd eat up anything you said, try everything.

"We played a preseason game in Louisville, where John had gone to school, and I was interviewed on the radio. Raymond and Jim Mutscheller were roommates then, and they happened to be listening. The guy on the radio said, 'Well, you got Unitas looking good now at quarterback, if you can get somebody to catch the ball you may have a football team.' I said, 'Well, I beg to differ. I think we have some fine young receivers,' and I named Raymond and Jim and said it was just a matter of time. Raymond told me later that it gave them both a lift, gave them some confidence when they needed it.

"Raymond made himself a great receiver, but he was so frail, you shuddered every time he got hit. Now the Sam Huff thing, that was in the championship game in '58. What happened, I thought Sam hit him late, about five yards out of bounds. He gave him a shove over near our bench and we all went at him. There was some

Alan Ameche

pushing and shoving, but I never actually took a swing at him. The newspapers played it up and I worried about what Bert Bell was going to do. The next day Bert called and said, 'Hell, forget it, Weeb, you were fighting for your players. I thought he hit late, too.'

"My whole career was different from most people's. You check and you'll see, every job I ever had, I had to build. You don't come in and win right away if the team isn't there. Nobody does. When I got to Baltimore I put the defense together first, mainly by moving people around. Joe Campanella, I moved to middle guard from offensive tackle. Gino Marchetti was an offensive tackle, I moved him to defensive end. Next we got John, and then our wide receivers developed, and it all came together. But when I first got there we had three teams, the one they had yesterday, the one that came in today, and the one leaving tomorrow. I forget how many kids went through our training camp that first year but it was well over a hundred.

"I had coached under Paul Brown five years when the Colts came to me. Paul was the same as any coach, he didn't like to lose a playbook. Every time you lose a coach to some other team there goes another playbook. It wasn't just what you had on paper, but in the coach's head. You could look at the book and say, 'Is that what they do on defense?' And you'd take all the doubt out of it. On the other hand, you have to feel proud when one of your assistants gets a head job. I took Don McCafferty and Chuck Knox out of college. I prided myself on having good people around me. It's the most necessary thing a coach can do.

"The Colts needed a whole new regime. Don Kellett had done a great job of public relations. I've never seen his equal. But as far as the football side, it had no organization whatsoever. The first thing I did was try to instill a businesslike attitude in them. I had to convince them that when we went to play another team, it wasn't social, it was a business trip. Keith Molesworth had been the coach the year before. Carroll wanted to fire him during training camp. Carroll was nervous anyway. I looked at what we had and told him it was going to take five years to be respectable. By the second year he wanted to get rid of me. It took us five years and eight minutes to win the first championship.

"Carroll was upset when I hired an assistant [John Bridgers] from a small school in Baltimore. He said, 'My God, Weeb, my people in New York think it's terrible you hired a coach from Johns Hopkins.' I said, 'I didn't hire a coach from Johns Hopkins. I hired a coach who knows football.' And he did a good job for me. In 1956, we were crippled up and the Bears beat us horribly [58-27], and Carroll went to Don Kellett, very distraught, and said, 'We have to make a change.' Don talked him out of it. He knew we were on the right track.

"Another time I met with Carroll at his home in Florida to discuss the team. He had made a survey of the players, how they felt about me. He said, 'Well, I checked the players'—he was honest and up front about everything—'and I'll say this, thirty-two of them are for you and there's only one against.' I said, 'Goddam, Carroll, I must not be doing a good job if I haven't made more than one mad at me. But I can tell you who that one is.' So I told him who it was. He said, 'How did you know?' I said, 'Well, dammit, Carroll, when he's talking to me he complains about you.' And that's the way this player was. He was a guy just trying to protect himself.

"I remember the game that convinced me we had a football team. The 49ers came to town, we were playing poorly, and they had us 14-7 with a few seconds to go in the half. John came to the sideline and I said, 'Dammit, let's run out the clock and get straightened out in the locker room and we'll beat 'em.' Well, hell, no sooner do I say that than I look up and he's putting the ball in the air. It gets tipped, goes into a linebacker's hand, and now we're behind 21-7 as the half ends. So we went inside, changed our defenses and came back and beat 'em 35-27. Our kids found they could come back strong, and that you can't take anything for granted. Every championship team has to learn those lessons.

"That was 1958 and, of course, everybody knows what happened in the game with the Giants. If we had lost, I guess I would have been second-guessed plenty. [Leading 14-3 with a fourth-and-goal at the 1, the Colts let Ameche sweep for it. He was nailed for a loss.] We were just cocky enough to think we could push it over. I didn't think they could stop Ameche, and we were running the play behind Jim Parker. What I didn't realize was that the footing was poor in that spot. It was in the third quarter, at the closed end of the stadium, and the ground had actually frozen. But I'll tell you, there is no perfect play in football. You can go for a field goal and sometimes you don't even catch the snapback.

"The other play that caused so much fuss, I didn't call. In fact, I nearly fainted. We were at the nine, on our winning drive, and the television cable went out and while they were fixing it John came over and said, 'What do you think?' I said, 'Let's keep it on the ground.' I told him to give the ball to Alan, who was surehanded, and keep it as much in front of the goal post as we could. Steve Myhra wasn't the most consistent kicker around, and if we had to go for the field goal I wanted to give him every edge. Well, dammit, John lobs it over a linebacker and right to Jim Mutscheller at the one, and if he had known where he was Jim could've fallen over the goal. After the game John said if he was covered he'd have thrown it out of bounds. That's why he was so great. He believed in himself. But a coach doesn't think that way. You think, what if he gets his arm hooked? What if the wind catches the ball? What if...

"The Giants were a helluva team that year. Conerly, Webster, Gifford, the fine defense. We were lucky to win the game. The next year [1959] *we* were a really fine team, and we beat the hell out of them [31-16 in the championship game].

"The thing I miss about the fifties, people seemed to have more respect for each other, even if they disliked you. There was more of a purpose, less selfishness. People talked about doing their share. Whatever happened to that? The players lived on what they made and they didn't worry about deferred payments and investments. Every dollar counted. I remember Ameche, he was like Namath, he hated to get up in the morning. I used to fine players ten dollars for being late to a meeting. Alan overslept a few times, but he usually made it. It killed him to pay that ten dollars.

"In those days they could find something funny in a broken leg. I remember when Big Daddy [Lipscomb] was with the Rams, he hit Unitas out of bounds, and I was standing right there. John was still on the ground. I looked up at Big Daddy—it must've been a sight, me coming to his shoulder—and I said, 'Lipscomb, you're the dirtiest football player in the National League.' He jumped back and put his hands in front of his face, like he was afraid, and said, 'Oh, man, don't you hit me.' I couldn't keep from laughing. He was such a big clown.

"When the Rams put him on waivers we grabbed him. I never found out why they let him go. But I liked him. He was a great guy. I'm one of those who never believed that story, about him taking the needle, and so forth. I still believe it was foul play.

Ewbank: "I said, 'Lipscomb, you're the dirtiest football player in the National League.' He jumped back and put his hands in front of his face, like he was afraid, and said, 'Oh, man, don't you hit me.'"

Carroll Rosenbloom

"He was such a character. He had an ex-wife in California, and whenever we went out there, whether we got in at seven in the morning or ten at night, there would be a summons waiting for him for not paying his alimony. He was always tied up with lawyers' fees and all. The club finally set it up so that it could be deducted from his check.

"He used to come up to me about a week before we'd go to the coast and he'd say casually, 'Has you had any, uh, letters from California?' I'd say, 'No, have you, Daddy?' He'd say, 'No, I was just wondering if the man's going to meet me.' Sure enough, whenever we got in, there would be the man with the summons.

"Those teams had a great *esprit de corps*. We had a net between the goal posts that Raymond and the receivers used, and one time Big Daddy just sort of spread himself across there—his arms were so wide he could darn near touch each post—and he shouted, 'Looky here, what Weeb done trapped in his net.' And one of the boys yelled, 'Yeah, a smoked herring.'

"Another time, we used the color system in our signals, and in practice Unitas was calling the plays and he called out 'black.' Big Daddy looked up and said, 'Hey, Unitas, watch yo'self with them empithets.' It just broke everyone up.

"Art Donovan was another character. He'd make up a story and it kept getting bigger and after a while he'd believe it himself. I'm not Catholic, but I used to go to services with Artie. He told everybody that I went with him so I could watch him kneel, and see if he could still get up and down and how fast he was aging. Fact is, he never did get down on his knees. He'd just sit there on his haunches."

Carroll Rosenbloom reminisced about the Colts in 1975.

"Baltimore was trying to get its franchise back in 1953. Bert Bell had told the town that if they could sell fifteen thousand season tickets, and get a proper owner, they could have it back. Bert had been after me for some time to have ownership in the National Football League and I wasn't anxious to do so, certainly not in Baltimore, where I didn't even live, although I had a business there. When my father died, I had merged his company with mine—we manufactured clothing—but I had also branched out into railroads, movie making, electronics, several things. When Bert came to me about taking a franchise I said, 'Bert, I just don't have time. And I really don't have that much interest.'

"To get away from Bert, I took my family to Palm Beach, where we kept a home, and while I was there Bert announced in Baltimore that if he could get Carroll Rosenbloom to accept the franchise, the city would have a team again. Well, that really put me on the spot. If I didn't take it, the folks in Baltimore would hate me, and if I did take it I'd hate myself. That's how I was forced into pro football.

"I had played football for Bert in college. He was my backfield coach at the University of Pennsylvania. That's how we had become good friends. I paid $200,000 for the franchise, something like that, with part of the money going to the Redskins. Bert gave me some advice. 'Carroll,' he said, 'please promise me two things. First, don't have any partners'—a rule I immediately violated, keeping fifty-two percent and taking in four other people, to my eventual sorrow. Bert was absolutely right, because a franchise becomes one man's team. Someone has to make the decisions. If you do it by committee, that's democracy, and we know that doesn't work. I finally got it all when two died and I bought out the other two.

"The other thing Bert told me was: 'Look out for the coaches. I've been an owner and a coach in the National Football League and now I'm the commissioner, and I'll tell you, coaches will ruin the league if they get the chance.'

"I violated the first and the second I watched very carefully. I did not let a coach get control of my ball club. Bert picked my first coach for me, who was Keith Molesworth, a wonderful guy but someone not cut out to be a head coach. During the middle of that year—1953—I started to look for a new coach and everybody told me the man I wanted was Blanton Collier. Well, Paul Brown didn't want Collier to leave and refused to give me permission to talk with him. I went to see Bert about that and he assured me I had a perfect right to do so, whether Brown wanted me to or not, as long as it was a step up. So I talked to Blanton, who was scared to death of Paul Brown and did not want to be a head coach at that time, which was strange.

"Mickey McBride, who owned the Browns, told me, 'Look, it's not Blanton you want anyway. The fellow you want is Weeb Ewbank.' I hadn't been around long enough to have much information on coaches. I knew nothing about Ewbank, but I had him meet me in New York and I was impressed with him—a cocky little son-of-a-bitch—and we got along famously. I liked him instantly. It was the saddest thing I ever had to do when I let Weeb go [in 1962], but I felt he had lost control of the team, which happens. But I still liked him and admired him. I told Sonny Werblin, who had taken over the Jets, that if he wanted a coach who would build him a football team, Weeb was the man. I wrote Weeb's Jets contract myself, and when I wrote it I included a clause that gave him the right to buy ten percent of the franchise. But he let Werblin talk him out of it after a few years.

"Whenever we lost, some of the other owners would talk and speculate, but there was never a time when I had any intention of letting Weeb go in the years before the championship. Never. Weeb was fine, always, until he won, and then, you know, coaches win and they cease to be coaches. They become apostles.

"We won the title first in 1958 and should have won it in '57. We had a great football team that year. We lost it on a bad call in San Francisco, when they shoved off on one of our receivers. We had knocked out [Y.A.] Tittle, and the other kid [John Brodie] threw a touchdown pass to beat us [17-13].

"When I got my football team they didn't give me much talent. It had been a swing team that the Texas millionaires, after they lost a little money, threw up their hands and let go. When I got the team, it was a sorry bunch. No discipline. No pride. And very few good players. I had to think of something, like you do in any business, to stimulate them. So the first time we got our group together, I talked to them and I told them we were going to try to build something in Baltimore, and if they would do it, it would mean financial rewards to them but, more important, they would always have boasting rights. We were going to be champions and be able to carry our heads high. I told them when we got beat in the early years, as I knew we would, all I asked of them was to let the other team know it had been in a game. If you do that, I said, I'll look after you financially.

"The first year I had an incentive system—if you intercepted a pass, or the defense played well...we weren't talking about much but in those days if a player got an extra twenty-five bucks a game it was like a celebration. At the end of the first year, whatever profits we had I split up among the players. It wasn't much, but they got about five-hundred dollars apiece as bonuses, which was unheard of. I gave them a basket at Thanksgiving and something at Christmas. I'd go to the league meeting—we only had twelve owners then and the others regarded me as a communist—and whatever I had done, well, at the next meeting they would vote it out and I'd have to think of something else. When we won the championship after just

Ewbank: "In practice, Unitas was calling the plays and he called out `black.' Big Daddy looked up and said, `Hey, Unitas, watch yo'self with them empithets.' It just broke everyone up."

143

Alex Hawkins

five years, when some of them had been trying for thirty and still hadn't made it, that really ticked them off.

"One of my great convictions was that a player should make his home wherever he played. That made for better team play, better exposure with the town, and more opportunity for the player. I set up an office with the Colts where they could come and talk about what they wanted to do when they were through playing football, and we'd help them get jobs, and help set them up in business. Some of them became millionaires.

"Of all the players I have known I can count on the fingers of one hand those I didn't like. You have to be a family. You have to be able to live together. The ones who didn't fit we got rid of. I don't think players have really changed. But I will say this, there were more characters then, and they were all lovable guys. Some of them would never listen. I'd tell them, 'Look, we'll find you a business, I'll put up the money, all you have to do is work at it. We want you to stay here and be successful.' Alex Hawkins, our Captain Who?, would look me right in the eye and say, 'Look, I'm no businessman. All I know is football. Don't worry about me. I'll find a way to live when I'm through playing.'

"Some didn't want help. It took me five years to convince Gino Marchetti to go into the restaurant business with Ameche and the others. He wanted to go back to Antioch and work with his father and brothers in the family gas station. That's all he ever wanted to do. Finally, I cornered him in a hotel in San Francisco one trip, with his wife, Flo, and I told him: 'Now, look, you dago s.o.b., you have an opportunity to make all the money you want, they love you so much in Baltimore. Why don't you go ahead and make your money and then go back to Antioch?' I stayed at him for an hour. Finally, he threw up his hands and said, 'All right, Carroll, you win.' By the time we finished, I had the feeling that Gino was helping *me*.

"There came a time when one of our veterans couldn't make it with the Colts anymore. He had given us long service, and I did for him what I had tried to do for all our players who had been with us a time and had done well. This one had gone through a divorce, had no savings—he would never take a job in the offseason—and I called him in and told him, 'The coaches say you can't make it here, but we're going to try to get you on with someone else. I want you to know that if you don't play any place this year you're going to get your full salary because you have been a damned good man for the Colts, and I wish you luck. If you do catch on later, you can return the salary when you're able.' He agreed to that and thought it was wonderful. We let him go and I sent him a year's pay. He caught on with a team and I was glad for him. I also waited to hear from him. He was let go by that team, then caught on with the other league and played two or three more seasons. But I never did hear from him. If he had called and said, 'I spent the money but I'll pay it back a dollar a week,' I'd have understood perfectly. But I never heard from him. It was my only disappointment.

"I was maybe the first fellow to come into the league, and stick, who was primarily a business guy. You go down the roster of the owners who were there in those days, and you'll find that football had been their whole life—Mara, Halas, Marshall, they were football people, they had never done anything else. The Morabitos, in San Francisco, were in the trucking business, but they became football men. Danny Reeves was all football.

"In those days, all of the power lay in the hands of Bert Bell. The strong people were those who had been in the league forever—Halas, Rooney, Marshall. They

144

did all the talking, but Bell made the moves. When he wanted to get something done, Bert would sit there in Philadelphia and, if he wasn't getting his way, he would take out his false teeth and lay 'em on the table. His face would pinch up and he would look sooo old, sooo tired, and he would start to cry. He was a great crier. Tears would come to his eyes and slowly roll down those weathered cheeks. George Preston Marshall would be walking up and down, screaming and exhorting everybody, and finally they would see that Bert was crying and somebody would say, 'For chrissakes, George, sit down, you're annoying Bert.'

"One day I said to him, 'Bert, it's got to come, there has to be a pension plan for the players. What the hell, every business I'm in has a pension plan. If you give a little now, you're going to avoid a lot of problems later.' I sold Bert on the idea and he proposed it to the other owners and Marshall said, 'What communist sumbitch thought of that idea?' They all knew it was me.

"We—Bert and I—were asking for fifteen thousand dollars from the league to have a survey done. They said, 'We won't give you a nickel.' It was really something. These were tough guys who had been around. But they really were happy days. We got along well. Everybody wanted to win, but you didn't screw anybody. They all were decent people.

"I stayed over after the meeting and the next night Bert and I went to dinner. He said, 'What are we going to do now? We don't have any money.' I said, 'Well, Bert, why don't you let me handle this, and I'll send someone to see you and draw up a plan and then you can decide if you want to do it.' I had in mind a young kid in Baltimore I thought was a comer, Sig Hyman, who was then in his father's insurance agency. I told the story to Sig and told him, 'Look, if you lose any money on this I'll see about it. But if it works you're going to be made.' He worked like hell, sold the league on it, and that's how the pension plan came into being.

"It was a tighter group of owners then and it wasn't all unselfish. We could talk things out. It would be just the twelve of us and Bert. He didn't allow coaches and office people in our meetings. You go to a meeting today and you're liable to have a hundred people in the room and you're afraid to talk.

"The meetings were always in Philadelphia. Bert didn't like to travel and he couldn't stand to fly. A train trip was all he would make and if you couldn't get there by train he wouldn't go.

"When I came in I thought it might take ten years for pro football to make it. The day I bought the ball club I put a million and a half dollars in the Chemical Bank, and I said to my partners, 'When I lose that, when it's gone, that's as far as I'm going to go.' I knew they wouldn't put up any money, if we needed some. Of course, the strange thing was, pro football turned around almost immediately. We never had a losing year, financially, and an interesting thing happened. I believe we began to convince people that pro football was a logical extension of college football, a way for them to continue to follow their college heroes, who otherwise would have graduated and never been heard from again. Take Alan Ameche. They wanted to keep seeing him, and now millions could, all over the country.

"At the same time, we convinced our players, 'Look, you guys dress up, wear a coat and a tie, and go out and conduct yourself in a proper way. You've had an education. Show it.' Pretty soon, everywhere we went, the Colts were considered a gentleman's football team. And a lot of players wanted to play for the Colts.

"I remember vividly when Unitas came in. He had been in camp a few days and Art Rooney called me about something or other. He said, 'Carroll, you have that

Rosenbloom: "If Bert wasn't getting his way, he would take out his false teeth and lay 'em on the table. His face would pinch up and he would look sooo old, sooo tired, and he would start to cry."

145

Johnny Unitas

boy Uni-TASS. I want to tell you something. My boys tell me that guy was the best looking quarterback we had in camp and my coach [Walt Kiesling] never let him throw the ball.' After that I watched John in practice. He was so relaxed, so loose, and a very likable kid. This whole time we were wondering if we needed to trade for another quarterback, or if Unitas could do the job backing up George Shaw. We went into Chicago, and we were leading that game by ten points. And in the middle of the second quarter, they ruined Shaw's career. The Bears were always dirty, and they hit him high and low and across the mouth, broke his nose and knocked out most of his teeth, and he was a sight. They really kicked the hell out of him and unnecessarily so. They had to carry Shaw off, and Unitas had to come into the game. I must say he looked horrible and we lost it.

"I went down to the locker room and John was never one to show his emotions, but he was sitting in front of his locker, still hadn't taken off his uniform and had his head hanging between his legs so that all you could see was the top of that crew cut. I walked over and got him under the chin and lifted his head up. I said, 'Now, look, John, that was not your fault. You haven't had an opportunity to play and no one is blaming you. You're not only going to be a good one in this league, you're going to be a great one.'

"Well, I was just trying to build him up, get him out of the dumps. I wasn't sure right then he'd even make the club. But many times over the years John would ask me about that, how I could be so sure he'd make it. I'd tell him, 'What the hell, John, I'm an old jock. I know talent.'

"He was always a gentleman and each year we'd go through a pleasant ritual when his contract ran out. I'd ask him what he wanted and he would say he didn't know. I'd say, 'Well, I don't know how much you should have.' And he'd counter, 'What do you think?' And I'd say, 'What do you think?' Then he would finally come up with a figure and I'd say, 'That's all right, but I think maybe you should have a little more,' and we'd work it out.

"As we came up to the 1958 sudden-death game, I didn't want to sit in the press box, and I didn't want to be around anyone I knew. I called Timothy Mara and asked him to find me two seats, off by myself, where I could see the football game and the only ones who would know where I'd be sitting would be Tim and myself. He said, 'Carroll, I know exactly how you feel in your first championship game and I'll take care of it.' He got me two seats, and Don Kellett went up there with me, they were way up high. I was in such a state of shock, just being in the game so soon, and playing in New York, that when it went to sudden death and we won it, I just went numb.

"When I came down to the locker room to congratulate the team—the place was insane—I got a message from Father Dudley, the priest who traveled with the Giants, that Tim Mara wanted to see me outside. I said to bring him in, but Father Dudley said Tim didn't feel he should and would like for me to come out. Here was this nice old gentleman, who wasn't feeling well, who had a heart condition and shouldn't even have been there—in fact, he died a few months later—and I went to him in the corridor in that dank old stadium.

"He came over and put his arm around me and said, 'Carroll, I wanted to congratulate you and I wanted to tell you something. You will win many important games, and more championships, but none will ever be as sweet as your first. Enjoy it. If we had to lose it, I'm pleased it was to you and your team.' It was one of the nicest gestures anyone ever made to me."

16

The 1950s: What, Them Worry?

Kids don't hop on the back of an ice truck and suck ice in the summer sun any more. Or catch fireflies in a Mason jar. Or wear khaki pants so stiff with Argo that they crackled when kids sat down. Worse yet, they can't imagine why anyone would.

Memory can be a tangled yarn. But for those who established pro football as the coming national madness, one thread seemed to run through the fifties: The simple pleasures were the best. Life—even unto football—was more fun, the teams had more esprit, and money and winning were not everything (although they still were way ahead of whatever came in third).

If there was any one condition the decade needed, or wanted, but in most cases lacked, it was the so-called killer instinct. Not just in football, mind you, but the whole country. In 1951, a lady in Los Angeles built America's first backyard bomb shelter (at a cost of $1,995), and even as Red Chinese troops were crossing the Yalu River, she blithely explained that it would make a wonderful playroom for the kids.

In pro football, if you did not have a killer instinct at least you could get by, sometimes, on audacity and luck. It happened that way once to Dick Nolan, the alert, young cornerback of the New York Giants.

This was in the Los Angeles Coliseum, and the Rams were threatening at the 8-yard line. The ball went to Deacon Dan Towler on a dive play over left tackle, and when the Deacon dived it was like trying to tackle a torpedo. The hole opened so wide no one even touched him. Helmet lowered like a billy goat, Towler launched himself at the end zone. Unfortunately, he banged headfirst into the lightly padded wooden goal post, which then was mounted on the goal line.

According to Nolan, who enjoyed a splendid view of the collision, the goal post quivered like a tuning fork. Towler staggered back to the 5. The ball bounced crazily out to the 13. The Giants recovered. Towler was in a weird, half-sitting position, legs spraddled, eyes glassy, waiting for his bones to begin obeying his brain. Nolan sized up the moment and found it irresistible. He walked over and glared down on the helpless Towler. "Yeah, Deacon," he growled. "You come through here again and I'll *really* stick you."

There was still time for a dialogue between the players, some of it angry, some of it kidding-on-the-square, some of it hilarious. But essentially it all reflected a feeling of warmth among men who belonged to the brotherhood of pain.

By every practical measure, the modern game is better—bigger players, bigger stadiums, bigger crowds, massive television coverage, better equipment, more coaching. Players make more in a year than Carroll Rosenbloom paid for the Baltimore Colts.

And yet. And yet...

Eddie LeBaron

Here is Tex Schramm, sitting in the office of the World League of American Football, fishing through the years. He pulls out an aging, yellowed sheet he happened to save as a memento of his days with the Los Angeles Rams. "Ah, here it is," he says with the satisfaction of a man who finds something where it ought to be. At the top of the sheet are typed the words SALARIES AND BONUSES. It is a payroll for the 1955 Rams, and two points are of immediate interest: (a) The Rams were a conference championship team that year and (b) there were no bonuses.

The highest paid player on the list was Norm Van Brocklin, $19,000...Big Daddy Lipscomb, $6,000...Don Paul, at the height of his career, $10,000...Crazylegs Hirsch and Tom Fears, two of the premier receivers of any time, made $14,000 and $12,000, respectively.

Schramm scans the list and smiles. "I can look at these and it doesn't strike a chord," he says. As an afterthought, he added, "Dan Reeves signed Van Brocklin."

The money mattered, of course (let's not be silly!). And we don't need an economist to tell us that nutmeg was only a nickel a ton and the dollar stretched a lot farther. In 1958, Eddie LeBaron, the Little General of the Washington Redskins, quarterbacked the East to a squeaky win over the West in the Pro Bowl, a game that meant $300, cold cash, to each winner. Still years before the boom, a player might not kill for $300 but he would think about maiming a little.

As LeBaron greeted his bride outside the locker room door, Big Daddy Lipscomb emerged from the other dressing room. "My wife hadn't been around football much," Eddie recalled. "Big Daddy walked over. He was six-seven, maybe three-hundred pounds. He had a little beard and he wore a porkpie hat. Sweat was dripping down his goatee. He loomed over me and said, 'You little son of a bitch. I'll get you next year.'

"Hell, my wife wanted me to retire on the spot."

LeBaron was an interesting case. At 5-7 and 160, he was not exactly what you would call classic quarterback dimensions. Yet the Redskins hand-picked him to succeed the nonpareil, Slingin' Sammy Baugh, who was tall and lean as whipcord and even chewed tobacco (a habit George Preston Marshall encouraged, figuring it would enhance Sammy's Texas image). In the huddle, dwarfed by his teammates, LeBaron looked like Johnny of Philip Morris. For all that, his size never was a real issue, except in a good-humored way. As one of his receivers put it: "You run your deep patterns and look back and nobody's there. You can't see him. And, suddenly, it looks like the ball is coming at you out of a silo." There were times, the rest of the decade, when Eddie was all the Redskins had going for them.

A couple decades later, LeBaron looked back and said, sadly, "The day of the little quarterback is gone forever. In my prime—twenty-eight to thirty-one—I could have played today. But I'd never have gotten a shot at it. Hell, I wouldn't have in college, either."

How long ago was that? As change is measured, not very. At MIT and Princeton, the scientists were working on machines that could perform the same calculations as the human brain, only faster. They called them computers. An atomic-powered submarine, the *Nautilus,* sailed under the polar icecap, fulfilling the vision of Jules Verne in *20,000 Leagues Under the Sea,* which was written in 1864. The Communists denounced Marilyn Monroe as a capitalist trick to make the U.S. masses forget how miserable they were. Josef Stalin died. Connie Mack retired, reluctantly, after 67 years in baseball.

The fifties were a mixed time for words and pictures. The *Brooklyn Eagle* published its last issue after 114 years. *Collier's*, an American reading favorite, folded after 38 years. But new periodicals sprang up to replace them, catering to more exclusive interests: *Sports Illustrated*, *TV Guide*, and *Mad*, a zany comic whose symbolic character, Alfred E. Neuman ("What? Me worry?") captured the pulse of the times. And it came to pass that another new magazine, *Playboy*, discovered sex, and found it good.

Names? You want more names? Try John Foster Dulles, Edd (Kookie) Byrnes, Bernard Goldfine, Autherine Lucy, Dave Garroway, Howdy Doody, Francis Gary Powers, and Bevo Francis.

The fifties nostalgia was not, as some at first suspected, a media hype. There simply arose, years later, a longing for a time that people remembered as more fun, a bridge between a world that had been at war and a time when we would be engulfed by our own new awareness. The fifties were like a teen-age girl in her first pair of high heels, looking into a mirror, feeling awkward and, yet, discovering for the first time that she was going to be beautiful.

Professional football was like that, too. It would make gigantic progress in the fifties, even as baseball watched its minor leagues wither and die, and basketball floundered, crippled by a college point-fix scandal, and boxing fell on lean times. Pro football thrived, and much of it was the work of a man born to Philadelphia Main Line society—de Benneville Bell, known as Bert.

He was the product of a political family. His father once was the attorney general of Pennsylvania. His brother sat on the State Supreme Court. And a grandfather served in Congress. But Bert Bell's mission in life was football, and he knew it from every side. In 1933, with six partners, he bought the Frankford Yellow Jackets for $2,500 and changed the name of the franchise to the Philadelphia Eagles. When his partners pulled out after three costly seasons, he bought the club back at a public auction for $4,500.

From 1938 through 1940, he sold tickets and advertising, handled publicity, and coached the Eagles to a record of 8 wins, 25 losses, and 1 tie. As a coach he suffered from a shortage of playing talent, but not of energy or enthusiasm. In one game, against Chicago, the Bears' Luke Johnsos tricked one of the Eagles into lateraling the ball to him, whereupon he fled down the field for a touchdown. Every step of the way, Bell raced with him down the sideline, screaming at Johnsos until his own wind and legs gave out.

After the 1940 season, Bell wound up with $50,000 in cash and a half-interest in the Pittsburgh Steelers, in a three-way transaction that resulted in Alexis Thompson acquiring the Eagles. In January, 1946, Bell sold his interest in the Steelers when his fellow owners hired him to succeed Elmer Layden as commissioner at a salary of $25,000 for three years. The owners gauged correctly that Bell had the toughness, and the incisiveness, to get them through the now escalating pro football war.

On December 9, 1949, Bell accepted the surrender of the All-America Football Conference on his—and the NFL's—terms. From that moment on, he began to implement the three actions that would most assure the prosperity of pro football in the decades to come:

(1) His policy of blacking out telecasts of home games,

(2) His decision to police the league, and thereby protect the integrity of the sport,

(3) His willingness to fight the powerful teams and owners on behalf of the weak.

The fifties were like a teen-age girl in her first pair of high heels, looking into a mirror, feeling awkward and, yet, discovering for the first time that she was going to be beautiful.

Bert Bell

Bell understood the hungriness of television better than most men of his time. "I'm a great believer in TV," he explained. "It creates interest, but it's only good as long as you can protect your home gate. You can't give a game to the public for free, on television, and expect them to pay to go to the ball park for the same game." Those words became the NFL doctrine with respect to television.

In December of his first year in office, Bell was confronted with a problem that threatened to shake the entire sport, a gambling scandal. On the eve of the championship game between the Bears and the Giants, the New York district attorney's office reported an attempted bribe of two New York players, Merle Hapes and Frank Filchock. They had been approached to fix the point spread.

Based on the evidence at hand, Bell declared Hapes, the fullback, out of the game, but allowed Filchock to play. He passed for New York's only touchdowns in a 24-14 loss. After a trial that sent a gambler, Alvin Paris, to prison, Bell suspended both players indefinitely. Neither had accepted money from Paris, nor agreed to his plot. But they had failed to report his offer and Bell came down hard. He made Filchock's suspension stick until 1950. Hapes never did return to the NFL.

Bell worked tirelessly to pass a sports anti-bribery law. He compiled a list of the country's most prominent gamblers. And he hired an ex-FBI man, Austin Gunsel, to oversee an intelligence loop that would operate in each league city.

He also established a system of listening posts, confidential sources who would tip him off when large amounts of money surfaced on any one team or any particular game. One night he got the price on a game between the Chicago Cardinals and the Cleveland Browns. The next day the spread dropped three points. Instantly, Bell called Cleveland, where he learned that the Browns had just announced that Otto Graham wouldn't play. That incident led to another Bell edict: Henceforth each team would announce, at least 48 hours before a game, if a player was injured and unable to play. "The gamblers know these things," he said. "I want the public to know them, too."

Bell was a short, round man with a foghorn voice, which had been trained to rise above the roar of the crowd when he quarterbacked Penn, in the years around World War I. The voice was stilled on October 11, 1959. While watching a game between the two teams closest to his heart, the Eagles and the Steelers, at Franklin Field, Bert Bell died of a heart attack. It was almost a storybook thing, ironic, even prophetic. Bell had often told friends that he would die happy, if he could die at a football game.

In a few months the decade was ended, and this would be the legacy of the fifties: It would bring pro football to the Age of Aquarius, to massive use of television, to the years of Pete Rozelle and Vince Lombardi, and the birth of a new enterprise, the American Football League, that would challenge and shake the establishment. Pete Rozelle took over a league office staffed by two clerks "and an 80-year-old Kelly Girl." Today the NFL office employs more than one hundred people.

But mostly the fifties would be remembered as a mood, a state of mind, a time when the pace was slower and pro football existed almost entirely on the field. Outside influences simply were not tolerated.

There is a story that makes the point about Art Rooney, one of the revered figures in the sport, who spent most of his adult lifetime waiting for the Pittsburgh Steelers to win a championship. It is also worth noting that Rooney, according to legend, bought the Steelers with winnings from the racetrack.

When Walt Kiesling was coaching the Steelers in the mid-fifties, Art grew impatient with Kiesling's custom of starting every game with the same play—a fullback plunge up the middle. Finally, wearily, Rooney went to Kiesling and ordered him to get some variety into the game plan. He ordered him, in fact, to attempt a pass on their very first play. It was one of the rare times on record that Rooney ever butted in on his coach's business.

As luck would have it, in their next game the Steelers called the boss man's play and, sure enough, the pass went for a touchdown. As fate would have it, however, a Steelers lineman was detected offside, and the touchdown was called back. It developed later that the offending lineman had been under instructions from Kiesling to commit the infraction. "If this pass play works," the coach had warned his team, "Rooney will be down here every week giving us plays."

And a final whiff of the 1950s, as recalled by Don Shula, erstwhile rookie cornerback with the Cleveland Browns: "In those years the veterans used to ignore the rookies, but Lou Rymkus, the big tackle, would take five or six of us to a bar where the owners gave out free cigars to all the players who came in. As soon as we got the cigars, Rymkus would collect them for himself and then go off to another table."

The offending lineman had been under instructions from Kiesling to commit the infraction. "If this pass play works," the coach had warned his team, "Rooney will be down here every week giving us plays."

151

NFL Rosters 1950-59

1950 Baltimore Colts
Owner
Abraham Watner
Coach
Clem Crowe
Players
Averno, Sisto, G
Blanda, George, QB
Blandin, Ernie, T
Brown, Hardy, LB
Buksar, George, B
Burk, Adrian, QB
Campbell, Leon, B
Collins, Rip, B
Colo, Don, T
Cooper, Ken, G
Crisler, Hal, E
Donovan, Art, T
Filchock, Frank, QB
Fletcher, Oliver, G
French, Barry, G
Grossman, Rex, B
Jenkins, Jon, T
Jensen, Bob, E
King, Ed, G
Kissell, Vito, B
Livingston, Bob, B
Maggiolo, Achille (Chick), B
Mazzanti, Gino, B
Murray, Earl, G
Mutryn, Chet, B
Nelson, Bob, C
North, John, E
Nowaske, Bob, E
Oristaglio, Bob, E
Owens, Jim, E
Perina, Bob, B
Rich, Herb, B
Salata, Paul, E
Schweder, John, G
Spaniel, Frank, B
Spavital, Jim, B
Spinney, Art, G
Stone, Billy, B
Tittle, Y. A., QB
Williams, Joel, C
Zalejski, Ernie, B

1953 Baltimore Colts
Owner
Carroll Rosenbloom
Coaches
Keith Molesworth
Weeb Ewbank
Players
Agase, Alex, G
Ameche, Alan, B
Averno, Sisto, G
Barwegen, Dick, G
Berry, Raymond, E
Bighead, Jack, E
Blandin, Ernie, T
Braase, Ordell, E
Brethauer, Monte, E
Brown, Ray, B
Bryan, Walter, B
Call, Jack, B
Campanella, Joe, G-T
Cheatham, Ernie, T
Chrovich, Dick, T
Colteryahn, Lloyd, G-E
Cooke, Ed, E
Coutre, Larry, B
Davidson, Frank (Cotton), QB
Davis, Milt, B
DeCarlo, Art, B
Del Bello, John, B
Donovan, Art, T
Dupre, L. G., B
Ecklund, Brad, C
Edwards, Dan, E
Eggers, Doug, LB-G
Embree, Mel, E
Enke, Fred, QB
Feamster, Tom, T
Finnin, Tom, T
Flowers, Bernie, E
Flowers, Dick, QB
Harness, Jim, B

Hawkins, Alex, B
Hermann, John, B
Horn, Dick, B
Hugasian, Harry, B
Huzvar, John, B
Jackson, Ken, T
James, Tommy, B
Joyce, Don, E
Kalmanir, Tom, B
Keane, Tom, B
Kerkorian, Gary, QB
Koman, Bill, G
Krouse, Ray, T
Langas, Bob, E
Lange, Bill, G
Leberman, Bob, B
Lesane, Jim, B
Lewis, Hal, B
Lipscomb, Gene (Big Daddy), T
Little, Jack, T
Lyles, Lenny, B
Marchetti, Gino, E
Matuszak, Marv, LB
McMillan, Chuck, B
McPhail, Buck, B
Mioduszewski, Ed, B
Moore, Henry, B
Moore, Lenny, B
Mutscheller Jim, E
Myers, Bob, T
Myhra, Steve, G
Nelson, Andy, B
Nutter, Buzz, C
Nyers, Dick, B
Owens, Luke, T
Parker, Jim, G-T
Patera, Jack, T-G
Pellington, Bill, LB-G
Pepper, Gene, G
Peterson, Gerry, T
Plunkett, Sherman, T
Poole, Barney, E
Preas, George, T
Pricer, Billy, B
Radosevich, George, C
Raiff, Jim, G
Rechichar, Bert, B-K
Renfro, Dean, B
Richardson, Jerry, E
Robinson, Charley, G
Sample, Johnny, B
Sandusky, Alex, G
Sanford, Leo, LB
Sharkey, Ed, G
Shaw, George, QB
Sherer, Dave, E
Shields, Burrell, B
Shinnick, Don, LB
Shula, Don, B
Simpson, Jackie, B
Sommer, Mike, B
Spinney, Art, E-G
Stone, Avatua, B
Szymanski, Dick, C-LB
Taliaferro, George, B
Taseff, Carl, B
Thomas, Jesse, B
Thurston, Fred (Fuzzy), G
Toth, Zollie, B
Unitas, John, QB
Vessels, Billy, B
White, Bob, B
Wingate, Elmer, E
Winkler, Jim, T
Womble, Royce, B
Young, Buddy, B
Young, Dick, B

Chicago Bears
Owner
George Halas
Coaches
George Halas
Paddy Driscoll
Players
Adams, John, B
Anderson, Bill, B
Anderson, Ralph, E
Atkins, Doug, E

Autrey, Bill, C
Aveni, John, E
Badaczewski, John, G
Barnes, Erich, B
Barwegen, Dick, G
Bauman, Alf, T
Bingham, Don, B
Bishop, Bill, T
Bishop, Don, B-E
Blanda, George, QB
Boone, J. R., B
Brackett, M. L., T
Bradley, Ed, G
Bratkowski, Zeke, QB
Bray, Ray, G
Brink, Larry, E
Brown, Ed, QB
Bukich, Rudy, QB
Campana, Al, B
Campbell, Leon, B
Carey, Bob, E
Carl, Harland, B
Caroline, J. C., B
Casares, Rick, B
Castete, Jesse, B
Clark, Herm, G
Clarkson, Stu, C
Cody, Ed, B
Cole, Emerson, B
Connor, George, T
Cooke, Ed, E
Cowan, Les, T
Cross, Bob, T
Daffer, Ted, E
Dambre, John, G
Damore, John, G
Davis, Art, T
Davis, Fred, T
Davis, Harper, B
Dempsey, Frank, T
Dewveall, Willard, E
Dimancheff, Boris (Babe), B
Dooley, Jim, E-B
Dottley, John, B
Douglas, Merrill, B
Drzewiecki, Ron, B
Falkenberg, Herb, B
Figner, George, B
Floyd, Bobby Jack, B
Fortunato, Joe, LB
Galimore, Willie, B
Garrett, Bill, G
George, Bill, LB
Gibron, Abe, G
Gilbert, Kline, T
Gorgal, Ken, B
Gulyanics, George, B
Haluska, Jim, B
Hansen, Wayne, G-C
Hatley, John, G
Healy, Don, G
Helwig, John, E-G
Hensley, Dick, E
Hill, Harlon, E
Hoffman, Jack, E
Hoffinan, John, B
Howley, Chuck, LB
Hugasian, Harry, B
Hunsinger, Chuck, B
Jagade, Harry (Chick), B
Jecha, Ray, G
Jeter, Perry, B
Jewett, Bob, E
Johnson, Jack, B
Johnson, Pete, B
Jones, Stan, G-T
Kavanaugh, Ken, E
Keane, Jim, E
Kilcullen, Bob, T
Kindt, Don, B
Klawitter, Dick, C
Klein, Dick, T
Knox, Ronnie, QB
Kreamcheck, John, T-G
Lee, Herman, T
Leggett, Earl, T
Lesane, Jim, B
Lipscomb, Paul, T

Livingston, Howard, B
Lowe, Lloyd, B
Luckman, Sid, QB
Lujack, Johnny, QB
Macon, Eddie, B
McAfee, George, B
McColl, Bill, E
McElroy, Bucky, B
Meadows, Ed, E
Mellekas, John, C-T
Moore, McNeil, B
Morris, Johnny, B
Morris, Larry, LB
Morrison, Fred (Curly), B
Moser, Bob, C
Mosley, Henry, B
Mucha, Charles, G
Neal, Ed, T
Negus, Fred, C
Nickla, Ed, T
O'Connell, Tommy, QB
O'Quinn, John, E
Perini, Pete, B
Petitbon, Richie, B
Proctor, Rex, B
Reid, Floyd, B
Roehnelt, Bill, G-LB
Roggeman, Tom, G
Romanik, Steve, QB
Rowland, Brad, B
Ryan, John, B-E
Rykovich, Julie, B
Schroeder, Gene, E
Serini, Wash, G
Shipkey, Jerry, B
Smith, J.D., B
Smith, Ray Gene, B
Sprinkle, Ed, E
Stautberg, Gerry, G
Stenn (Stenko), Paul, G
Stone, Billy, B
Strickland, Larry, C
Sumner, Charley, B
Taylor, Lionel, E
Thrower, Willie, QB
Turner, Clyde (Bulldog), C
Wallace, Stan, B
Watkins, Bob, B
Weatherly, Gerry, C
White, Wilford, B
Whitman, S. J., B
Whittenton, Jesse, B
Wightkin, Bill, E-T
Williams, Bob, QB
Williams, Fred, T
Zucco, Vic, B

Chicago Cardinals
Owners
Mrs. Walter Wolfner
Charles Bidwill, Jr.
William V. Bidwill
Coaches
Curly Lambeau
Joe Kuharich
Joe Stydahar
Ray Richards
Phil Handler
Cecil Isbell
Frank (Pop) Ivy
Players
Anderson, Charley, E
Anderson, Cliff, E
Andros, Plato, G
Angle, Bob, B
Angsman, Elmer, B
Apolskis, Ray, G-C
Arterburn, Elmer, B
Bagdon, Ed, G
Banonis, Vince, C
Barni, Roy, B
Barry, Paul, B
Bates, Ted, LB
Bernardi, Frank, B
Bienemann, Tom, E
Blackburn, Bill, C
Bock, Wayne, T
Boydston, Max, E
Brancato, George, B

Bredde, Bill, B
Brettschneider, Carl, LB
Brosky, Al, B
Brown, Hardy, LB
Brubaker, Dick, E
Burl, Alex, B
Campana, Al, B
Carr, Jimmy, B
Carter, Willie, B
Chickillo, Nick, G
Childress, Joe, B
Cochran, Red, B
Compton, Ogden, QB
Conrad, Bobby Joe, B
Cook, Ed, T-G
Cowhig, Jerry, B
Crittendon, Jack, E
Cross, Billy, B
Cross, Bob, T
Crow, John David, B
Crow, Lindon, B
Culpepper, Ed, T
Curcillo, Tony, QB
Dahms, Tom, T
Davis, Jerry, B
Delavan, Burt, G-T
Dimancheff, Boris (Babe), B
Dittrich, John, G
Dove, Bob, E
Eggers, Doug, LB
Embree, Mel, E
Fanucchi, Ledio, T
Ferry, Lou, T
Finnin, Tom, T
Fischer, Bill, G-T
Fugler, Dick, T
Fuller, Frank, T
Gasparella, Joe, QB
Gay, Bill, B
Gehrke, Fred, B
Geri, Joe, B
Gilchrist, George, T
Gillis, Don, C
Glick, Freddy, B
Goldsberry, John, T
Goble, Les, B
Gordon, Bob, B
Gray, Ken, G
Groom, Jerry, C-T
Hall, Ken, B
Hammack, Mal, B
Harder, Pat, B
Hardy, Jim, QB
Hartshorn, Larry, G
Hatley, John, G
Hauser, Art, G
Hennessey, Jerry, E
Hickman, Larry, B
Higgins, Tom, T
Hill, Jimmy, B
Hill, King, QB
Hock, John, G
Hogland, Doug, G
Houghton, Jerry, T
Husmann, Ed, G
Jackson, Charley, B
Jagielski, Harry, T
Jankovich, Keever, E
Jennings, Jack, T
Joyce, Don, T
Karras, Johnny, B
Keane, Tom, B
Kinek, George, B
King, Emmett, B
Kingery, Ellsworth, B
Klimek, Tony, E
Knafelc, Gary, E
Koman, Bill, LB
Konovsky, Bob, G
Kutner, Mal, E
Ladd, Jim, E
Lane, Dick (Night Train), B
Lander, Lowell, B
Lange, Bill, G
Larson, Paul, QB
Lauro, Lindy, B
Leggett, Dave, QB
Lewis, Mac, T
Lewis, Woodley, B
Lipinski, Jim, T
Lipostad, Ed, G
Lunceford, Dave, T

Lynch, Lynn, G
Mann, Dave, B
Marchibroda, Ted, QB
Matson, Ollie, B
McCusker, Jim, T
McDermott, Lloyd, T
McHan, Lamar, QB
McPhee, Frank, E
Meinert, Dale, LB
Memmelaar, Dale, G
Mergen, Mike, T
Morgan, Bob, T
Nagel, Ray, QB
Nagler, Gern, E
Nolan, Dick, B
Norton, Jerry, B
Nussbaumer, Bob, B
Oakley, Charley, B
Olszewski, Johnny (0), B
Owens, Luke, T
Panciera, Don, QB
Panelli, John, B
Panfil, Ken, T
Pasquariello, Ralph, B
Pasquesi, Tony, T
Patera, Jack, LB
Patton, Cliff, G
Paul, Don, B
Pelfrey, Ray, E
Peters, Volney, T
Petrovich, George, T
Philpott, Dean, B
Polofsky, Gordon, G
Polsfoot, Fran, E
Popa, Eli, B
Psaltis, Jim, B
Putman, Earl, C
Ramsey, Garrard (Buster), G
Ramsey, Knox, G
Ramsey, Ray, B
Randle, Sonny, E
Reynolds, Mack, QB
Richards, Perry, E
Roach, John, QB
Romanik, Steve, QB
Root, Jim, QB
Rushing, Marion, LB-E
Sagely, Floyd, E
Sandifer, Dan, B
Sanford, Leo, G-C
Schleicher, Maury, LB
Schmidt, George, E
Schwall, Vic, B
Sears, Jim. B
Shaw, Bob, E
Sikora, Mike, G
Simmons, Jack, C
Sitko, Emil, B
Spence, Julian, B
Spinks, Jack, G
Stacy, Billy, B
Stonesifer, Don, E
Sugar, Leo, E
Suminski, Dave, G
Summerall, Pat, E-K
Svobada, Bill, LB
Swistowicz, Mike, B
Taylor, Jim, C-LB
Teeuws, Len, T
Thomas, Ralph, E
Thompson, Harry, G
Toogood, Charley, G
Tracey, John, E
Triplett, Wally, B
Trippi, Charley, B
Tripucka, Frank, QB
Tubbs, Jerry, LB
Ulrich, Chuck, T
Wagstaff, Jim, B
Wallner, Fred, G
Watford, Gerry, E
Watkins, Bobby, B
Weber, Chuck, LB
West, Stan, G
Wham, Tom, E
Whitman, S.J., B
Yablonski, Ventan, B
Cleveland Browns
Owners
Mickey McBride
Dave Jones
Coach

Paul Brown
Players
Adamle, Tony, B
Agase, Alex, G
Amstutz, Joe, C
Atkins, Doug, E
Bassett, Maurice, B
Bolden, Leroy, B
Borton, John, QB
Bradley, Hal, G
Brewster, Darrell, E
Brown, Jim, B
Bumgardner, Rex, B
Campbell, Milt, B
Carpenter, Ken, B
Carpenter, Lew, B
Carpenter, Preston, B-E
Catlin, Tom, LB-C
Clarke, Frank, E
Cole, Emerson, B
Colo, Don, T
Costello, Vince, LB
Davis, Willie, E-T
Deschaine, Dick, E
Donaldson, Gene, G
Fiss, Galen, LB
Ford, Henry, B
Ford, Len, E
Forester, Herschel, G
Freeman, Bobby, B
Gain, Bob, T
Gatski, Frank, C
Gaudio, Bob, G
Gibron, Abe, G
Gillom, Horace, E-P
Gorgal, Ken, QB
Goss, Don, T
Graham, Otto, QB
Grigg, Forrest (Chubby), T
Groza, Lou, T-K
Hanulak, Chet, B
Helluin, Jerry, T
Herring, Hal, C
Hickerson, Gene, G
Houston, Lin, G
Howard, Sherm, B
Howton, Billy, E
Humble, Weldon, G
Hunter, Art, C
Jagade, Harry (Chick), B
James, Tommy, B
Jones, Dub, B
Jones, Tom, T
Jordan, Henry, T
Kinard, Bill, B
King, Don, T
Kissell, John, T
Konz, Ken, B
Kreitling, Rich, E
Lahr, Warren, B
Lavelli, Dante, E
Lewis, Cliff, QB
Lloyd, Dave, LB-C
Macerelli, John, T
Martin, Jim, G-E
Massey, Carlton, E
McClung, Willie, T
McCormack, Mike, T
Michaels, Walt, LB
Mitchell, Bobby, B
Modzelewski, Ed, B
Morrison, Fred (Curly), B
Moselle, Dom, B
Motley, Marion, B
Ninowski, Jim, QB
Noll, Chuck, G
O'Brien, Fran, T
O'Connell, Tommy, QB
Oristaglio, Bob, E
Palmer, Darrell, T
Palumbo, Sam, C
Parilli, Vito (Babe), QB
Parrish, Bernie, B
Paul, Don, B
Perini, Pete, B
Peters, Floyd, T
Petitbon, John, B
Phelps, Don, B
Plum, Milt, QB
Ptacek, Bob, QB
Quinlan, Bill, E
Quinlan, Volney (Skeet), B

Ratterman, George, QB
Rechichar, Bert, B
Renfro, Ray, B
Reynolds, Billy, B
Robinson, Fred, G
Rymkus, Lou, T
Sandusky, John, T
Schafrath, Dick, T
Sharkey, Ed, G
Sheriff, Stan, LB
Shofner, Jim, B
Shula, Don, B
Skibinski, Joe, G
Smith, Bob, B
Smith, Jim Ray, G
Speedie, Mac, E
Steinbrunner, Don, T
Taseff, Carl, B
Thompson, Tommy, C
Weber, Chuck, LB
White, Bob, B
Wiggin, Paul, E
Willis, Bill, G
Wooten, John, G
Wren, Junior, B
Young, George, E
Youngelman, Sid, T
1952 Dallas Texans
Owners
Connell and Giles Miller
Coach
Jimmy Phelan
Players
Averno, Sisto, G
Baggett, Billy, B
Campanella, Joe, T
Cannamela, Pat, G
Celeri, Bob, QB
Colo, Don, T
Davis, Jerry, B
Donovan, Art, T
Ecklund, Brad, C
Edwards, Dan, E
Felker, Gene, E
Flowers, Keith, C
Gandee, Sonny, E
Gregg, Forrest, T
Hoerner, Dick, B
Humble, Weldon, G
Jackson, Ken, T
Jankovich, Keever, E
Keane, Tom, B
Lansford, Jim , T
Lauricella, Hank, B
Marchetti, Gino, E
McKissack, Dick, B
Ortman, Chuck, QB
Pelfrey, Ray, E
Petitbon, John, B
Poole, Barney, E
Reid, Joe, C
Robison, George, G
Sherman, Will, B
Soboleski, Joe, G
Tait, Art, E
Taliaferro, George, B
Tanner, Hamp, T
Toth, Zollie, B
Tripucka, Frank, QB
Wilkins, Dick, E
Williams, Stan, E
Wozniak, John, G
Young, Buddy, B
Detroit Lions
Owner
Edwin J. Anderson
Coaches
Bo McMillin
Buddy Parker
George Wilson
Players
Ane, Charley, T-C
Atkins, George, G
Bailey, Byron, B
Banonis, Vince, C
Barr, Terry, B
Berrang, Ed, E
Bingaman, Les, C
Bowman, Bill, B
Box, Cloyce, E
Brown, Howard, G
Brown, Marv, B

Bulger, Chet, T
Cain, Jim, E
Campbell, Stan, G
Carpenter, Lew, B
Cassady, Howard (Hopalong), B
Christiansen, Jack, B
Cifelli, Gus, T
Cline, Ollie, B
Clowes, John, T
Cook, Gene, E
Creekmur, Lou, T
Cronin, Gene, E
Cunningham, Leon, C
D'Alonzo, Pete, B
David, Jim, B
Davis, Milt, B
Dibble, Dorne, E
Doll, Don, B
Doran, Jim, E
Dove, Bob, E-G
Dublinski, Tom, QB
Earon, Blaine, E
Enke, Fred, QB
Flanagan, Dick, C
French, Barry, G
Fucci, Dom, B
Gandee, Sonny, E
Gatski, Frank, C
Gedman, Gene, B
Gibbons, Jim, E
Gilmer, Harry, QB
Girard, Earl (Jug), B
Glass, Bill, C-E
Gordy, John, G
Greene, John, E
Grossman, Rex, B
Grottkau, Bob, G
Hafen, Bernie, E
Harder, Pat, B
Hardy, Jim, QB
Hart, Leon, E-B
Hill, Jim, B
Hoernschemeyer, Bob, B
Hogland, Doug, G
Jaszewski, Floyd, T
Jenkins, Walt, E-T
Johnson, John Henry, B
Junker, Steve, E
Karilivacz, Carl, B
Karras, Alex, T
Kercher, Dick, B
Koepfer, Karl, G
Krall, Gerry, B
Krouse, Ray, T
Lary, Yale, B-P
Layne, Bobby, QB
LeBeau, Dick, B
Lewis, Dan, B
Lininger, Ray, C
Long, Bob, LB-E
Lowe, Gary, B
Lusk, Bob, C
Magnani, Dante, B
Mains, Gil, T
Martin, Jim, E-G-LB-K
McCord, Darris, T
McDermott, Lloyd, T
McGraw, Thurman (Fum), T
McIlhenny, Don, B
Middleton, Dave, B-E
Miketa, Andy, C
Miller, Bob, T
Momsen, Bob, G
Morrall, Earl, QB
Murakowski, Art, B
Panciera, Don, B
Panelli, John, B
Paolucci, Ben, T
Pearson, Lindell, B
Perry, Gerry, T
Pietrosante, Nick, B
Prchlik, John, T
Rabold, Mike, G
Reichow, Jerry, B
Ricca, Jim, G
Richards, Perry, E
Rifenburg, Dick, E
Riley, Lee, B
Rogas, Dan, T
Rote, Tobin, QB
Russell, Ken, T
Rychlec, Tom, E

Salsbury, Jim, G
Sandifer, Dan, B
Schmidt, Joe, LB
Schroll, Charles, B
Scott, Clyde (Smackover), B
Self, Clarence, B
Sewell, Harley, G
Simmons, Jack, G-C
Smith, J.R. (Bob), B
Smith, Robert L. (Bob), B
Soboleski, Joe, G
Spencer, Ollie, G
Stanfel, Dick, G
Steffen, Jim, B
Stits, Bill, B
Summerall, Pat, E-K
Swiacki, Bill, E
Topor, Ted, LB
Torgeson, LaVern, LB-C
Tracy, Tom, B
Triplett, Wally, B
Turner, Hal, E
Walker, Doak, B-K
Walker, Wayne, LB-K
Watson, Joe, C
Weatherall, Jim, T
Webb, Ken, B
Whitsell, Dave, B
Woit, Dick, B
Womack, Bruce, G
Yowarsky, Walt, E
Zatkoff, Roger, LB
Green Bay Packers
Board Chairman
Dominic Olejniczak
Coaches
Gene Ronzani
Lisle Blackburn
Scooter McLean
Vince Lombardi
Hugh Devore
Players
Afflis, Dick, G
Aldridge, Ben, B
Amundsen, Norm, G
Bailey, Byron, B
Baldwin, Al, E
Barnes, Emery, E
Barry, Al, G
Barton, Don, B
Beck, Ken, T
Bettis, Tom, G-LB
Boedeker, Bill, B
Bookout, Billy, B
Boone, J. R., B
Borden, Nate, E
Brackins, Charley, QB
Bray, Ray, G
Brown, Bill, G
Brown, Tim, B
Bullough, Hank, G
Burris, Paul, G
Butler, Bill, B
Canadeo, Tony, B
Cannava, Tony, B
Capuzzi, Jim, QB
Carpenter, Lew, B
Carmichael, Al, B
Christman, Paul, QB
Cifelli, Gus, T
Clemens, Bob, B
Cloud, Jack, B
Collins, Rip, B
Cone, Fred, B
Cook, Ted, E
Coutre, Larry, B
Currie, Dan, LB
Dahms, Tom, T
DanJean, Ernie, G
Davis, Harper, B
Dawson, Gib, B
Dees, Bob, T
Deschaine, Dick, E
Dillon, Bobby, B
DiPierro, Ray, G
Dittrich, John, G
Dowden, Steve, T
Dowler, Boyd, E
Drulis, Chuck, G
Dreyer, Wally, B
Ecker, Ed, T
Elliott, Carleton, E

Faverty, Hal, C
Felker, Art, E
Ferguson, Howie, B
Floyd, Bobby Jack, B
Ford, Len, E
Forester, Bill, T-G-LB
Forte, Bob, B
Francis, Joe, QB
Freeman, Bobby, B
Fritsch, Ted, B
Garrett, Bobby, QB
Girard, Earl (Jug), B
Gorgal, Ken, B
Gregg, Forrest, G-T
Gremminger, Hank, B
Grimes, Billy, B
Hanner, Dave, T
Hays, George, E
Held, Paul, QB
Helluin, Jerry, T
Hornung, Paul, B-K
Howton, Billy, E
Hunter, Art, T
Jansante, Val, E
Jennings, Jim, E
Johnson, Joe, B
Johnson, Marv, B
Johnson, Tom, T
Jordan, Henry, T
Keane, Jim, E
Kimmel, J. D., T
Kinard, Billy, B
King, Don, T
Knafelc, Gary, E
Knutson, Gene, E
Kramer, Jerry, G
Kramer, Ron, E
Lauer, Larry, C
Logan, Dick, T
Loomis, Ace, B
Losch, Jack, B
Lucky, Bill, T
Manley, Bill, G-T
Mann, Bob, E
Martinkovic, John, E
Massey, Carlton, E
Masters, Norm, T
Matuszak, Marv, LB
McGeary, Clarence (Clink), T
McGee, Max, E
McHan, Lamar, QB
McIlhenny, Don, B
Meilinger, Steve, E
Michaels, Walt, G
Miller, Don, B
Moje, Dick, E
Moselle, Dom, B
Neal, Ed, C
Nichols, Ham, G
Nitschke, Ray, LB
Nix, Doyle, B
Nussbaumer, Bob, B
O'Donahue, Pat, E
O'Malley, Bob, B
Orlich, Dan, E
Palumbo, Sam, C
Papit, Johnny, B
Parilli, Vito (Babe), QB
Pearson, Lindell, B
Pelfrey, Ray, B-E
Petitbon, John, B
Pritko, Steve, E
Psaltis, Jim, B
Purnell, Frank, B
Quinlan, Bill, E
Reichardt, Bill, B
Reid, Floyd (Breezy), B
Rhodemyre, Jay, C
Ringo, Jim C
Roberts, Bill, B
Robinson, Bill, B
Romine, Al, B
Rote, Tobin, QB
Ruetz, Howard, T
Rush, Clive, E
Ruzich, Steve, G
Salsbury, Jim, G
Sandifer, Dan, B
Sandusky, John, T
Schmidt, George, C
Schroll, Chuck, G
Schuette, Carl, C

Self, Clarence, B
Serini, Wash, G
Shanley, Jim, B
Skibinski, Joe, G
Skoronski, Bob, T
Smith, Jerry, G
Spencer, Joe, T
Spencer, Ollie, T
Spinks, Jack, G
Stansauk, Don, T
Starr, Bart, QB
Steiner, Rebel, E
Stephenson, Dave, G-C
Summerhays, Bob, B
Switzer, Veryl, B
Symank, John, B
Szafaryn, Len, G-T
Taylor, Jim, B
Temp, Jim, E
Teteak, Deral, G
Thomason, Bobby, QB
Thurston, Fred (Fuzzy), G
Timberlake, George, G
Tonnemaker, Clayton, C
Tunnell, Emlen, B
Vereen, Carl, T
Walker, Val Joe, B
White, Gene, B
Whittenton, Jesse, B
Wildung, Dick, T
Williams, A. D., E
Wimberly, Abner, E
Wizbicki, Alex, B
Young, Glenn, B
Zatkoff, Roger, T
Los Angeles Rams
Owner
Dan Reeves
Coaches
Joe Stydahar
Hamp Pool
Sid Gillman
Players
Agajanian, Ben, K
Arnett, Jon, B
Baker, John, T-E
Barry, Paul, B
Bighead, Jack, E
Bouley, Gil, T
Bowers, Bill, B
Boyd, Bob, E-B
Braatz, Tom, E
Bradshaw, Charley, T
Bravo, Alex, B
Brink, Larry, E
Brito, Gene, E
Bruney, Fred, B
Bukich, Rudy, QB
Burroughs, Don, B
Carey, Bob, E
Casner, Ken, T
Cason, Jim, B
Castete, Jesse, B
Champagne, Ed, T
Clarke, Leon, E
Collier, Bob, T
Cothren, Paige, K
Cross, Bob, T
Dahms, Tom, T
Daugherty, Dick, G-C-LB
Davis, Glenn, B
Dickson, Paul, T
Doll, Don, B
Dougherty, Bob, LB-E
Dwyer, Jack, B
Ellena, Jack, G
Fears, Tom, E
Ferris, Neil, B
Finlay, Jack, G
Fournet, Sid, T
Franckhauser, Tom, B
Fry, Bob, T
Fuller, Frank, T
Griffin Bob, C
Guzik, John, LB
Halliday, Jack, T
Harris, Jimmy, B
Hauser, Art, G-T
Haynes, Hall, B
Hecker, Bob, B
Hecker, Norb, E-B
Hirsch, Elroy (Crazylegs), B-E

Hock, John, G
Hoerner, Dick, B
Holladay, Bob, B
Holtzman, Glenn, T-E
Houser, John, G
Huffman, Dick, T
Hughes, Ed, B
Humphrey, Buddy, QB
Iglehart, Floyd, B
Jobko, Bill, LB-C
Johnson, Marv, B
Jones, Jim, B
Kalmanir, Tom, B
Karilivacz, Carl, B
Keane, Tom, E-B
Klosterman, Don, QB
Lane, Dick (Night Train), B
Lange, Bill, G
Lansford, Buck, G
Lazetich, Milan, G
Lewis, Woodley, B-E
Lipscomb, Gene (Big Daddy), T
LoVetere, John, T
Lundy, Lamar, E
Marconi, Joe, B
Matson, Ollie, B
Mayes, Carl, B
McCormick, Tom, B
McFadin, Bud, G-T
McLaughlin, Leon, C
Meador, Ed, B
Michaels, Lou, E-T
Miller, Paul, E
Miller, Ron, E
Morris, Jack, B
Morris, Larry, LB-B
Morrow, John, G-C
Myers, Brad, B
Myers, Jack, B
Naumetz, Fred, C
Panfil, Ken, T
Pardee, Jack, LB
Pasquariello, Ralph, B
Paul, Don, C-LB
Phillips, Jim (Red), E
Pitts, Hugh, LB
Putnam, Duane, G
Quinlan, Volney (Skeet), B
Reid, Joe, C
Reinhard, Bob, T
Rich, Herb, B
Richter, Les, LB-G
Robustelli, Andy, E
Ryan, Frank, QB
Selawski, Gene, T
Sherman, Will, B
Shiver, Ray, B
Shofner, Del, E-B
Sims, George, B
Simensen, Don, T
Smith, Billy Ray, T-E
Smith, Verda (Vitamin T), B
Smyth, Bill, E
Statuto, Art, C
Stephenson, Dave, G
Strugar, George, T
Svare, Harland, LB-G
Taylor, Cecil, B
Teeuws, Len, T
Thomas, Clendon, B
Thompson, Harry, G
Toogood, Charley, T
Towler, Dan, B
Van Brocklin, Norm, QB
Vasicek, Vic, G
Wade, Bill, QB
Waller, Ron, B
Wardlow, Duane, E
Waterfield, Bob, QB
West, Stan, G
Whittenton, Jesse, B
Wilkins, Roy, E-LB
Williams, Jerry, B
Williams, Sam, E
Wilson, Tom, B
Winkler, Jim, T
Younger, Paul (Tank), B
Zilly, Jack, E
New York Giants
Owner
John V. Mara
Coaches

Steve Owen
Jim Lee Howell
Players
Agajanian, Ben, K
Albright, Bill, G
Amberg, John, B
Anderson, Cliff, E
Austin, Bill, G
Avinger, Butch, B
Baker, Jon, G
Barry, Al, G
Barzilauskas, Fritz, G
Bauer, John, G
Beck, Ray, G
Benners, Fred, QB
Berry, Wayne, B
Biscaha, Joe, E
Boggan, Rex, T
Bookman, John, B
Brackett, M. L., T
Broussard, Fred, C
Brown, Roosevelt, T
Burnine, Hank, E
Cannaday, John, LB-C
Carroccio, Russ, G
Chandler, Don, K
Clatterbuck, Bobby, QB
Clay, Randy, B
Collins, Ray, T
Conerly, Charlie, QB
Coulter, DeWitt (Tex), T-C
Crawford, Ed, B
Crow, Lindon, B
DeRogatis, Al, T
Dess, Darrell, G
Douglas, Everett, T
Dublinski, Tom, QB
Duncan, Jim, E
Epps, Bobby, B
Ettinger, Don, G
Filipski, Gene, B
Galiffa, Arnold, QB
Gifford, Frank, B
Grandelius, Sonny, B
Grier, Roosevelt, T
Griffith, Forrest, B
Guy, Mel (Buzz), T-G
Hall, John, E
Hannah, Herb, T
Hauser, Art, T
Heap, Joe, B
Heinrich, Don, QB
Hermann, John, B
Hodel, Merwin, B
Hudson, Bob, E
Huff, Sam, LB
Hughes, Ed, B
Huth, Gerry, G
Jackson, Bob, B
Jelacic, Jon, E
Johnson, Herb, B
Karilivacz, Carl, B
Katcavage, Jim, E
Kelly, Ellison, G
Kennard, George, G
Kimber, Bill, E
King, Phil, B
Knight, Pat, E-B
Krouse, Ray, T
Lagod, Chet, G
Landry, Tom, B
Livingston, Cliff, LB-E
Long, Buford, B
Lott, Billy, B
Lynch, Dick, B
MacAfee, Ken, E
Mackrides, Bill, QB
Mangum, Pete, B
Maronic, Duke, G
Martinkovic, John, E
Mastrangelo, John, G
Maynard, Don, B
McChesney, Bob, E
Menasco, Don, B
Miles, Leo, B
Milner, Bill, G
Mischak, Bob, G
Mitchell, Hal, T
Modzelewski, Dick, T
Moore, Henry, B
Morrison, Joe, B
Mote, Kelly, E

Murray, Earl, G
Nolan, Dick, B
Ostendarp, Jim, B
Patton, Bob, G
Patton, Jim, B
Pelfrey, Ray, E
Peviani, Bob, G
Poole, Barney, E
Poole, Ray, E
Price, Eddie, B
Pritchard, Bosh, B
Ramona, Joe, G
Rapacz, John, C
Rich, Herb, B
Roberts, Gene, B
Robustelli, Andy, E
Roman, George, T
Rote, Kyle, B-E
Rowe, Harmon, B
Sanchez, John, T
Schmidt, Bob, T
Schnelker, Bob, E
Schnellbacher, Otto, B
Scott, George, B
Scott, Joe, B-E
Scott, Tom, LB
Shaw, George, QB
Sherrod, Horace (Bud), E
Shipp, Bill, T
Skladany, Leo, E
Spinks, Jack, G
Stits, Bill, B
Stribling, Bill, E
Stroud, Jack, G
Sulaitis, Joe, B-C-G-E
Summerall, Pat, K-E
Sutherin, Don, B
Svare, Harland, LB
Svoboda, Bill, LB
Swiacki, Bill, E
Thomas, George, B
Tidwell, Travis, QB
Topp, Bob, E
Triplett, Mel, B
Tunnell, Emlen, B
Weaver, Larrye, B
Webster, Alex, B
Weinmeister, Arnie, T
West, Stan, G
White, Jim, T
Wietecha, Ray, C
Wilkins, Dick, E
Wilkinson, Bob, E
Williams, Ellery, E
Woodward, Dick, C
Yelvington, Dick, T
Youso, Frank, T
Yowarsky, Walt, E
1950-51 New York Yanks
Owner
Ted Collins
Coach
Norman (Red) Strader
Players
Adams, Chet, T
Aldridge, Ben, B
Alford, Bruce, E
Averno, Sisto, G
Brown, George, G
Celeri, Bob, QB
Champion, Jim, G
Clowes, John, T
Colo, Don, T
Crowe, Paul, B
Cullom, Jim, G
Domnanovich, Joe, C
Donovan, Art, T
Ecklund, Brad, C
Edwards, Dan, E
Garza, Dan, E
Golding, Joe, B
Griffin, Bob, B
Howard, Sherm, B
Iverson, Chris, B
Jenkins, Jon, T
Johnson, Harvey, B
Johnson, Nate, B
Kennedy, Bob, B
Kissell, Vito, B
Kusserow, Lou, B
Layden, Pete, B
McCormack, Mike, T

Meisenheimer, Darrell, B
Mitchell, Paul, T
Nagel, Ross, T
Nolan, John, G
O'Connor, Bill, E
Pollard, Al, B
Poole, Barney, E
Ratterman, George, QB
Rauch, John, QB
Ruby, Martin, T
Russell, Jack, E
Sanders, Orban (Spec), B
Sharkey, Ed, G
Siegert, Wayne, G
Signaigo, Joe, G
Soboleski, Joe, T
Stroschein, Brock, E
Swistowicz, Mike, B
Tait, Art, E
Taliaferro, George, B
Toth, Zollie, B
Vogelaar, Carroll, T
Wallace, Bev, QB
Weiner, Art, E
Wozniak, John, G
Yonaker, John, E
Young, Buddy, B
Philadelphia Eagles
Owners
Jim Clark
Frank McNamee
Coaches
Earle (Greasy) Neale
Bo McMillin
Wayne Millner
Jim Trimble
Hugh Devore
Buck Shaw
Players
Armstrong, Neil, E
Aschbacher, Darrell, G
Barnes, Billy Ray, B
Barnes, Walter (Piggy), G
Barni, Roy, B
Bawel, Ed (Bibbles), B
Bednarik, Chuck, C-LB
Bell, Eddie, B-E
Berzinski, Bill, B
Bielski, Dick, B-E
Boedecker, Bill, B
Bradley, Hal, G
Bredice, John, E
Brewer, John, B
Brookshier, Tom, B
Burk, Adrian, QB
Burnine, Hank, E
Campbell, Marion, T
Campbell, Stan, G
Carr, Jimmy, B
Carroccio, Russ, G
Catlin, Tom, LB
Cifelli, Gus, T
Cooke, Ed, E
Cothren, Paige, K
Cowhig, Jerry, B
Craft, Russ, B
D'Agostino, Frank, G
DeLucca, Gerry, T
Dimmick, Tom, G
Dorow, Al, QB
Dowda, Harry, B
Enke, Fred, QB
Farragut, Ken, C
Ferrante, Jack, E
Ferris, Neil, B
Gambold, Bob, B
Gaona, Bob, T
Giancanelli, Skip, B
Giannelli, Harold, G
Gibron, Abe, G
Goldston, Ralph, B
Goode, Rob, B
Grant, Harry (Bud), E
Green, Johnny, E
Hansen, Roscoe, T
Harris, Jimmy, B
Higgins, Tom, T
Hix, Billy, E
Horrell, Bill, G
Hudson, Bob, B
Huth, Gerry, G
Huxhold, Ken, G

Huzvar, John, B
Irvin, Bill, E
Jacobs, Proverb, T
Jarmoluk, Mike, T
Johnson, Don, B
Johnson Gene,B
Jurgensen, Sonny, QB
Keller, Ken, B
Kelley, Bob, C
Khayat, Eddie, T-E
Kilroy, Frank (Bucko), G-T
King, Don, T
Koman, Bill, LB
Kowalczyk, Walt, B
Laack, Galen, G
Lansford, Buck, G-T
Ledbetter, Toy, B
Lindskog, Vic, C
Louderback, Tom, LB
Luft, Don, E
MacAfee, Ken, E
MacDowell, Jay, T
Mackrides, Bill, QB
Magee, John, G
Maronic, Duke, G
Mavraides, Menil, G
McCusker, Jim, T
McDonald, Tommy, B-E
McHugh, Pat, B
Meadows, Ed, E
Michels, John, G
Miller, Don, B
Mitcham, Gene, E
Moselle, Dom, B
Muha, Joe, B
Murley, Dick, T
Mrkonic, George, T
Myers, Brad, B
Myers, Jack, B
Nacrelli, Andy, E
Nipp, Maurey, G
Nocera, John, LB
Norton, Jerry, B
O'Quinn, John (Red), E
Oristaglio, Bob, E
Owens, Don, T
Pagliei, Joe, B
Parmer, Jim, B
Patton, Cliff, G
Peaks, Clarence, B
Pellegrini, Bob, LB-G
Peters, Volney, T
Pihos, Pete, E
Pollard, Al, B
Powell, Art, B
Pritchard, Bosh, B
Ramsey, Knox, G
Rauch, John, QB
Reagan, Frank, B
Restic, Joe, E
Retzlaff, Pete, E
Ricca, Jim, T
Richardson, Jess, T
Riley, Lee, B
Robb, Joe, E
Robinson, Wayne, LB-C
Roffler, Bill, B
Rogas, Dan, G
Romero, Ray, G
Ryan, John, B
Saidock, Tom, T
Sandifer, Dan, B
Sapp, Theron, B
Schaefer, Don, B
Schnelker, Bob, E
Scott, Clyde (Smackover), B
Scott, Tom, E-LB
Sears, Vic, T
Sharkey, Ed, G
Simerson, John, C
Smith, Bob, B
Smith, Jess, T
Snyder, Lum, T
Steere, Dick, T
Stevens, Don, B
Stickel, Walt, T
Stribling, Bill, E
Striegel, Bill, G
Stringer, Bob, B
Sutton, Bud, B
Szafaryn, Len, T
Taliaferro, George, B

Thomason, Bobby, QB
Thompson, Tommy, QB
Tyrrell, Joe, G
Van Buren, Ebert, B
Van Buren, Steve, B
Van Brocklin, Norm, QB
Walston, Bobby, E
Weatherall, Jim, T
Weber, Chuck, LB
Wegert, Ted, B
Wells, Billy, B
Willey, Norm (Wildman), E
Williams, Jerry, B
Wilson, Jerry, E
Wistert, Al, T
Wojciechowicz, Alex, C
Worden, Neil, B
Wydo, Frank, T
Youngelman, Sid, T
Ziegler, Frank, B
Zilly, Jack, E

Pittsburgh Steelers
Owner
Art Rooney, Sr.
Coaches
John Michelosen
Joe Bach
Walt Kiesling
Buddy Parker
Players
Alban, Dick, B
Alderton, John, E
Allen, Lou, T
Andabaker, Rudy, G
Baldacci, Lou, B
Balog, Bob, C
Barker, Ed, E
Barnett, Tom, B
Beams, Byron, T
Beatty, Ed, C
Bernet, Ed, E
Bishop, Don, E-B
Bolkovac, Nick, T
Bowman, Bill, B
Brady, Pat, QB
Brandt, Jim, B
Brewster, Darrell, E
Broussard, Fred, C
Brundage, Dewey, E
Bruney, Fred, B
Butler, Jack, B-E
Call, Jack, B
Calvin, Tom, B
Cameron, Paul, B
Campbell, Leon, B
Campbell, Dick, LB
Cenci, John, C
Chandnois, Lynn, B
Cheatham, Ernie, T
Christy, Dick, B
Cichowski, Gene, B
Cifelli, Gus, T
Craft, Russ, B
Davis, Art, B
Davis, Bob, E
Dawson, Len, QB
DeCarlo, Art, B
Derby, Dean, B
Dess, Darrell, G
Dial, Buddy, E
Dodrill, Dale, G
Dougherty, Bob, LB
Doyle, Dick, B
Eaton, Vic, QB
Elter, Leo, B
Evans, Jon, E
Feher, Nick, G
Ferry, Lou, T
Finks, Jim, QB
Fisher, Ray, T
Flanagan, Dick, G
Ford, Henry, B
Fournet, Sid, G
Fugler, Dick, T
Fullerton, Ed, B
Gage, Bob, B
Gaona, Bob, T
Gasparella, Joe, QB
Geri, Joe, B
Girard, Earl (Jug), B
Glatz, Fred, E
Glick, Gary, B

Gunderman, Bob, E
Hall, Ron, B
Harkey, Lem, B
Hartley, Howard, B
Hays, George, E-T
Hayes, Dick, LB
Hegarty, Bill, T
Held, Paul, QB
Hendley, Dick, QB
Henry, Mike, LB
Hensley, Dick, E
Hill, Jim, B
Hipps, Claude, B
Hogan, Darrell, G
Hollingsworth, Joe, B
Hughes, Dick, B
Hughes, George, G
Jansante, Val, E
Jecha, Ralph, G
Jelley, Tom, E
Karras, Ted, T
Kemp, Jack, QB
Kerkorian, Gary, QB
Kissell, Ed, QB
Krisher, Bill, G
Krupa, Joe, T
Krutko, Larry, B
Ladygo, Pete, G
Lasse, Dick, E-LB
Lattner, Johnny, B
Layne, Bobby, QB
Lea, Paul, T
Leahy, Gerry, T
Lee, Herman, T-G
Levanti, Lou, C-G
Lewis, Joe, T
Liddick, Dave, T
Long, Bill, E
Luna, Bobby, B
Mackrides, Bill, QB
Marchibroda, Ted, QB
Matesic, Joe, T
Mathews, Ray, B-E
Matuszak, Marv, LB-G
McCabe, Richie, B
McClairen, Jack, B-E
McClung, Willie, T
McConnell, Dewey, E
McFadden, Marv, G
McPeak, Bill, E
McWilliams, Tom, B
Meadows, Ed, E
Mechelich, Charley, E
Michael, Bill, G
Michalik, Art, G
Minarik, Henry, E
Miner, Tom, E
Modzelewski, Dick, T
Modzelewski, Ed, B
Momsen, Tony, C
Morrall, Earl, QB
Motley, Marion, B
Murley, Dick, T
Murray, Earl, G
Nagler, Gern, E
Nickel, Elbie, E
Nicksich, George, G
Nisby, John, G
Nuzum, Jerry, B
O'Brien, Jack, E
O'Malley, Joe, E
O'Neil, Bob, G
Oniskey, Dick, G
Orr, Jimmy, E
Ortman, Chuck, QB
Palmer, Tom, T
Perry, Lowell, E
Priatko, Bill, LB
Reger, John, LB-G
Reynolds, Billy, B
Richards, Perry, E
Rogel, Fran, B
Rozelle, Aubrey, LB
Sandusky, Mike, G
Samuel, Don, B
Samuelson, Carl, T
Scarbath, Jack, QB
Schweder, John, G
Seabright, Charley, QB
Shepard, Charley, B
Sheriff, Stan, G-C
Shields, Burrell, B

Shipkey, Jerry, B
Simerson, John, C
Sinkovitz, Frank, C
Smith, Billy Ray, T
Smith, Truett, QB
Spinks, Jack, G-B
Stautner, Ernie, T
Stock, John, E
Sulima, George, E
Sutherin, Don, B
Szot, Walt, T
Tarasovic, George, E-LB-C
Taylor, Jim, C
Tepe, Lou, C
Tomlinson, Dick, G
Tracy, Tom, B
Varrichione, Frank, T
Walsh, Bill, C
Watson, Sid, B
Weed, Tad, K
Wells, Billy, B
Wiley, John, T
Wydo, Frank, T
Young, Dick, B
Younger, Paul (Tank), B
Zombek, Joe, E

San Francisco 49ers
Owners
Tony Morabito
Vic Morabito
Coaches
Buck Shaw
Norman (Red) Strader
Frankie Albert
Howard (Red) Hickey
Players
Albert, Frankie, QB
Aldridge, Ben, B
Arenas, Joe, B
Atkins, Billy, B
Babb, Gene, B
Babcock, Harry, E
Bahnsen, Ken, B
Baker, Dave, B
Banducci, Bruno, G
Barnes, Larry, B
Beals, Alyn, E
Beatty, Ed, C
Berry, Rex, B
Boone, J. R., B
Bosley, Bruce, G
Brodie, John, QB
Brown, Hardy, LB
Brown, Pete, C
Bruce, Gail, E
Brumfield, Jack, E
Bruney, Fred, B
Burke, Don, B-G
Campbell, Marion, T
Campora, Don, T
Carapella, Al, T
Carr, Paul, LB-B
Cason, Jim, B
Cassara, Frank, B
Cathcart, Royal, B
Cathcart, Sam, B
Clark, Monte, T
Collins, Ray, T
Connolly, Ted, G
Conner, Clyde, E
Cross, Bob, T
Dahms, Tom, T
Davis, Tommy, K
Dove, Eddie, B
Dow, Harley, G
Downs, Bob, G
Dugan, Fred, E
Duncan, Maury, QB
Endriss, Al, E
Evans, Ray, T
Feher, Nick, G
Galiffa, Arnold, QB
Garlin, Don, B
Gehrke, Fred, B
Goad, Paul, B
Gonzaga, John, T
Grgich, Visco, G
Hantla, Bob, G
Hardy, Carroll, B
Harkey, Lem, B
Harrison, Bob, LB
Hazeltine, Matt, LB